Visual Geography

9780333151051
D1744397

Western Europe

Grahame H. C. Waters
W. J. Hayes

Contents	Page

Macmillan Education

First published 1974
Reprinted 1977, 1979
Published by
MACMILLAN EDUCATION LIMITED
Houndmills Basingstoke Hampshire RG21 2XS
and London
Associated companies in Delhi Dublin Hong Kong Johannesburg Lagos Melbourne New York Singapore and Tokyo

Cartography by Lovell Johns Ltd., Oxford

Printed in Hong Kong by
Dai Nippon Printing Co., (H.K.) Ltd.

How to use this book

The aim of this book is to provide a very wide range of information in visual form, capable of use at widely different levels of age and ability and within the financial reach of school geography departments. The material is carefully placed so that geographical relationships are suggested and may be discovered. Throughout the book there is frequent reference to the U.K. in order to bring out comparisons and contrast in scale, occupations and developments in general.

It is clear that to make the best use of this book the teacher must make a careful selection from the great wealth of information presented. The authors have so designed the layout as to make such selection as easy as possible – each illustration and each question is numbered and topics are dealt with on a single or double page basis as far as is practicable. Although a traditional sequence is used for each country and may be followed if required, the lack of numbered chapters as such makes it easier for the teacher to select topics in any order desired. The book may be used in a traditional regional study of any of the countries of North West Europe or, by a choice of topics, may be used, for example, to show similarities or contrasts in the physical and/or human geography of similar or different regions, and reasons for these differences or similarities may also be indicated.

The use of the illustrations is completely flexible and the questions vary widely in difficulty, offering the teacher the widest possible scope and control over the material presented here.

NB. Metric Conversion Tables are provided on the inside back cover.

Other titles in this series are:
The British Isles   North America
Southern Continents

In this book North and West Europe are taken to comprise the following countries, one of which—the British Isles—has been dealt with in a separate book in this series: Norway, Sweden, Denmark, Switzerland, France, W Germany, Belgium, the Netherlands, Luxembourg, and the British Isles. Special reference is also made to Italy—the European Economic Community country of Southern Europe.

Fig.3 The countries of Europe

3a Name countries A - I.
3b Name water areas J - M
3c Of which country was Iceland a part until 1944?

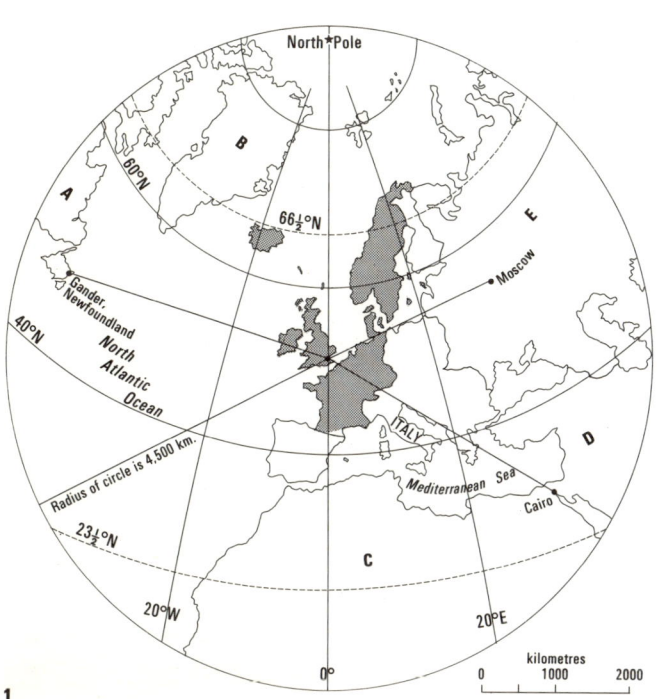

1

▨ Area taken as N and W Europe in this book.   Distances in straight lines are correct

Fig.1 Position of N & W Europe

The map is centred on London, England.

1a What is radius of the circle in miles/kilometres?
1b What is the distance between London and (i) Moscow (ii) Gander (iii) Cairo?
1c What is the (i) continent A (ii) island B (iii) continent C (iv) political area D (v) country E?
1d What is the approximate length of N & W Europe from N-S?

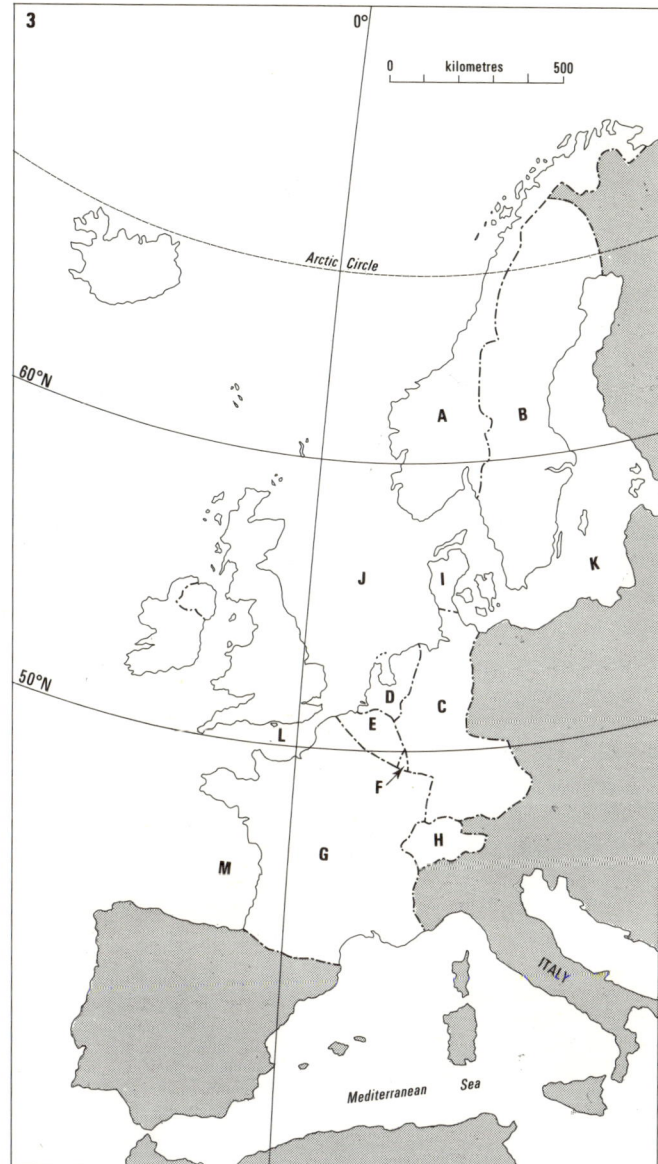

Fig.2 Areas and populations of N & W European countries

2a Which country has (i) the highest density of population per sq km? (ii) the lowest density of population per sq km?
2b About how many times larger than Belgium is the British Isles?
2c About how many times larger is the population of the British Isles than that of Belgium?

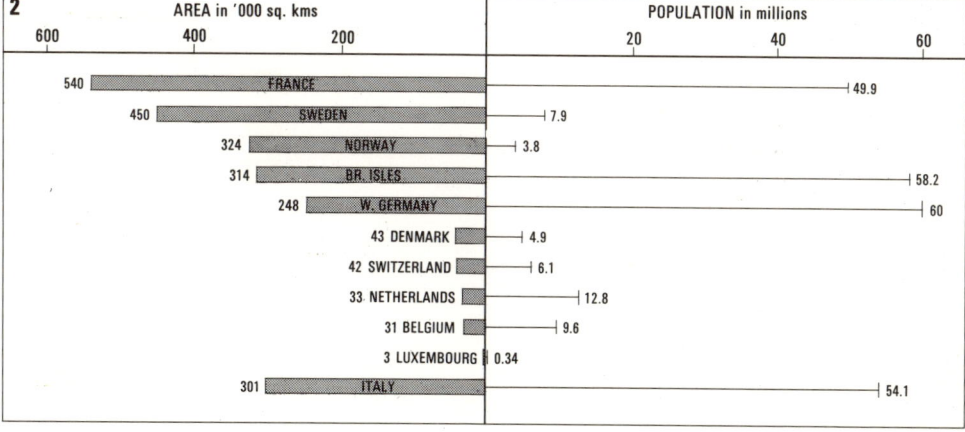

	AREA in '000 sq. kms	POPULATION in millions
FRANCE	540	49.9
SWEDEN	450	7.9
NORWAY	324	3.8
BR. ISLES	314	58.2
W. GERMANY	248	60
DENMARK	43	4.9
SWITZERLAND	42	6.1
NETHERLANDS	33	12.8
BELGIUM	31	9.6
LUXEMBOURG	3	0.34
ITALY	301	54.1

The present shape and relief of Europe is the result of:
(a) earth movements (i) horizontal, i.e. the work of three folding periods; (ii) vertical (the vertical depression and/or uplift of the lands);
(b) denudation (erosion and deposition) i.e. the work of weather, wind, rivers, waves and moving ice;
(c) the fall and rise in sea level caused by the expansion and contraction of the ice sheets—how?—

The three main folded systems developed in widely separated geological periods between each of which fresh layers of sedimentary deposits (sandstones, clays, limestones) were laid down on the sea beds:

   A The Caledonian: c. 320 million years ago
   B The Hercynian: c. 240 million years ago
   C The Alpine: c. 35 million years ago

Mountains formed during the two earlier foldings (orogenies) have long since been eroded away, and today uplands from these systems only occur because:
   (a) they have been re-uplifted vertically;
or (b) some of their rocks are very resistant and remain like the stumps of rotted teeth;
or (c) both (a) and (b).
The Alpine folds have also been eroded and re-uplifted but they are, of course, very much younger and have not been so severely reduced. The Baltic Shield and Russian Platform form relatively stable areas of ancient rocks which have been overlaid with various glacial deposits of the recent Ice Age. Volcanic activity and earthquakes occurred during each mountain building period (orogeny), e.g. Antrim lava plateau, Etna, Vesuvius, Stromboli, and Mt. Hekla. Note the sequences of rocks by age (oldest 1, youngest 8).

Fig.4 The structural zones of Europe

4a In which countries are remnants of the Caledonian system to be seen?

4b The Hercynian Blocks (re-uplifted and often tilted and cracked by the pressures from the Alpine waves to the South) are numbered 1 - 7. Find out the names of those not identified below:

      3 Vosges, 4 Black Forest, 6 Harz Mts,
      7 Bohemian 'diamond'.

4c Identify fold mountains A - E.

4d Which upland areas show evidence of glacial (ice) erosion?

4e Find the derivation of the words 'Caledonian' and 'Hercynian'.

Fig.5 Surface rock and loose deposits (drift) of Europe

5a Is much of the Caledonian system covered by later deposits?

5b (Look also at Fig. 6) What is loess? (Note the areas of this deposit.)

5c What rocks form the old Hercynian surfaces?

5d What deposit covers most of the North European Plain?

5e Most of the coalfields are in basins within, or on the edges of which old fold system?

5f Look at figs 4, 5, and 7 together and note any similarities in the distributions they show, e.g. folds, relief, surface deposits.

5g Find the volcanic features named from above in your atlas.

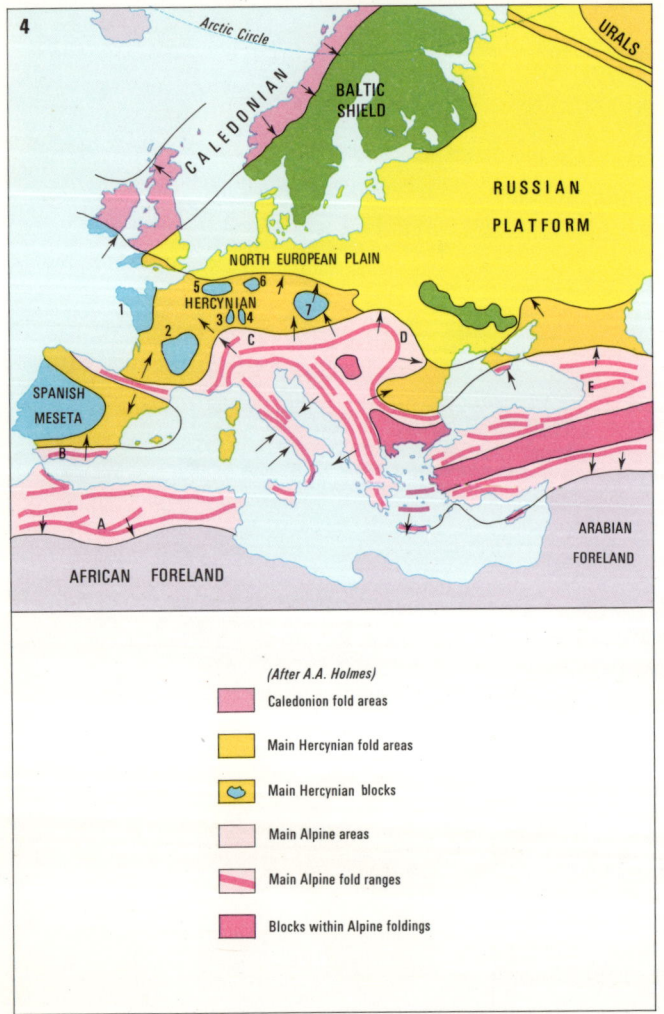

(After A.A. Holmes)

- Caledonian fold areas
- Main Hercynian fold areas
- Main Hercynian blocks
- Main Alpine areas
- Main Alpine fold ranges
- Blocks within Alpine foldings

(Collins-Longmans 'Visible Regions Atlas')

8 LOOSE SURFACE DEPOSITS
  Recent ALLUVIUM; Lowlands
7b
  LOESS: Light wind-blown soil; plains
7a
  GLACIAL CLAYS, with boulders and sand; hillocks, sandy plains and marshy valleys. These also overlie much of the Baltic Shield and lower parts of the Caledonian system.

6 ROCKS NEWER THAN COAL
  Intensely folded high mountains
5
  Gently tilted; scarped uplands and vales
4
  Coalfields

SANDSTONE
LIMESTONES
AND CLAYS

3 ROCKS OLDER THAN COAL
  Old GRITS and SLATES: resistant low plateaus.
2
  Very old GNEISS and SCHIST: resistant high plateaus.
1
  Oldest GNEISS and SCHIST: resistant lowlands

Fig.6 Maxmium extent of main Ice Caps in Europe

The Great Ice Age came to an end in Europe about 20,000 years ago and lingers today only in the tiny remains of Ice Cap in Norway and the Alpine System. Its importance lies in the influences the moving ice and glacial melt-water had upon the scenery—eroding *uplands* to form much deepened U shaped valleys, cirques, hanging valleys, arêtes and truncated spurs, and *depositing* various types of moraine, particularly in lowland areas, in sheets, ridges and mounds: boulder clay; sandy outwash plains, drumlins, eskers, terminal, medial and lateral moraines.

6a Name all the European countries which were wholly beneath the maximum Ice Cap.

6b Which mountains produced the three smaller ice caps shown?

6c Where was the 'centre of dispersion' of the ice?

6d Describe the location of loess.

6e Find out and write notes about all the glacial features listed above under headings 'Features of Ice Erosion' and 'Features of Ice Deposition'.

6f Look at fig. 5. In which areas were glacial clays deposited in particular?

Fig.7 Relief and routeways of W. Europe

Examine this figure together with figs. 3 and 4, and your atlas map of European relief. Routeways into and through W. Europe have traditionally followed lowland—and still follow the same relatively easy routes of communication.

7a With which folding period is most of the upland associated in Europe?

7b Is most of the northern coast of mainland Western (not including Northern) Europe upland or lowland?

7c The main gaps and corridors of W. Europe are numbered 1-6. Find out and list the names of those not identified below.
   1 The Perpignan Gap,   2 The Gate of Carcassone
   3 Gate of Poitou,   4 is the Corridor of which river?
   5 Belfort Gap,   6 is the Corridor of which river?

7d Find all the named parts in your atlas.

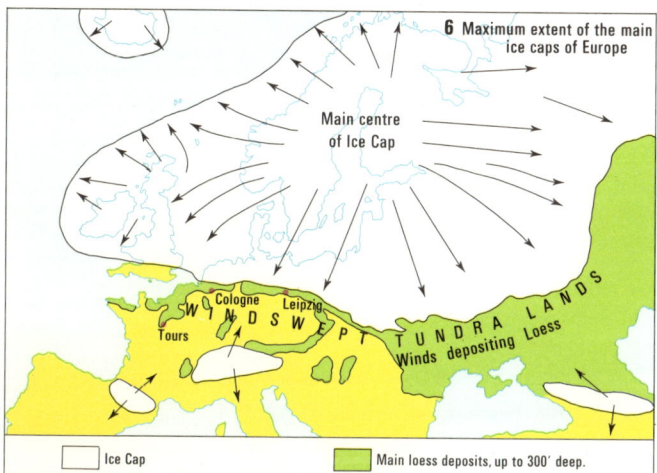

6 Maximum extent of the main ice caps of Europe

Main centre of Ice Cap

W I N D S W E P T
Cologne Leipzig
Tours
T U N D R A   L A N D S
Winds depositing Loess

Ice Cap | Main loess deposits, up to 300' deep.

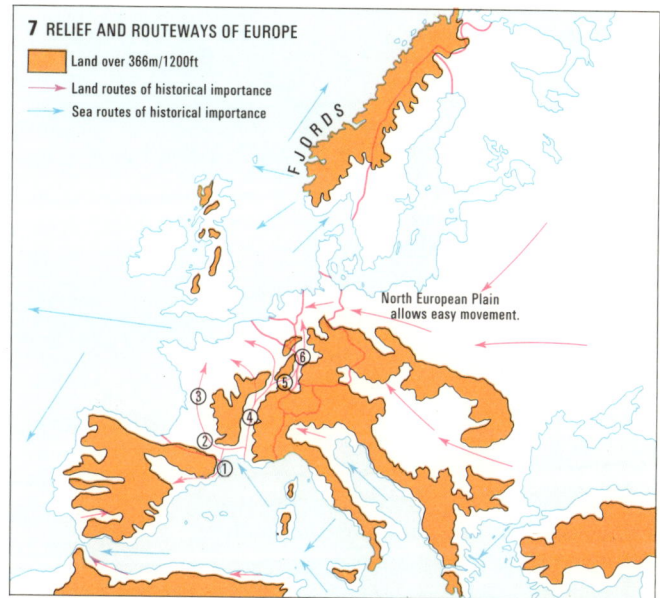

7 RELIEF AND ROUTEWAYS OF EUROPE

Land over 366m/1200ft
Land routes of historical importance
Sea routes of historical importance

F J O R D S

North European Plain allows easy movement.

Fig.8 Drainage of Europe

8a Name the rivers 1-10.

8b Name water areas A-E.

8c What do you notice about the rivers of Scandinavia?

8d Which countries are served by each of the following:
   Rhine, Elbe, Loire, Rhone?

8e On which rivers do the following ports stand:
   Rotterdam, Hamburg, Goteborg, Bremen, Le Havre, Bordeaux, Antwerp?

Fig.9 A typical valley glacier

9a Note the over-deepened U shaped valley and all the other glacial features illustrated. Name 2 areas in Europe where these might be seen.

9b Find photographs of uplands in your example areas.

9c Where would you go in Great Britain to find such examples?

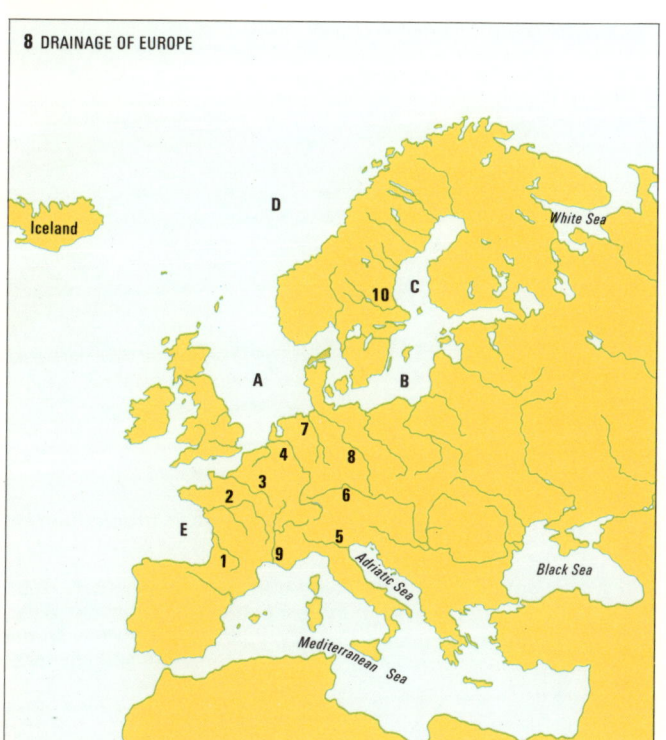

8 DRAINAGE OF EUROPE

Iceland

White Sea

D

10   C

A   B

7
4   8
3
2   6
E
1   9   5
Adriatic Sea
Black Sea
Mediterranean Sea

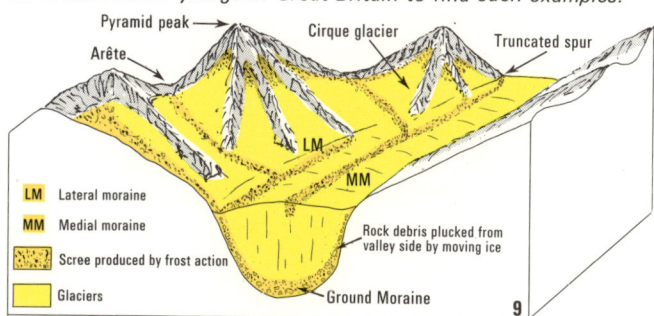

Pyramid peak
Cirque glacier
Truncated spur
Arête
LM
MM

LM Lateral moraine
MM Medial moraine
Scree produced by frost action
Glaciers
Rock debris plucked from valley side by moving ice
Ground Moraine
9

The climate of any area is the average of weather conditions (temperature, rainfall, winds, atmospheric pressure, sunshine hours, clouds) over a period of at least 35 years.

The controls of climate are latitude (position in relation to sun and world wind system), altitude, distance from the warming or cooling influence of (and dampness of winds from) the sea, air masses of the region. Air masses are great cells of air having distinctive characteristics of dampness (humidity) and temperature. Climate will depend very much on the frequency of various air masses over the given region (see figs. 14 and 16).

Special controls in Europe:
(1) The peninsularity of Europe (imagine that Africa were not there and this will be clear). Thus the sea has much influence.
(2) The uplands which are concentrated in the NW and South and which are very varied.
(3) The presence of the large landmass of Asia to the East which warms readily in summer and cools in winter.
(4) The position of the Polar and Arctic Fronts where air masses of different characteristics meet. Depressions form along the fronts.
(5) The prevailing westerly winds—warm, humid.
(6) The warm North Atlantic Drift.
Remember that high pressures tend to be stable weather zones. Low pressures attract winds and unstable conditions.

10 JANUARY: PRESSURE, WINDS AND RAIN

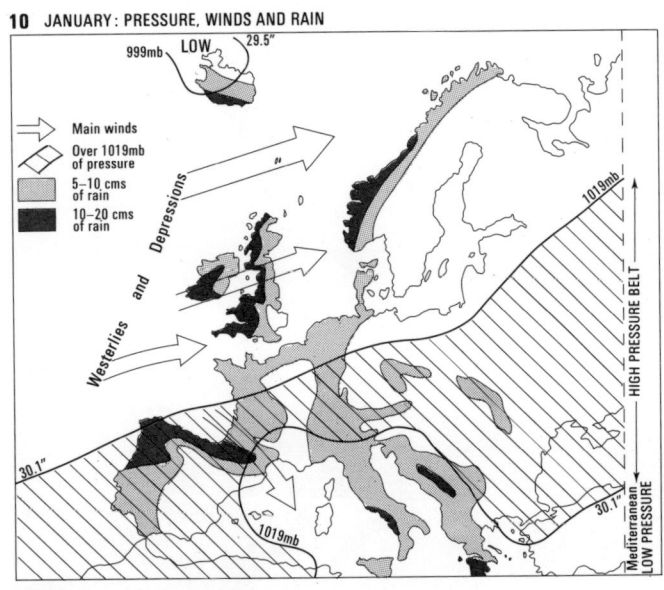

Fig.10 January. Pressures, winds, rainfall

10a Which areas have 10-20 cms of rain?
10b What are the sources of the rain?
10c Name three rain-shadow areas.
10d Describe the location of the high pressure belt.
10e What influence has relief on the rainfall of N and W Europe?

12 JULY: PRESSURE, WINDS AND RAIN

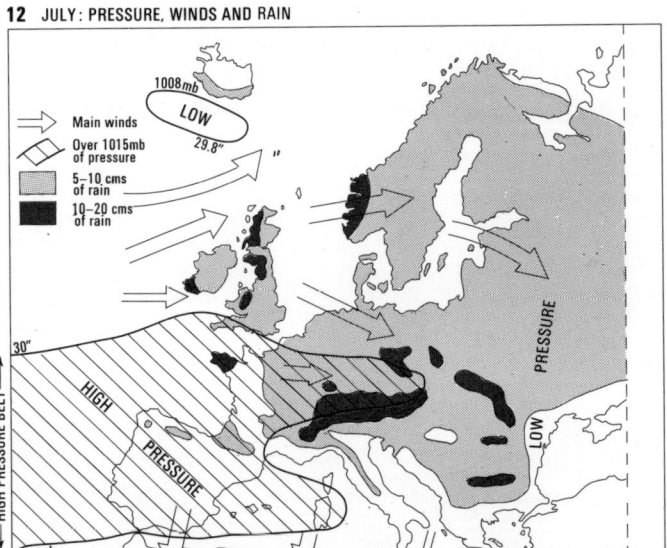

Fig.12 July. Pressures, winds, rainfall

12a Describe the main differences between (i) winds (ii) rainfall - in the January and July conditions. (E.g. do winds blow further inland? Why? Does Eastern Europe receive most rain in July or in January? Why? Does the Mediterranean area have most rain in July or January? Why?)

11 JANUARY

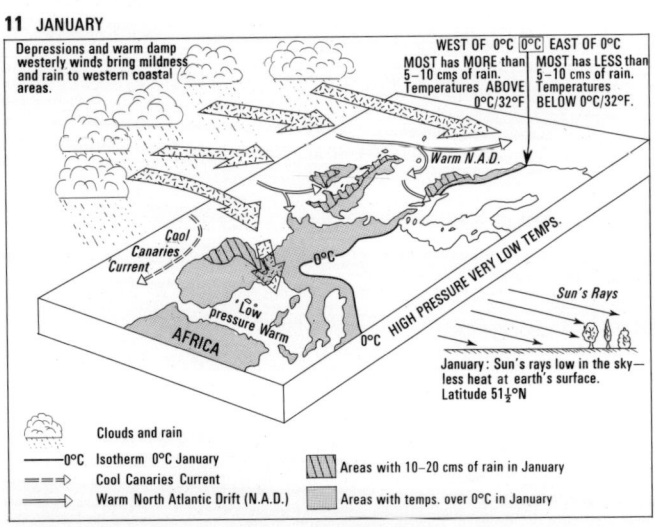

Fig.11 January. Pressures, winds and rainfall in block diagram form

11a Describe the influence of the sea and N.A.D. on the temperature of Maritime Europe.
11b Why is there high pressure in Continental Europe?

13 JULY

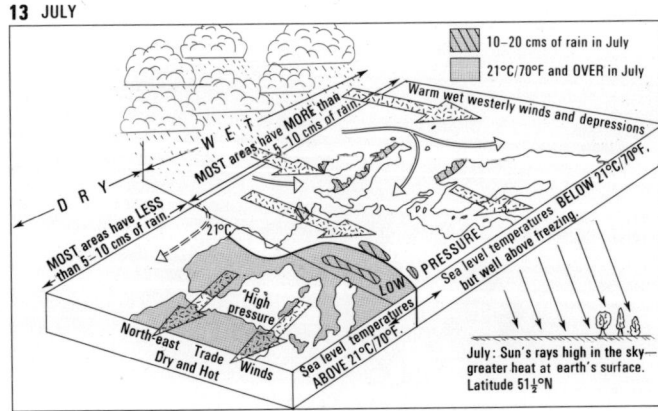

Fig.13 July. Pressures, winds and rainfall in block diagram form

13a Which is warmer, Southern Europe or the rest of Europe? Why?
13b Which is wetter, Southern Europe or the rest of Europe? Why?
13c Find a map in your atlas showing annual total rainfall for Europe. Broadly, which parts of Europe have rainfall of 150cms (60") per year?

North West coastal Europe experiences a Maritime Climate. That is, it is very much under the influence of airstreams from over the sea. As the sea warms and cools more slowly than the land it has a warming influence in winter and a cooling influence in summer.

Winds from over the sea tend to be warm and of high relative humidity: rain is brought to coastal areas, and is especially heavy on uplands (relief rain).

East Interior Europe is away from these maritime influences from sea winds, and has a Continental Climate. It experiences little warming or cooling influence from sea winds, and therefore winters are cold and summers are hot. Rain falls mainly in summer and declines in total from West to East.

Fig.14 Climates of Europe
Arctic. Long severe winters. Cold winds from the North (Polar). Short, warm summers. Slight rain (summer). Snow in winter.
Cold. Similar.
W. Margin Cool Temperate. Mild winters, warm summers. Plentiful rain all year round.
Cool Temperate transitional. Between the Maritime West Coast and the Continental Interior is a half-way area where both types of climate mingle, and it is shown as the 'Cool Temperate Transitional' on fig. 14. Colder winters than W Margin. Summers warmer. Rainfall (20-25", 508-635 mm, per year) especially in summer. Snow in winter.
'Mediterranean'—W Margin Warm Temperate. Warm wet winters. Hot dry summers.
Cool Temperate Continental

14a Describe the location of (i) the Arctic (ii) the Western Margin Cool Temperate climates.
14b What climates are experienced in Norway and Sweden?
14c Which part of the area we are taking as North Western Europe has a Mediterranean climate?
14d Describe the Cool Temperate Continental climate.

Fig.16 Air masses of Europe
The climate of a place may be described as the average of the air masses it experiences. Europe is influenced by five air masses, and three frontal zones of which two—Arctic and Polar—are especially important. The cyclones or *depressions* which dominate much of N and W European climate form along the Polar Front.

	AIR MASS	SOURCE	CHARACTERISTICS
1	Arctic (A)	Arctic Ocean	very cold
2	Polar Maritime (Pm)	North Atlantic	wet, cold
3	Polar Continental (Pc)	Siberia	winter dry, cold. summer dry, warm
4	Tropical Maritime (Tm)	Central Atlantic	wet, warm
5	Tropical Continental (Tc)	Africa	dry, warm (summer only)

16a Describe the changes in the positions of Arctic and Polar Fronts from winter to summer.

Fig.17 Natural vegetation of Europe
Little remains of the natural vegetation of the deciduous forest and Mediterranean lands, and most of the Steppe has been farmed.
17a Find out the names of four deciduous and four coniferous trees.
17b Examine the climate map fig.14 and the relief map fig.7 and note any relationships you may observe.
17c Try to find pictures of (i) tundra (ii) coniferous forest land.
17d Why are coniferous trees found at high altitudes in warm climates as well as at high latitudes in colder climates?

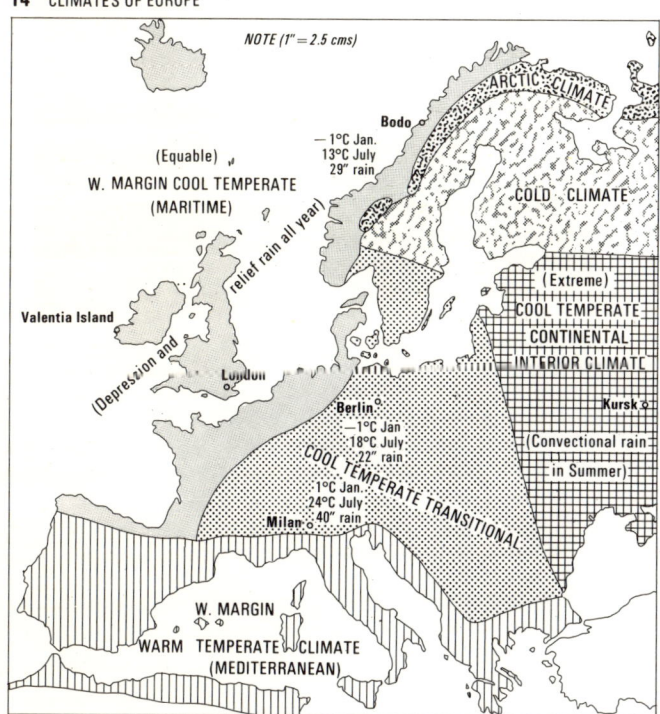

14 CLIMATES OF EUROPE

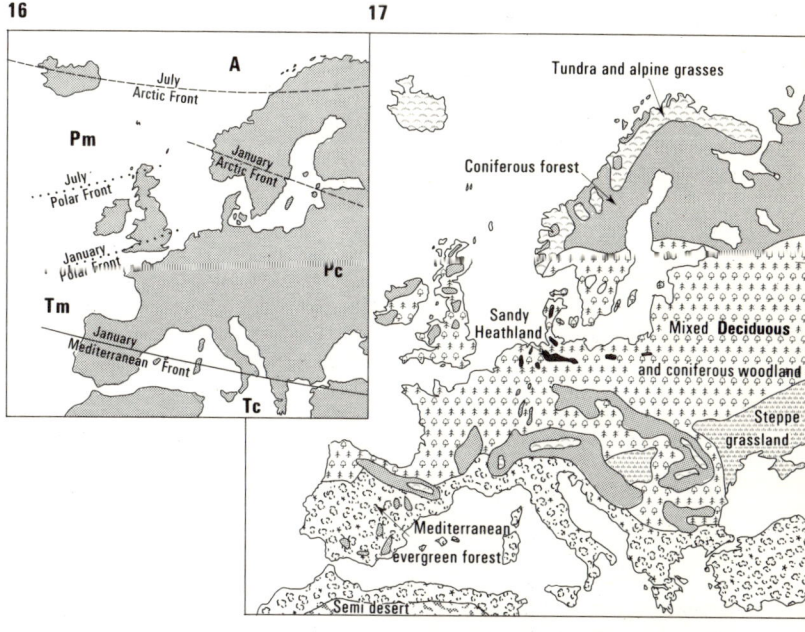

16   17

Fig.15 illustrates important characteristics and differences between Maritime and Continental European Climates

15a Does temperate range increase or decrease towards the East?
15b Which place receives most rainfall?
15c Why is temperature range only 8°C at Valentia Island?
15d What are the temperature figures for January and July for London?
15e Illustrate and describe the differences between the January and July temperatures for Bodo, Berlin and Milan. (see fig.14).

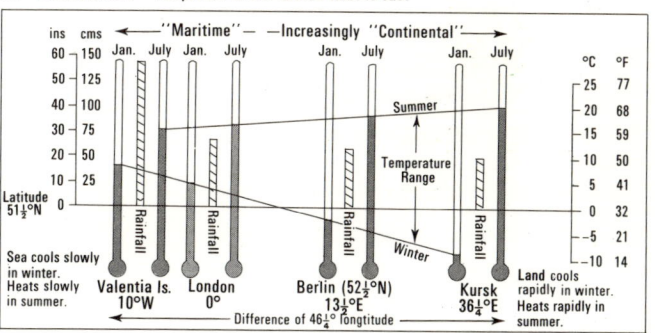

15 COMPARISON — Temperatures and rainfall west to east

The way in which farmers use their land—the crops they grow and the livestock they rear—depends on a considerable number of factors which we might divide into factors of physical geography and sociological factors, i.e. to do with Human Society.

Under Physical Factors or Controls would come—
(i) climate (especially length of growing season with temperatures over 6°C, and the season and quantity of precipitation i.e. rain and/or snow);
(ii) soil (whether thin or deep, rich or poor in valued plant minerals, its drainage);
(iii) relief and aspect (flat, steep, high/low, facing North, South, East or West).

All these influence what it is physically possible to grow or rear anywhere, and to what extent particular crops or livestock could be developed profitably under any given system of farming.

Under Human Factors would come:
(1) The legacy of past land use and systems of farming.
(2) The expected prices of various crops and farm animals (the results of the demands for them and the supplies of them—and therefore competition from other parts of the country and the world).
(3) The transport system and methods.
(4) Any government controls and subsidies.
(5) The skill and knowledge of the farmers.

It is not therefore by any means a simple task to describe and account for the pattern of farming which is found today in any part of the world, and it is especially difficult where physical and human factors are varied and complicated as they are in Europe.
The maps on this page indicate only the broad agricultural pattern of N and W Europe and the crude controls of physical geography may be discerned by studying them together with earlier maps of relief and climate. It is not possible to make much useful comment on the human factors at this stage but some ideas for you to consider are suggested by some of the questions.

Fig.18 emphasises the climatic differences between North and South, East and West in Europe which have strong influences on agriculture

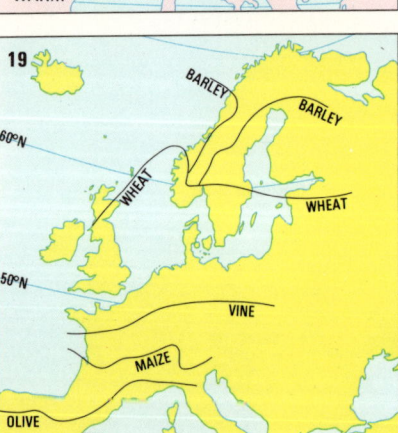

18a Why (i) does the length of time with temperatures above the base temperature required for plant growth (6°C/43°F) decrease from South to North and to the East?
(ii) does rainfall decrease to the East?
18b What is the main climatic disadvantage of the Mediterranean region?

Fig.19 shows the northern limits of reasonable cultivation

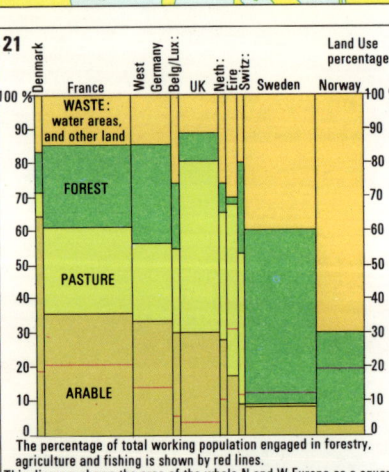

19a Relate figs.18 and 19 to each other.

Fig.20 Main areas by crops
20a The climatic controls for wheat and oats are shown. Find out the ideal physical conditions for the other crops named.

Fig.21 Land Use in West and North Europe
21a Which country has by far the greatest percentage of its land under (i) arable farming (ii) forests (iii) no form of agriculture? (Three different countries should be named.)
21b Which country has not even 1% under pasture?
21c Why has UK so small a percentage of its working population in agriculture?
21d Which country has as much as 30% of its working population in agriculture?
21e Which country has most arable land?
21f Suggest why the UK has so much pasture.

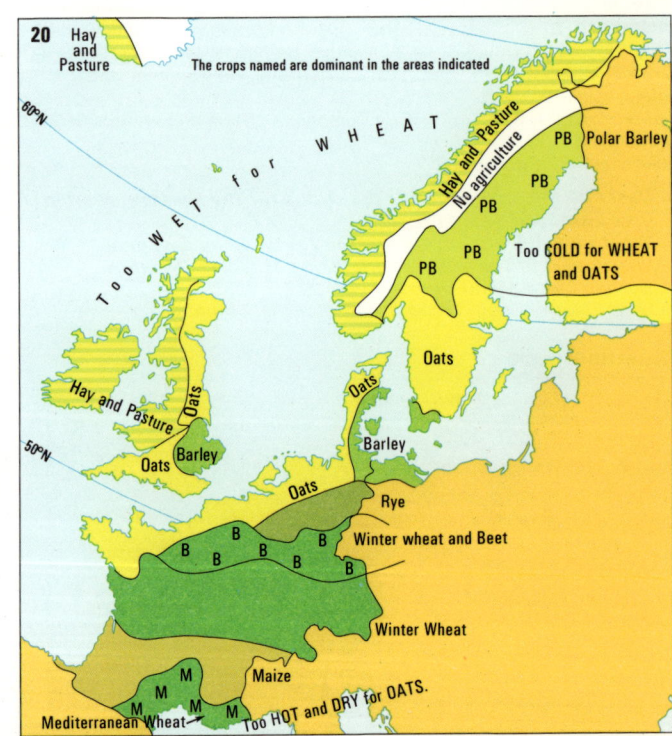

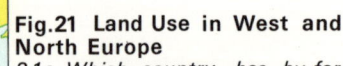

The crops named are dominant in the areas indicated

Fig.22 Agricultural statistics (look also at fig.21)
A great deal can be learned by examining these statistics—below are a few questions for you to start with. Invent ten more and answer them.

22a Which is the chief cereal producer?
22b Which is the chief potato producer?
22c Why has Norway so very little wheat output?
22d Which country has more pigs than people?

22	Production of selected crops and livestock in N and W Europe and in Italy								
	Crops in million metric tons : Animals in millions								
	PRODUCT								
	Wheat	Barley	Oats and mixed cereals	Potatoes	Sugar Beet	Wines	Cattle	Pigs	Sheep
Germany	6.0	4.9	4.2	18.8	13.4	5.9	14.2	19.3	0.9
France	14.5	9.4	3.0	9.8	16.0	62.5	21.8	10.6	10.6
Italy	9.5	0.2	0.4	3.9	11.8	68.2	9.6	9.2	9.1
Netherlands	0.6	0.4	0.3	4.8	5.0	–	3.8	5.2	0.3
Belgium	0.8	0.5	0.3	1.6	3.9	–	2.7	3.0	–**
Luxembourg	–*	–*	–*	–*		0.1	0.1	0.1	–**
E.E.C. Totals	31.4	15.4	8.2	38.9	50.1	136.7	52.2	47.4	20.9
UK ☆	3.6	8.7	1.2	6.8	6.8	–	12.1	7.3	28.0
Denmark ☆	0.4	4.5	0.8	0.8	2.2	–	3.1	7.9	0.1
Sweden	0.9	1.5	1.3	1.3	1.7	–	2.0	2.0	0.3
Norway	–*	0.5	0.1	0.9	–	–	1.0	0.6	2.0
Switzerland	0.3	0.1	–*	1.0	0.4	0.8	1.8	1.8	0.3

☆ New E.E.C. members   ** fewer than 100,000 animals   * Less than 100,000 metric tons

The percentage of total working population engaged in forestry, agriculture and fishing is shown by red lines.
This diagram shows the area of the whole N and W Europe as a square. The area of each country is shown correctly. The percentages of each country in each of four categories of Land Use are shown by colours. NOTE 64% of Italy is agricultural land of which 74% is arable. 20% of her labour is in farming

LAND USE IN NORTH AND WEST EUROPE

The Industrial Revolution, which developed first in England in the mid 18th century, led on from the development of water-powered machinery in the textile industries to steam-powered production of many articles in factories on a large scale, and to canals, railways and steamships in the 19th century. It depended, among other things, on the opening up of wide markets at home and overseas.

At first the basis of industrial power was coal, and Europe was well-supplied with rich coalfields. Since 1920, however, it has been necessary to import oil and natural gas and to develop more hydro-electric and atomic power.

Iron ore was also plentiful and, with the discovery of a way of smelting it with coke in place of charcoal, a large iron and steel industry soon blossomed.

Industries grew, inventions multiplied possibilities, new raw materials were imported and manufactured goods exported. Certain areas developed specialities of production as advantages of local raw materials and local skills exerted themselves, e.g. Sheffield for steel.

First in England, and then across the Channel in the extensive coalfield of NE France and Belgium, thick smoke began to pour from the chimneys of ever-increasing numbers of factories and industrial home-steads, and large areas of industrial landscape spread around the main source of power (coal) and metal (iron ore).

Not until the many separate kingdoms of what is now Germany were united in a single Prussian State in 1870 did this type of landscape develop there. After that date however the German Government, anxious to join the 'Steel Age', encouraged rapid industrial growth and soon the German coalfields (find them) were as smoke covered and grimy as any—especially the Ruhr which drew on the enormous local coalfield, and the iron-ores of Lorraine which Germany then controlled. The new sources of power, developed mainly in this century, of electricity (thermal and h.e.p.), natural gas, oil and atomic power, together with distribution by cable (e.g. National Grid in UK) and pipe line, have released industry from the necessity of a raw material or coal location, so that factories are now widespread and practically no town is without industrial development of some kind.

23 COAL AND IRON ORE (Excluding Italy)

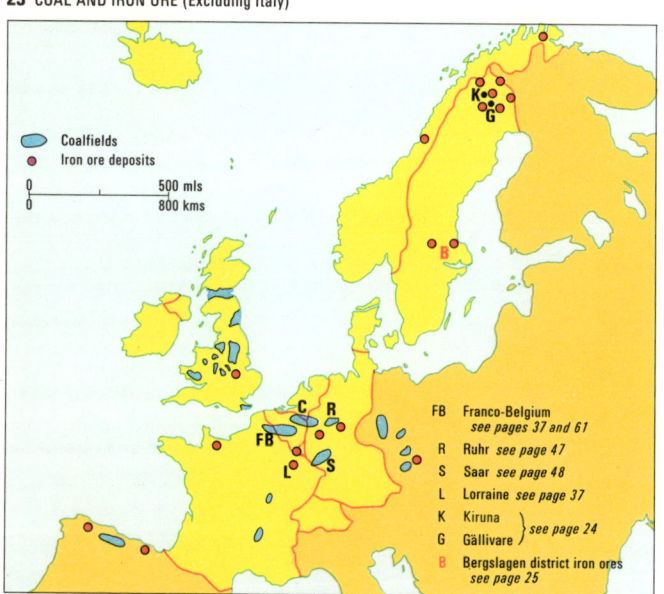

Fig.23 Coal and iron ore fields of N and W Europe

23a Find and note the name and location of all the lettered coal-fields of mainland Western Europe.
23b In which countries is iron ore found?
23c By which letter is the Campine (Belgium), Limburg (Netherlands), Aachen (German) coalfield indicated on the map?
23d Which countries have (i) iron but no coal?
(ii) coal but no iron?

Fig.24 Main industrial areas (very broadly shown)

24a In which country lacking coal is there a considerable 'industrial area'?
24b Suggest a likely source of power in Norway, Sweden and Switzerland.

In these three countries the grimy industrial landscape common with coal-based industry has never developed. The siting of their industry is less concentrated and their industrial areas are more like 'garden cities'.

Fig.25 Main areas with high population densities

NB Exclude references to British Isles in questions 25a and 25b.

25a Can any relationships be seen between the three Figs., 23, 24 and 25? Describe these.
25b Are any areas with high population density also areas without high industrial activity? (Figs. 24 and 25.)
25c Name (i) 2 countries which have only small parts of their total area under high population density
(ii) 2 countries which have very little of their total area which is not densely populated.

24

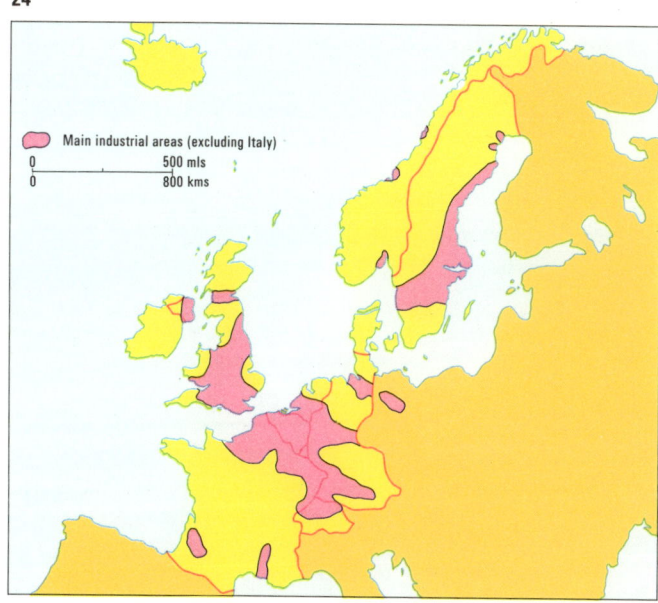

25 POPULATION – Main areas (Excluding Italy)

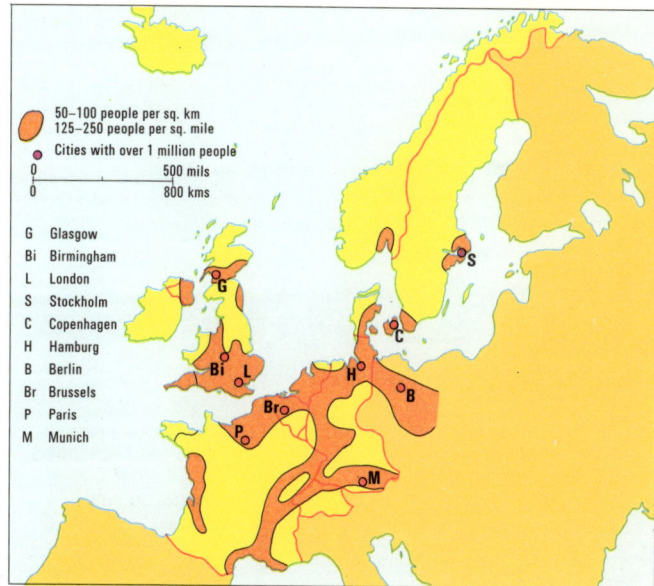

The development of the great industries was based on the possession of large reserves of two vital raw materials—coal and iron ore.

Fig. 26 (i-iv) illustrates the importance of these in N and W Europe and in products largely dependent upon them—crude steel and electric power. (Note that 100% of Norway's, 96% of Switzerland's, 87% of Sweden's and 44% of France's total electric power was h.e.p. and not thermal.)

What is h.e.p? How is thermal electricity produced?

Fig.26 Coal, iron ore, crude steel and electric power

26a *By what percentage did the N and W European share of total world production of the following increase or decrease since 1960? Coal, iron ore, crude steel, electric power.*

26b *Did the total output of each of these increase or decrease and by how much? (Deal with each separately.)*

26c *(i) Which had its output very nearly doubled? (ii) Why?*

26d *Was the output of coal in N and W Europe greater in 1960?*

26e *For which products did the output of Japan increase as percentages of World Total Production?*

26f *Which of the four products are more important in output total in UK than in (i) Germany (ii) France (iii) Sweden (iv) Japan?*

26g *In which products do the combined outputs of N and W European countries exceed those of (i) USA (ii) USSR?*

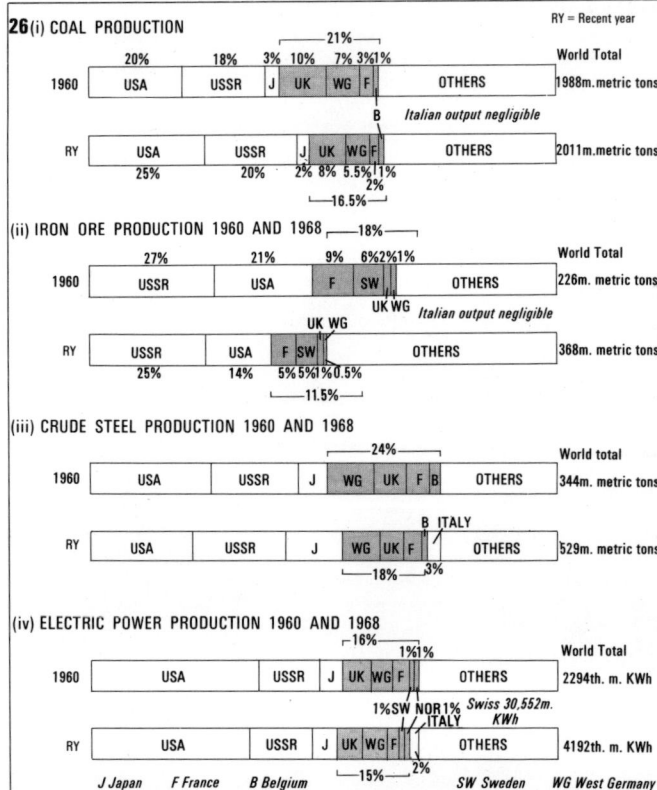

26(i) COAL PRODUCTION — RY = Recent year

1960: USA (20%), USSR (18%), J (3%), UK (10%), WG (7%), F (3%)(1%) [21%], OTHERS — World Total 1988m. metric tons — B Italian output negligible

RY: USA (25%), USSR (20%), J (2%), UK (8%), WG (5.5%)(1%)(2%), OTHERS — 2011m. metric tons — [16.5%]

(ii) IRON ORE PRODUCTION 1960 AND 1968

1960: USSR (27%), USA (21%), F (9%), SW (6%)(2%)(1%) [18%], OTHERS — World Total 226m. metric tons — UK WG — Italian output negligible

RY: USSR (25%), USA (14%), F (5%), SW (5%)(1%)(0.5%), UK WG, OTHERS — 368m. metric tons — [11.5%]

(iii) CRUDE STEEL PRODUCTION 1960 AND 1968

1960: USA, USSR, J, WG, UK, F, B [24%], OTHERS — World total 344m. metric tons

RY: USA, USSR, J, WG, UK, F, B ITALY, OTHERS — 529m. metric tons — [18%] 3%

(iv) ELECTRIC POWER PRODUCTION 1960 AND 1968

1960: USA, USSR, J, UK, WG, F (1%)(1%) [16%], OTHERS — World Total 2294th. m. KWh — 1%SW NOR 1% Swiss 30,552m. ITALY KWh

RY: USA, USSR, J, UK, WG, F (1%)(2%) [15%], OTHERS — 4192th. m. KWh

J Japan   F France   B Belgium   SW Sweden   WG West Germany

Fig.27 Development of North Sea oil and gas Resources

Until very recently W and N Europe depended almost entirely on imports for oil and natural gas. Today new resources of both are being discovered and exploited in the North Sea and parts of its coastal lands as shown in fig. 27.

27a *In which sections have (i) natural gas wells (ii) oil wells been developed?*

27b *Why was the pipeline from Ekofisk laid to the refinery at Teeside instead of Norway?*

27c *If you have natural gas in your area (i) when did it come (ii) where is it from (iii) how is it brought (iv) is it more powerful (i.e. has it a higher calorific value) than coal-gas? (Ask at your local gas office.)*

Fig.28 Natural gas output

COUNTRY	1965 in million metric tons	RY in million metric tons
United Kingdom	189	2200
Belg/Lux	79	65
France	5048	5682
West Germany	3219	7064
Netherlands	1827	14056

28a *Plot the above figures as bar-graphs using different colours for the two years.*

28b *By how many millions of metric tons has each country increased or decreased its output?*

28c *What influence do, and will, such changes have on coal outputs?*

28d *The bulk of European oil demands (200 million metric tons per year) are met by imports mainly from Middle Eastern and N. African countries. What influences might big oil finds in the North Sea have on European trade and relations with Middle Eastern lands?*

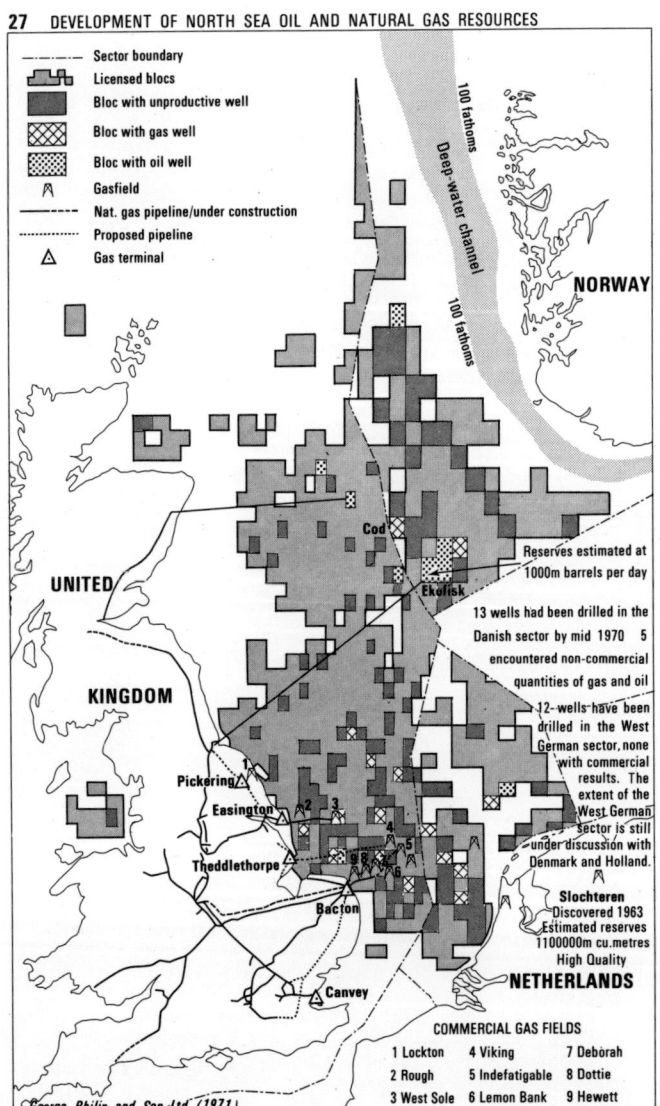

27 DEVELOPMENT OF NORTH SEA OIL AND NATURAL GAS RESOURCES

- —— Sector boundary
- Licensed blocs
- Bloc with unproductive well
- Bloc with gas well
- Bloc with oil well
- Gasfield
- —— Nat. gas pipeline/under construction
- .... Proposed pipeline
- △ Gas terminal

100 fathoms
Deep-water channel
100 fathoms

NORWAY

Cod

UNITED

Ekofisk

Reserves estimated at 1000m barrels per day

13 wells had been drilled in the Danish sector by mid 1970 5 encountered non-commercial quantities of gas and oil

KINGDOM

12 wells have been drilled in the West German sector, none with commercial results. The extent of the West German sector is still under discussion with Denmark and Holland.

Pickering △

Easington △

Theddlethorpe △

Bacton △

Slochteren Discovered 1963 Estimated reserves 1100000m cu.metres High Quality

Canvey △

NETHERLANDS

COMMERCIAL GAS FIELDS

1 Lockton   4 Viking   7 Deborah
2 Rough   5 Indefatigable   8 Dottie
3 West Sole   6 Lemon Bank   9 Hewett

George Philip and Son Ltd. (1971)

EEC (European Economic Community) and EFTA (European Free Trade Assn.) are basically economic groupings. The EEC grew out of the Coal and Steel Community proposed by R. Schuman of France in 1950 and formally created by treaty in August 1952. This original idea was for the formation of a Common Market in steel, iron and coal in which obstacles to free trade (such as tax on imports or on exports, called 'tariffs' or 'duties'), should be removed, and, as a result, over the years since 1952 these tariffs and other restrictions have in fact been taken off. Members of the C and S Community (the Six) were: Belgium, Netherlands, and Luxembourg (the Be-ne-lux countries), W Germany, Italy and France.

In 1957 more extensive economic co-operation was agreed by The Six at the Treaty of Rome—all barriers to trade among themselves were to be removed for all commodities, and all members were to have the same tariffs and other controls over trade with countries beyond the Six. Political ties were also established, and the EEC came into being (see fig. 29).

Since 1961 Great Britain, Norway, Denmark (all EFTA members) and the Irish Republic expressed wishes to join the Six—thus making a Community of Ten—especially in order to enjoy free access to its enormous market of about 188 million people. In 1972, however, one of these countries voted against joining the EEC (now the community of Nine): the others joined on January 1st 1973.

Fig.29. West European Economic and Strategic Groups

29a Identify and list the original members of (i) EFTA (ii) EEC
29b Which members of EFTA have not applied for entry to EEC?
29c What do the letters EEC and EFTA mean?
29d Which of the EFTA countries maintain statutory neutrality and therefore would not wish to join NATO?
29e List the 'Ten'. Which one voted in 1972 against joining the EEC?

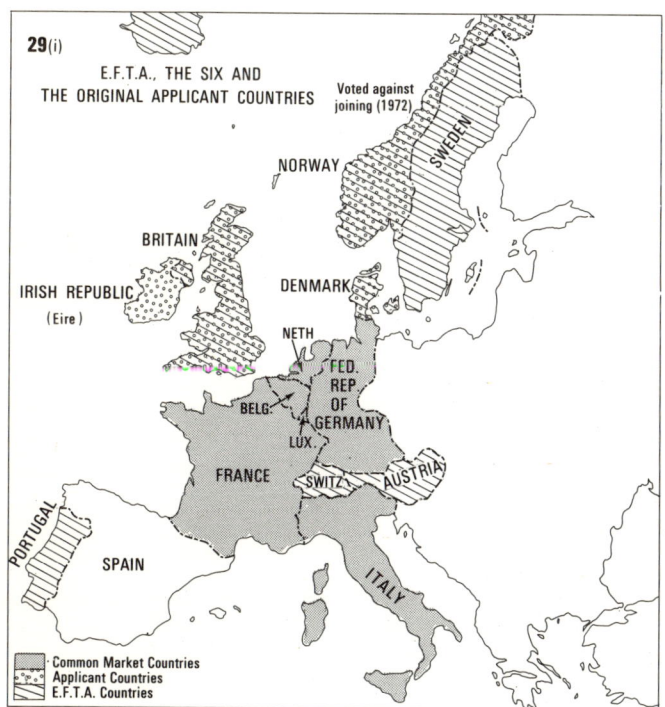

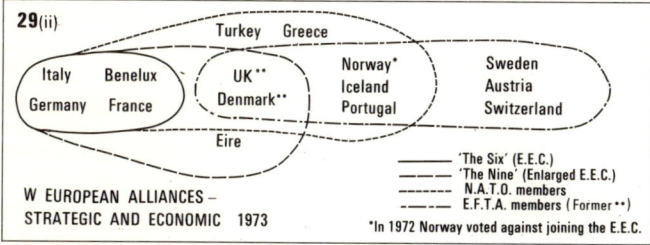

Fig. 30 The Community of 'Nine' compared with the USA, USSR and Japan

The arguments against joining the EEC have usually been concerned with a fear that national control over a country's political life as well as much of its economic life would be lost and that effective control would pass to the Council of Ministers. The Council, it is argued, would not necessarily have the special interests of any single country so strongly in mind as would the national government of that country.

Examine the bar-graphs 30 (i) - (v)

30a What is the combined population of the Nine? Is it greater than (i) the USSR, (ii) the USA, (iii) Japan?
30b How much larger is the population (the 'market') of the Nine than that of EFTA?
30c Compare the outputs of the Nine with those of the USSR, USA and Japan (each separately) of (i) steel, (ii) motor vehicles (iii) energy.

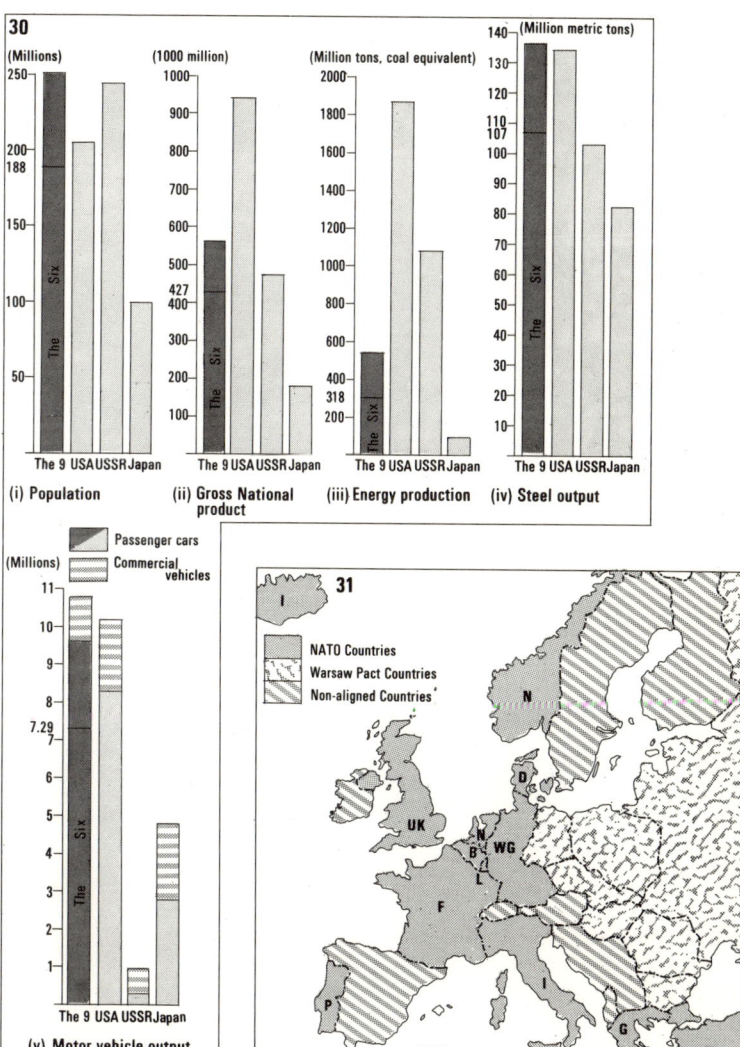

Fig.31 NATO Countries [see also fig 29. (ii)]

NATO (North Atlantic Treaty Organisation) was created in 1949 in order to organise a common system of defence among its members against any attack from any quarter on any member. Its headquarters are now in Brussels.

31a Name the member countries of NATO as shown in fig.31 Non-European members are USA and Canada.
31b Which European countries belong neither to NATO nor the Warsaw Pact (which was set up in 1955 as a Communist counterpart for NATO)?

Fig.32 Area and population

32a By how many sq. km. is (i) Sweden larger than Denmark, (ii) Norway smaller than Sweden, (iii) UK larger than Denmark, (iv) Norway larger than UK?
32b Work out and compare the population densities for each.

Fig.33 Relief

The physical landscape owes its present features to (i) the early Caledonian folding (ii) the prolonged erosion which reduced the folds to near sea-level (iii) the fracturing, tilting and sinking in various parts during the Alpine folding period, when, in particular, the west side of the Scandinavian block was raised to form a steep west face and gentler slope to the east (see fig. 33 inset) (iv) the volcanic outpourings of the Alpine period in the northern islands, Iceland and the Kjölen Mountains (v) the advances and retreats of the ice sheets and valley glaciers during the recent Ice Age. Uplands were eroded and stripped bare of soil: lowlands were strewn with glacial deposits (boulder clay, sands and gravels) (vi) the adjustments in levels of land and sea which have taken place (and still do) as a result of first the great downward pressure of ice caps, and then its release on melting. Sea levels fell and rose as water was removed as snow, and returned later as melt-water.

33a Describe the distribution of highland in Scandinavia.
33b List 5 features of glacial erosion and 3 of deposition.
33c When ice sheets melt (i) does sea level rise or fall, (ii) does land level rise or fall?
33d Find out about and describe the formation of raised beaches using diagrams.

Raised beaches fringe the shores and offer flat fertile shelves for settlement and farming.

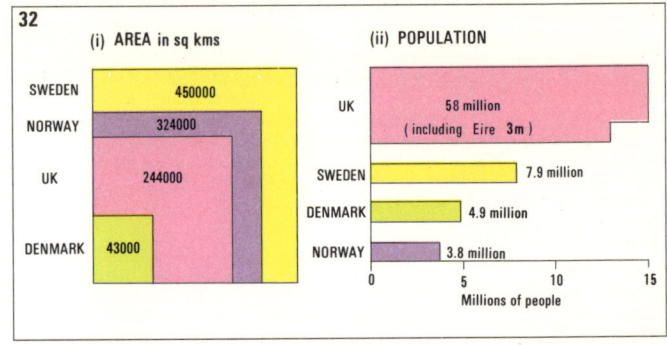

Fig.34 Isotherms for January and July

34a What is the chief characteristic of the North Atlantic Drift (NAD)?
34b State and give reasons for the ranges of temperature at (i)X (ii) Y (iii) Z
34c The Baltic Sea is low in salt content particularly in the Gulf of Bothnia. How does salinity influence the period of frozen seas?

Fig. 35 Effective rainfall

35a Which part of Scandinavia is characterised by mild temperatures and a considerable amount of effective rain per annum?
35b How is rainfall related to relief in Scandinavia (West and East sides)?

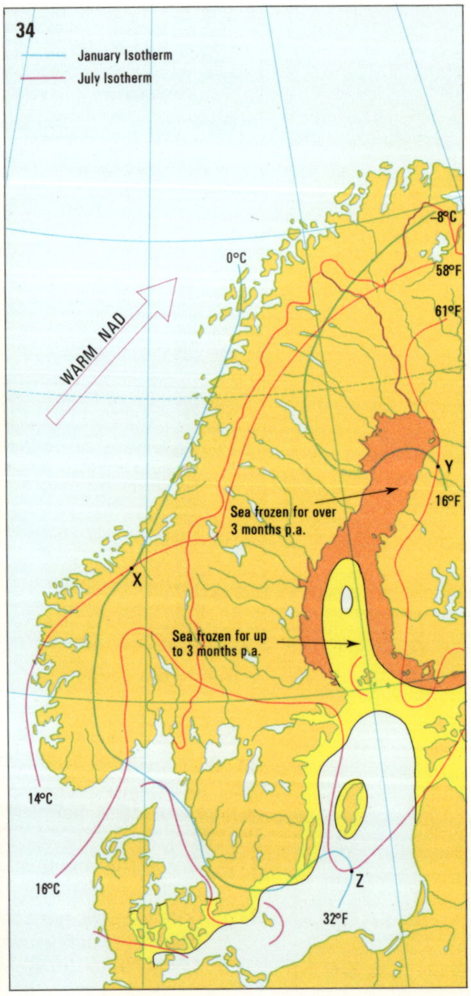

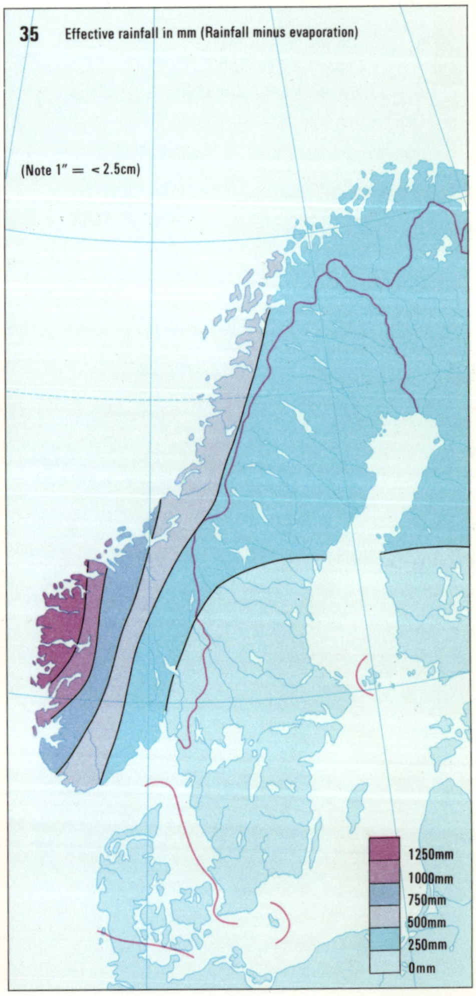

Fig.36 Drift and lake deposits

The ice, the melt-water from melting ice, and the post-glacial lakes of Scandinavia have provided a wide range of deposits which mask the solid geology beneath.

36a Which part is largely devoid of such deposits?
36b Find out and write a description about (i) boulder clay, (ii) drumlins, (iii) 'fluvio-glacial' deposits e.g. eskers.

Figs 37 and 38 Land Use   (See note under fig. 82)

The two figures illustrate the same data and reinforce each other.

37/38a What is the relief of the Tundra (waste) area?
37/38b Which of the three countries has the greatest percentage of its area (i) as arable land, (ii) under forest, (iii) as Tundra?
37/38c 1% of Norway is pasture. Is this a greater or smaller actual area than the 7.5% of Denmark which is pasture
37/38d Sweden has 8% arable and Denmark 65%. What does each equal in sq. km?
37/38e Describe the location of arable land, country by country.
37/38f What relationships do you notice between land use, relief and surface deposits (fig.36)?
37/38g Describe the inset diagram fig.37.

Fig.39 Distribution of population and main minerals

39a Describe as clearly as you can the location of areas of most people, country by country.
39b What land use is there in areas of low population?
39c Name the 2 'millionaire' cities St and C.
39d Which important mineral is most widespread in Scandinavia?
39e All the main towns are increasing in population though not all at the same rates. Among those increasing most rapidly are Copenhagen, Malmö, Oslo and Stockholm. The populations of all 3 countries are also increasing, yet in some areas population is declining. Suggest where the people from declining areas are moving to.
39f Identify towns lettered B, O, T, S, G, E, N. Note how settlements tend to line the valleys.

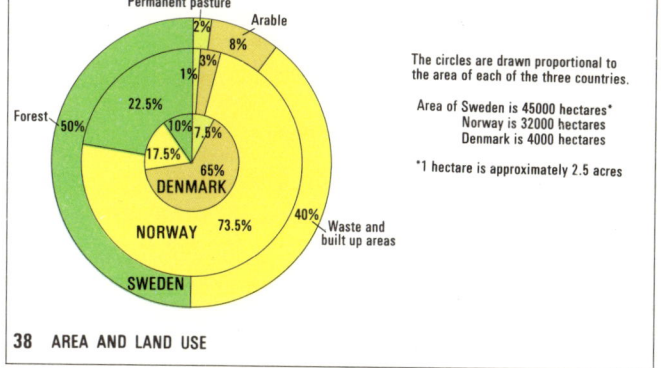

The circles are drawn proportional to the area of each of the three countries.

Area of Sweden is 45000 hectares*
Norway is 32000 hectares
Denmark is 4000 hectares

*1 hectare is approximately 2.5 acres

38   AREA AND LAND USE

---

36   DRIFT DEPOSITS OF THE ICE AGE

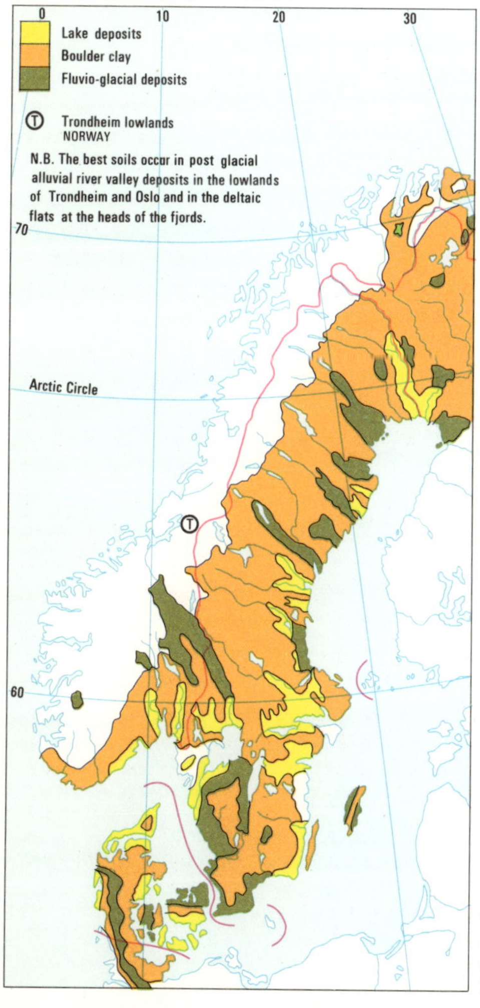

- Lake deposits
- Boulder clay
- Fluvio-glacial deposits

Ⓣ Trondheim lowlands
NORWAY

N.B. The best soils occur in post glacial alluvial river valley deposits in the lowlands of Trondheim and Oslo and in the deltaic flats at the heads of the fjords.

Arctic Circle

---

37   DOMINANT LAND USES

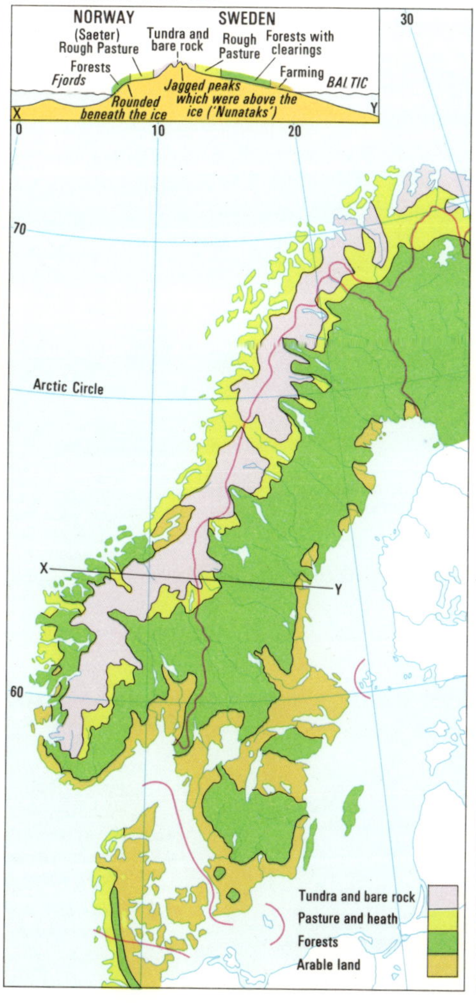

NORWAY   SWEDEN
(Saeter)   Tundra and   Rough   Forests with
Rough Pasture   bare rock   Pasture   clearings
Forests   Farming   BALTIC
Fjords   Jagged peaks
            which were above the
        Rounded   ice ('Nunataks')
    beneath the ice

X   Y

Arctic Circle

- Tundra and bare rock
- Pasture and heath
- Forests
- Arable land

---

39   POPULATION AND MINERALS

- Areas of decreasing population
- Areas of increasing population
- ○ 0–16% increase in town size
- ☐ 16% plus " " "
- Each dot represents
  200000 metric tons of iron ore
- ○ Cu Copper
- ○ S Silver
- ○ L Lead
- ○ Z Zinc
- ○ Mg Magnesium
- ○ Ti Titanium

St and C have over 1 million people

Sydvaranger
2.5 mill. met. tons

N   Kiruna
Sulitjelma
Z ○○ Cu   ○ Cu
Rana   Gallivare
0.8 mill met tons
○ Cu
SL
○ Z   ○ Cu
                  ○ S L
○ Cu   ○ S L   Cu S L Z
Cu ○ T ○ Z

Arctic Circle

○ L

B   LZ
                        ○ Cu
O
                        ☐ St
S ○ Mg   ○ S L Z
○ Ti

G

E   C

Fig.40 Position

40a Identify longitudes 1 and 2 and latitudes 3 and 4.
40b Name a town in Canada, a town in Alaska and a town in Scotland all of which occur within the same latitudes as Norway.

40

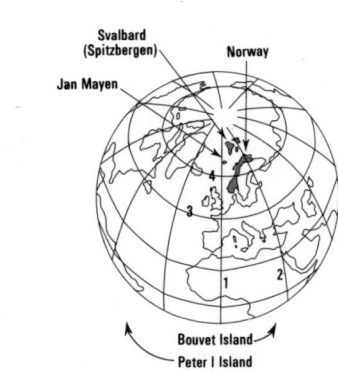

Fig.41 Dimensions

41a Find the latitude and longitudes shown on Fig.41. Through how many degrees of latitude does Norway stretch?
41b Norway has large fishing and merchant shipping industries. In what ways might the coastal features have encouraged this?
41c Find out, describe, and try to illustrate the features of fjords and how they are formed.
41d Examine an atlas map of UK. What are the maximum and minimum widths of UK?
41e How many degrees latitude is London South of Oslo?
41f Name any English town which lies as far from London as the Sogne fjord is long (182½km or 114 miles).
41g The midnight sun (what does this mean?) is visible at North Cape from 15 May to 31 July. Why is the sun above the horizon for so long a period in summer?

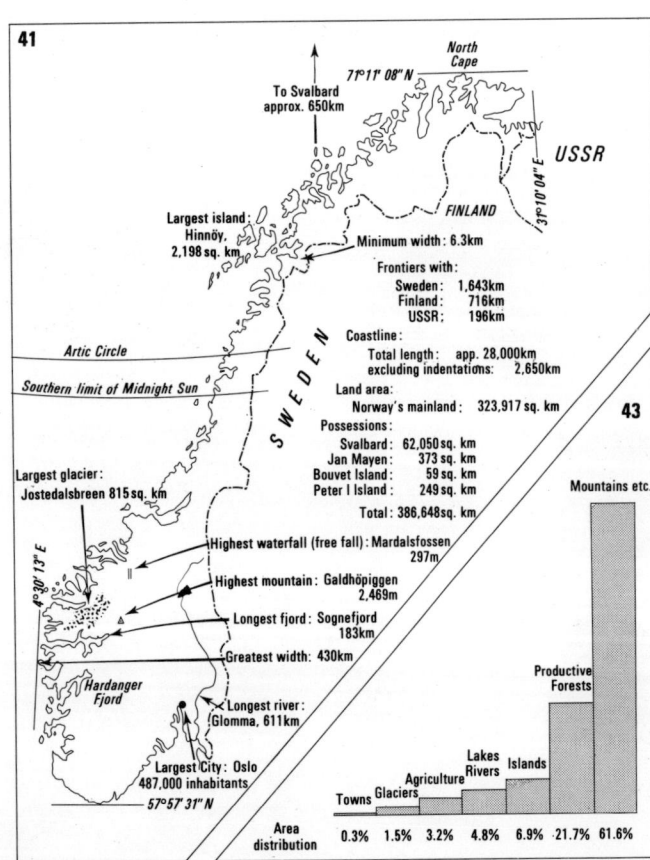

Fig.42 Climate

Typical Maritime climates are characterised by small temperature ranges, and rain all year: typical continental climates by high temperature ranges and maximum rain in summer.

42a What is the temperature range (Jan-July 'Means') (i) at Oslo, (ii) at Bergen, (iii) at Trondheim, (iv) at Bodo?
42b Which 2 places have the greater ranges and the smaller rainfall totals?
42c Which 2 places have maritime climates?
42d Which place has the mildest winters?
42e Suggest a reason for the relatively low rainfall of (i) Rorös in the deep Glomma Valley (ii) Oslo.
42f Do the figures for precipitation show that it (i) decreases or increases from South to North, (ii) decreases or increases from West to East? Though the East side is drier than the West, some precipitation is experienced at all times of the year. Is the East side also warmer than the West in summer?

Note A.   Temperature is influenced by position in relation to the sea and to altitude.
B.   Precipitation varies with the degree of exposure to the warm, wet, westerly winds and the frequent depressions which move in from the West. The heads of fjords may be sheltered and have less rain than their mouths (see Bergen and the head of Hardanger Fjord).
C.   The plateaux and mountains have a rather bleak difficult climate with cold snowy winters and cool summers.

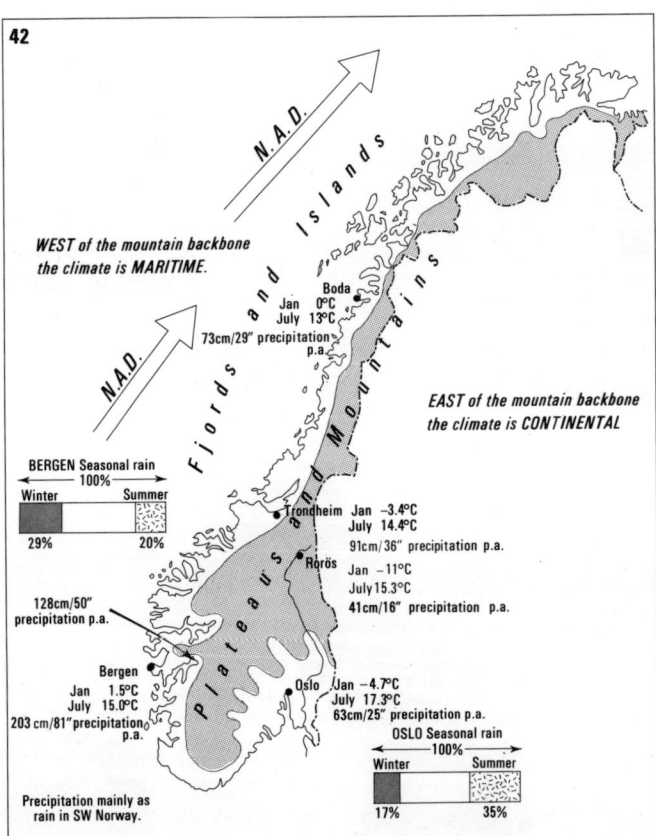

Fig.43 Land use (left)

43a Examine a relief map of Norway (fig.33) the climate maps and statistics given on figs 34, 35 and 42 and the surface deposits map fig. 36. Suggest reasons for (i) the small percentage of agricultural land (ii) the relatively large area of lakes and rivers.
43b What percentage of UK is agricultural land?
43c The islands are known as 'skerries'. Find out how they were (probably) formed.
43d In which area of Norway would you expect to find the most agricultural activity? Why?

The economy of Norway is based on (i) farming, (ii) fishing, (iii) forestry, (iv) industries (mainly metallic) using hydro-electric power (HEP). The increasing growth of industry using HEP has encouraged the drift of population to the SE where better paid jobs are easier to obtain. This increasing development of industry and the general attractions of urban life have led to changes in the distribution of the labour force between occupations and in the way in which the Gross National Product is made up.

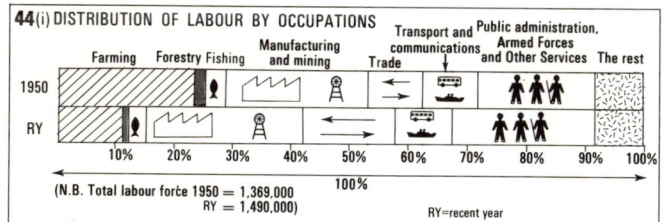

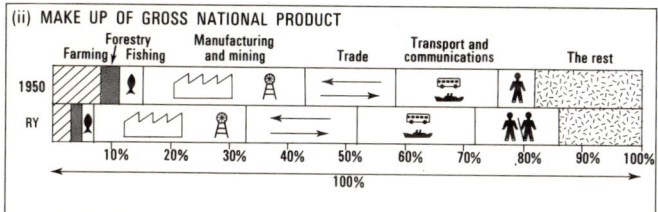

Fig.44 Labour distribution and the Gross National Product

44a   Describe the changes in percentages of total labour engaged in (i) agriculture, (ii) fishing, (iii) forestry, (iv) trade. Suggest reasons for the changes.
44b   Has industry (manufacturing) increased?
44c   Which categories in G N P have decreased in importance since 1950? Suggest reasons for the decreases.
44d   Has the share produced by trading increased? Why?

Fig.45 Typical fjord-side farm and general barn

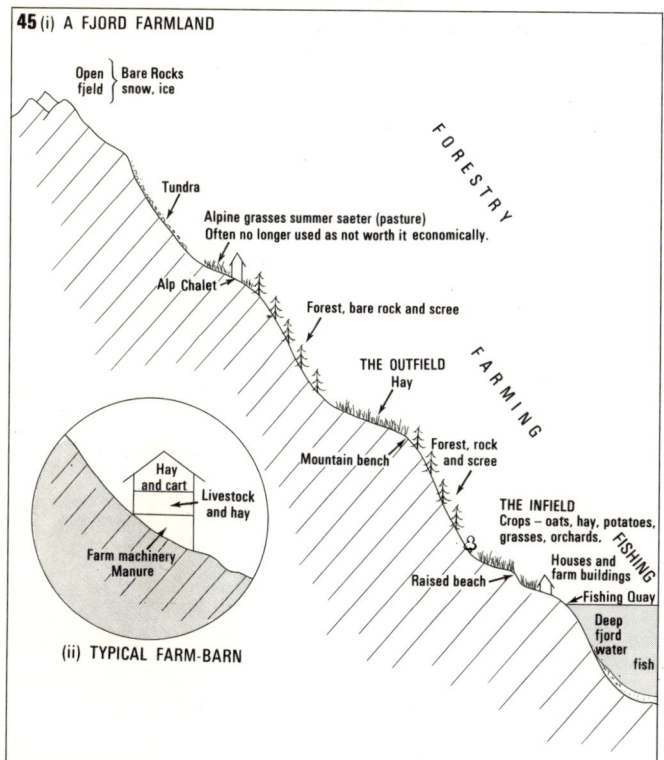

Fig.46 shows the increase In Norway's G N P since 1958

46a   Has the G N P doubled since 1968?
46b   Total population in 1958 was about 3·5 million and in 1968 was about 3·9 million. What was the G N P per head for each year?
GNP per head in 1974 was 5,950 US dollars

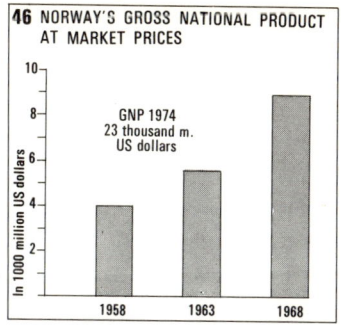

Farming

Traditionally, farming and other primary industries have been of greatest importance in Norway—we have already shown how this has not been true for many years and is becoming less and less true as industry and commerce increase. There are 3 main farming areas in Norway—these are shown on fig. 47 (v). Each is an area of better soil with flat areas capable of arable farming.

Fig.47 (i-iv) Distribution of some crops and livestock

47a   Describe as well as you can the distribution of (i) cattle, (ii) sheep, (iii) potatoes and oats.   About half the cattle are dairy animals in both Norway and UK.
47b   Norway is larger than UK. Compare the livestock totals and outputs shown on fig.47.
47c   What are the main disadvantages in farming over much of Norway? (Think of relief, soil, climate, transport.)

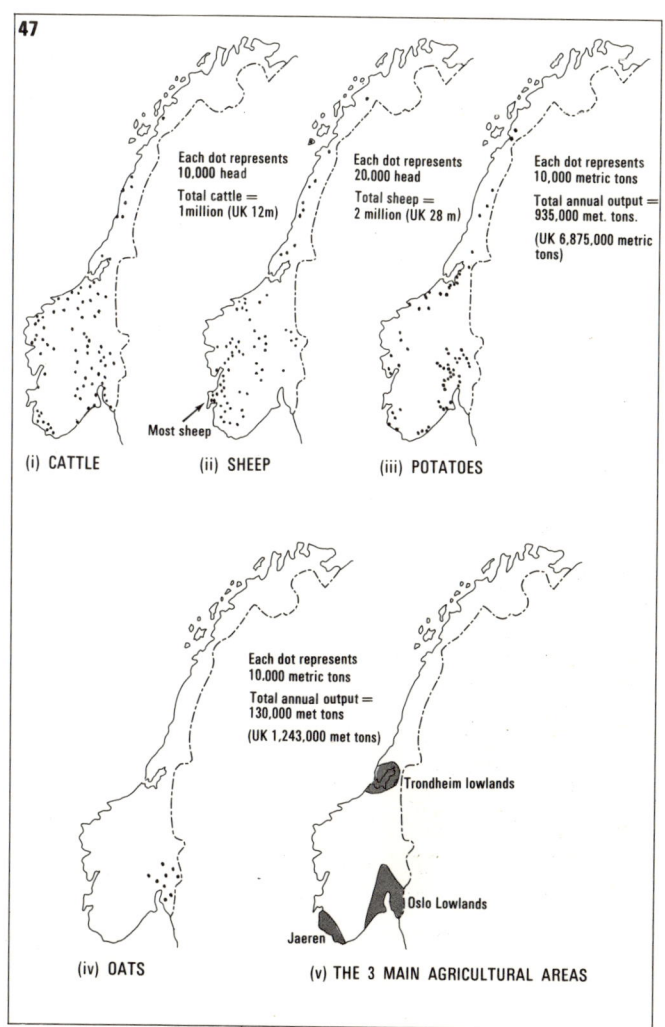

Fig.48 Manpower engaged in farming
48a What does the figure indicate?

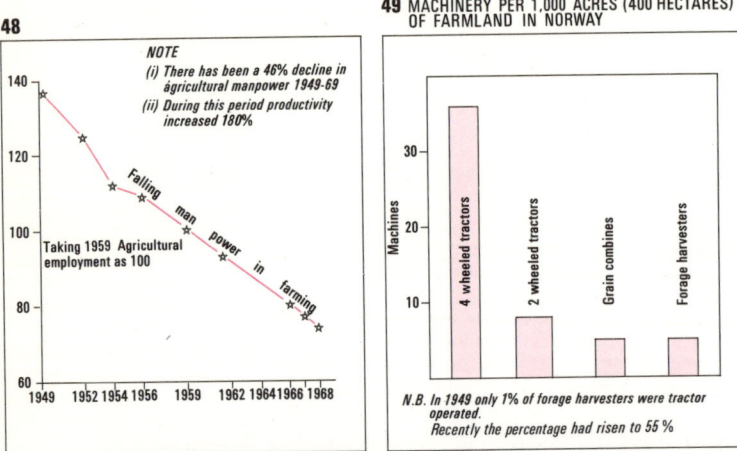

48

NOTE
(i) There has been a 46% decline in agricultural manpower 1949-69
(ii) During this period productivity increased 180%

Taking 1959 Agricultural employment as 100

Falling man power in farming

49 MACHINERY PER 1,000 ACRES (400 HECTARES) OF FARMLAND IN NORWAY

Machines — 4 wheeled tractors, 2 wheeled tractors, Grain combines, Forage harvesters

N.B. In 1949 only 1% of forage harvesters were tractor operated.
Recently the percentage had risen to 55%

Fig 49 Farm mechanisation
49a The figure suggests why it is possible for the numbers engaged in farming to fall although productivity has risen. Explain.

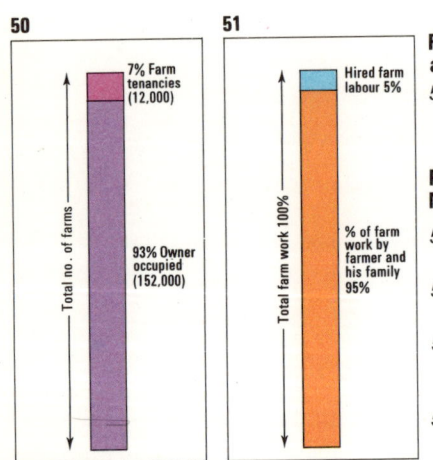

50
7% Farm tenancies (12,000)
Total no. of farms
93% Owner occupied (152,000)

51
Hired farm labour 5%
Total farm work 100%
% of farm work by farmer and his family 95%

Figs.50 and 51 The ownership and working of farms
50/51a Describe what the figure indicates about (i) farm ownership (ii) farm working in Norway.

Fig. 52 Changing farm size in Norway (1 hectare=2.4 acres)
52a Is the number of farms increasing or decreasing?

52b Are farms tending to increase or decrease in area?

52c Is mechanisation easier on a small or a large consolidated farm?

52d Are there many or few farms of less than 10 hectares in Norway?

52e Would you expect a farmer to be able to make a decent living out of a farm of less than 10 hectares?

52f UK has about twice as many farm-holdings as Norway. What is the major difference between size of holdings in general in these two countries ?

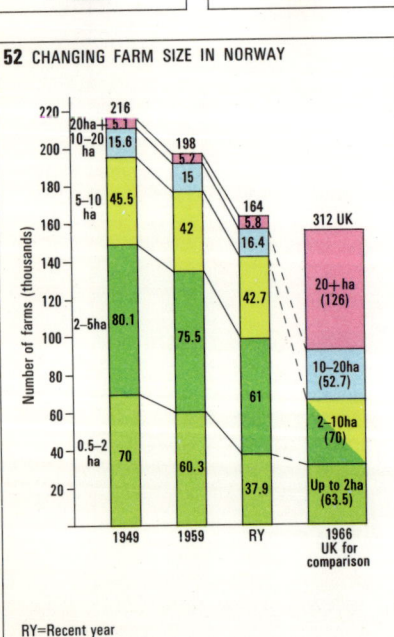

52 CHANGING FARM SIZE IN NORWAY

Number of farms (thousands)

1949: 216 — 20ha+ 5.1, 10–20 ha 15.6, 5–10 ha 45.5, 2–5ha 80.1, 0.5–2 ha 70
1959: 198 — 5.7, 15, 42, 75.5, 60.3
RY: 164 — 5.8, 16.4, 42.7, 61, 37.9
1966 UK for comparison: 312 UK — 20+ha (126), 10–20ha (52.7), 2–10ha (70), Up to 2ha (63.5)

RY=Recent year

55 MILK CONSUMPTION per head in various European countries

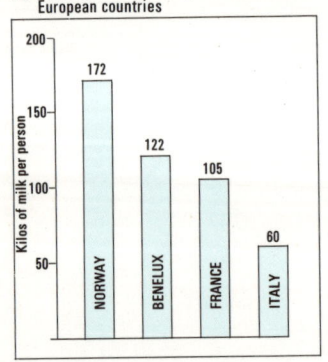

Kilos of milk per person
NORWAY 172, BENELUX 122, FRANCE 105, ITALY 60

Total of all home-run farms (100%)

In 45% of all home-run farms, farming is a SECONDARY occupation.

In 20% of all home-run farms, farming is the MAIN BUT NOT THE ONLY occupation.

In 35% of all home-run farms farming is the MAIN AND ONLY occupation.

Fig. 53 Farm Work
Because farms are so small, and good rich flat land so scarce in most of Norway, the farmers have for the most part to engage in a second occupation — frequently the farmer is also a fisherman or forester.

53a In what percentage of all home-run farms is a second occupation necessary?

Fig. 54 The main uses of farming land
54a What percentage is used for meadowland of any kind? Suggest what conditions make for so much pasture?

54b (i) Do the figures suggest that Norway is an arable farming country as well as pastoral?

(ii) What percentage is under crops?

54 PERCENTAGE OF TOTAL FARMED AREA ACCORDING TO USE (Total 2.5 million acres)

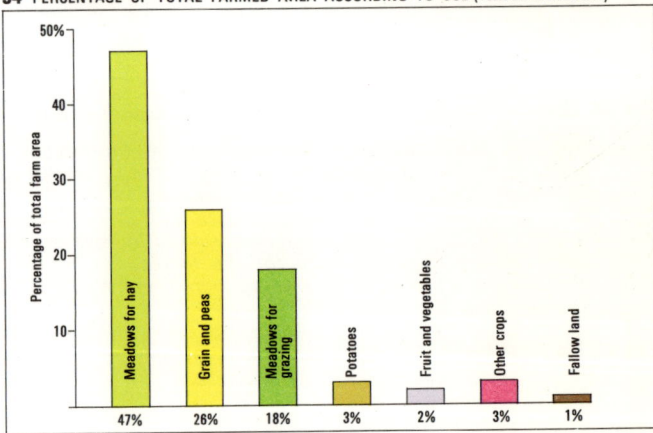

Percentage of total farm area
Meadows for hay 47%, Grain and peas 26%, Meadows for grazing 18%, Potatoes 3%, Fruit and vegetables 2%, Other crops 3%, Fallow land 1%

Fig. 55 Milk consumption per head
55a Is the consumption of milk per head in Norway higher than in other European countries? Why is this so?

Fig. 56/57 Agricultural production and degree of self-sufficiency in Norway
56/57a In which areas is livestock production of greatest local importance?

56/57b What are the main crops of Norway?

56/57c What is the money value of the livestock products?

56/57d List (i) the main food imports of Norway (ii) the products in which she is largely self-sufficient.

56 AGRICULTURAL PRODUCTION - crops and livestock items.

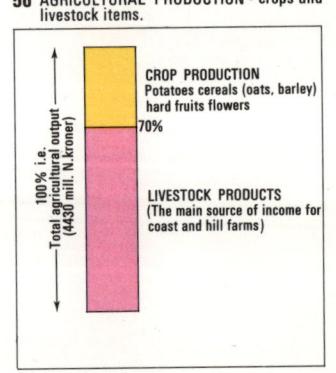

100% i.e. Total agricultural output (4430 mill. N.kroner)

CROP PRODUCTION
Potatoes cereals (oats, barley) hard fruits flowers
70%

LIVESTOCK PRODUCTS
(The main source of income for coast and hill farms)

57 DEGREE OF SELF-SUFFICIENCY IN FOOD OUTPUTS IN NORWAY

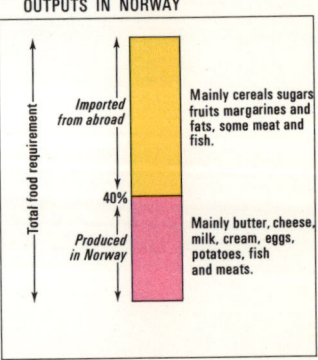

Total food requirement

Imported from abroad
Mainly cereals sugars fruits margarines and fats, some meat and fish.

40%

Produced in Norway
Mainly butter, cheese, milk, cream, eggs, potatoes, fish and meats.

The harshness of the physical conditions in much of coastal Norway (i.e. the lack of flat land and deep soil, the general background of high glaciated uplands with thin acidic soils exposed to heavy rains and winter snows) has encouraged the people to look for a living beyond their severely limited farming. They have looked up the slopes to the forests and out to the seas—to the inner waters around the strandflats, skerries and the deeper fjords and out again into the North Sea, to Icelandic fisheries, to the banks of Newfoundland and to the whale-waters of Antarctica. The inner waters and the North Sea are the most important areas for Norwegian fishermen.

The coast offers many advantages for the industry—the NAD provides warm waters and ice-free ports, and the mixing of this ex-tropical water with the colder fjord and Arctic waters provides ideal conditions for the growth of plankton and other marine organisms (flora and fauna) on which fish may feed. The fjords themselves—deep and steep-sided—offer excellent shelter where the boats may lay up, and the forests have provided timber for the traditional fishing vessels.

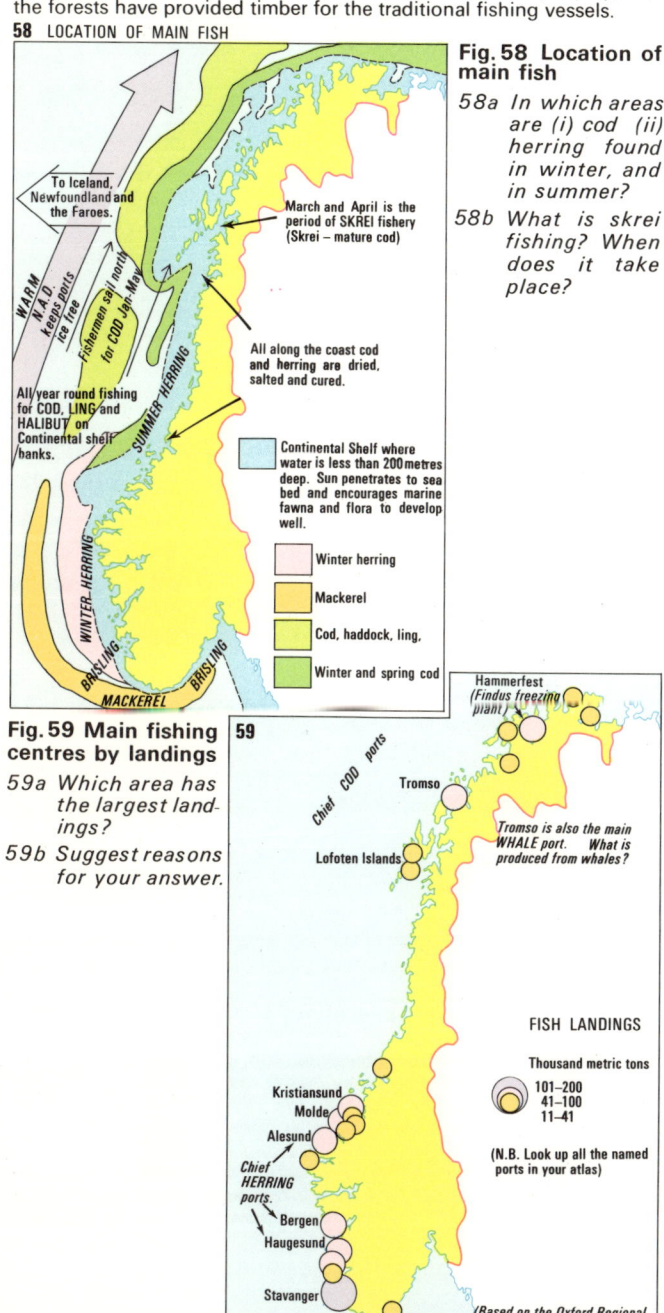

Fig. 58 Location of main fish

58a In which areas are (i) cod (ii) herring found in winter, and in summer?

58b What is skrei fishing? When does it take place?

Fig. 59 Main fishing centres by landings

59a Which area has the largest landings?

59b Suggest reasons for your answer.

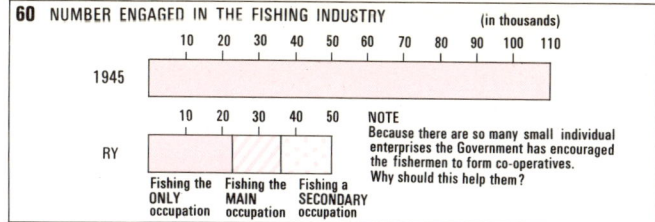

Fig. 60 Employment in the fishing industry

Examine this figure together with fig. 65.

60a By how many has the labour force engaged in fishing decreased since 1945?

60b Suggest two other occupations in which fishermen may engage to support themselves.

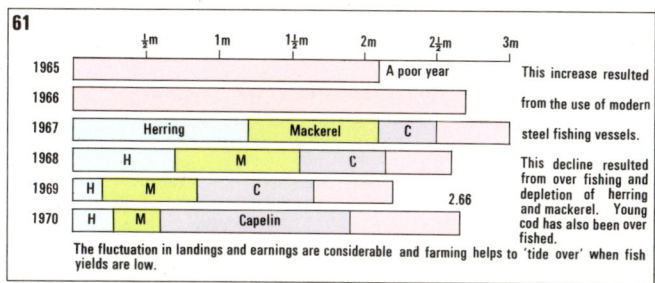

Fig. 61 Fish landings in millions of metric tons

61a Describe the relative importance of each of the following fish since 1967 (i) herring (ii) mackerel (iii) capelin.

61b Had the landings of capelin remained constant since 1967, what would the total landing have been in 1970? How would this have compared with 1965?

61c Why do the Norwegians in particular wish to keep a 10 mile fishing limit all along their coasts?

Although there has been an increase in the modernisation of vessels and a growth in the use of large trawlers, Norway does not solely concentrate her fishing on a few large ports (with fish factories). If she did so, many small ports would suffer.

61d If the fishermen in small ports could not make a living, what would happen (i) to them (ii) to their ports (iii) to the population totals especially in the North?

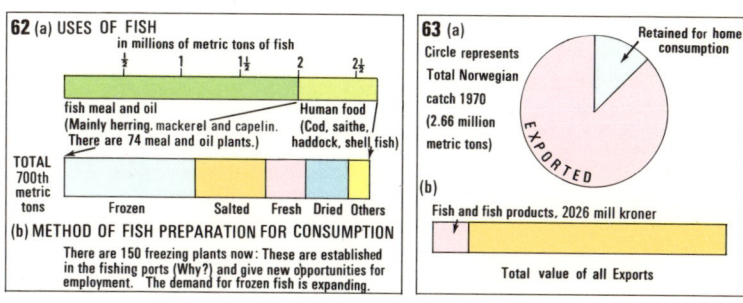

Fig. 62 Uses of Norwegian fish (1970 as example year)

62a Find out the uses to which the following may be put (i) fish meal (what is it?) (ii) fish oil.

62b What are the main fish for human consumption?

62c Which method of fish preparation is now most important? Salted cod (klipfish) and dried cod (stockfish) is sent to Mediterranean and tropical Roman Catholic countries. (Why?)

Fig.63 Fish exports

63a What fraction of total fish landings is exported in some form?

63b What is the approximate value of Norwegian fish and fish products in her export income?

Fig. 64 Area of forest in Norway

64a What is the total area of forest in Norway?
64b About what fraction of this is exploitable?
64c What is the area of forest in (i) Sweden (ii) UK?

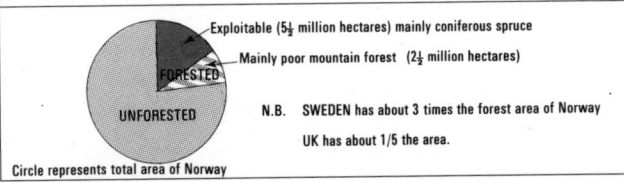

64 AREA OF FOREST

Exploitable (5½ million hectares) mainly coniferous spruce
Mainly poor mountain forest (2½ million hectares)
FORESTED
UNFORESTED
N.B. SWEDEN has about 3 times the forest area of Norway
UK has about 1/5 the area.
Circle represents total area of Norway

Fig. 65 Ownership of the forests of Norway

The Government supervises all forests in Norway regardless of ownership and ensures that some 27,000 hectares (65,000 acres) are planted with trees each year. The trees are cut when 50-100 years old. Main stands of spruce and pine are where valleys converge in the Trondheim area and towards the Oslo lowlands.

65a How does the figure suggest that Norwegian farmers cannot make a living out of farming alone?

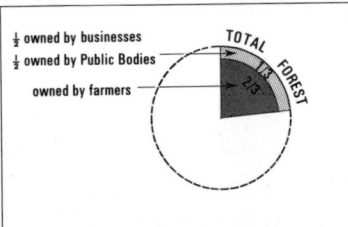

65 OWNERSHIP OF FORESTS IN NORWAY

⅙ owned by businesses
⅙ owned by Public Bodies
owned by farmers
TOTAL FOREST
2/3

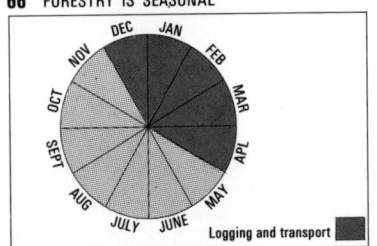

66 FORESTRY IS SEASONAL

DEC JAN FEB MAR APL MAY JUNE JULY AUG SEPT OCT NOV
Logging and transport

Fig. 66 Forestry is seasonal

66a Why should forestry work be concentrated in the winter and spring?
66b What work is there on the farms at these seasons?
The logging is by motor-saws and transport mainly by tractors, trucks and funiculars.
66c What is a funicular?
66d The main pulp, paper and sawmills are found at coastal ports e.g. Trondheim, Drammen, Larvik, Kristiansand. Why?

The 120,000 small producers find working conditions and transport difficult—why? Prices tend therefore to be higher than in the price-setting market leaders Canada and USA, and in Sweden also.

Fig.67 Uses of Norwegian timber

The pulp and paper plants need more timber than Norway can supply herself and 2-3 million cubic metres may be imported for them each year. Output of this industry is 1.3 million metric tons which is 1% of world output. It accounts however for 12% by value of all Norway's exports. 72% of the paper and paperboard products go to W European lands.

67a About how many million cubic metres of timber are used as sawn wood and how many for pulp and paper?

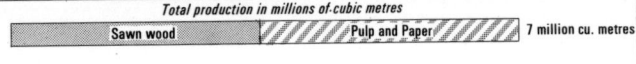

67 USES OF NORWEGIAN TIMBER

Total production in millions of cubic metres
Sawn wood | Pulp and Paper | 7 million cu. metres

Fig. 39 shows main minerals and mining areas of Norway. Outputs are not large apart from iron ore (crude iron ore output: 3,374,000 metric tons 1967; 3,704,000 metric tons 1968; 4,286,000 metric tons 1969.)

Fig. 68 Purity of iron ore (Fe content)

Norway has some of the purest iron ore in the world as the figure shows.
68a What was the iron content of the Norwegian production of crude iron ore in 1969?

68 PURITY OF THE IRON ORE (Fe content)

	20%	40%	60%	80%	100%
Canada			62		
Sweden			61		
USA					
Norway			59		

Sweden produces nearly nine times as much iron ore as Norway, and the UK output (by Fe content) is also higher (total 3,902,000 metric tons). Norway lies 20th in fact in the list of world producers. The bulk of her iron is used in the steel plant of Mo-i-Rana (see fig. 76).
68b Find the two main areas of iron ore mining on fig.39 and list the other minerals mined in Norway and shown on the that figure.

The development of industry depends on the development of energy resources.

Fig.69 Shows the sources of primary energy in Norway

69a Which source predominates?
69b Coal output is very small and is from 1 mine in Spitzbergen (see fig. 100). In 1967 only 427 000 metric tons was produced and this fell to 346 000 in 1968. The coal is sent to a coking plant for the Mo-i-Rana iron and steel works. Find out the output of coal in UK in a recent year.
69c Has Norway any oil and natural gas of her own? (See figure 27)

69 SOURCES OF PRIMARY ENERGY IN NORWAY

Coal 6%
Petroleum 40% (all imported)
Electricity 54%
The circle represents the total primary energy used in Norway

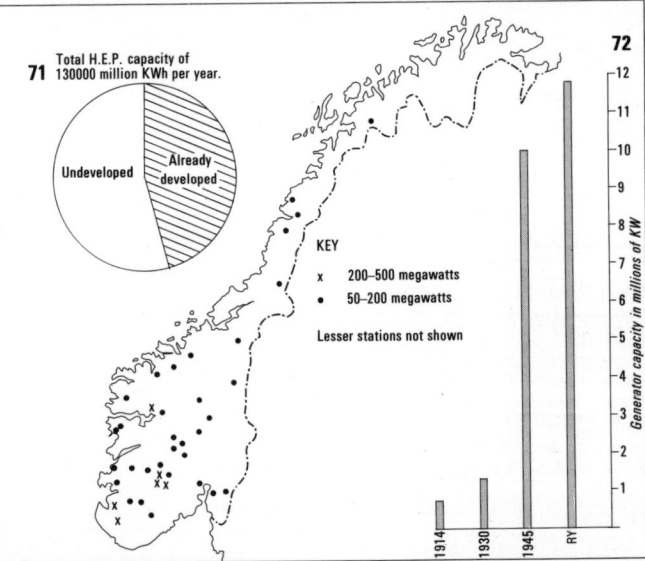

70 HYDRO-ELECTRICAL POWER STATIONS IN NORWAY

71
Total H.E.P. capacity of 130000 million KWh per year.
Undeveloped
Already developed

KEY
x 200–500 megawatts
• 50–200 megawatts
Lesser stations not shown

72
Generator capacity in millions of KW
12 11 10 9 8 7 6 5 4 3 2 1
1914 1930 1945 RY

Figs 70 and 73 show the locations of major HEP stations in Norway

Production depends (among other things) on climate, rainfall and relief
70/73a Which part of Norway has most HEP stations? Which has the least?
70/73b In what ways do climate and relief aid HEP development in Norway?
70/73c Demand for energy is greatest in winter. Why?
70/73d Output is often less in winter. What holds up the flow of water to the storage basins for use in the HEP plants there?

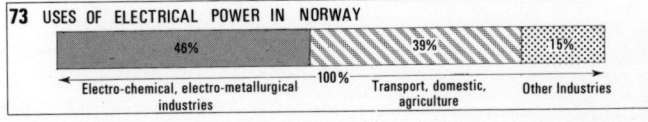

73 USES OF ELECTRICAL POWER IN NORWAY

46%	39%	15%
Electro-chemical, electro-metallurgical industries	Transport, domestic, agriculture	Other Industries
100%		

The basis of Norwegian manufacturing industries is hydro-electric power. To avoid loss in energy resulting from the transport of electricity by cable, those industrial plants which use much electric power have often been built near the HEP stations themselves e.g. electro-metallurgical and electro-chemical plants, using imported raw materials which use 45% of Norway's electrical output.

Manufacturing industries can be put into two main categories—those which largely supply the home market and those which are concerned with trade. The former include food and drink, textiles, clothing, iron and steel. The latter are dominated by the electro-metallurgical and electro-chemical industries, and ship-building.

Fig. 74 Development of industrial production in Norway 1961-69

74a What does the diagram show?

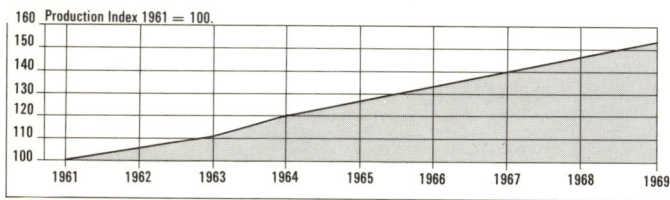

74 DEVELOPMENT OF INDUSTRIAL PRODUCTION IN NORWAY 1961-69

Electro-metallurgical industry

This was based on the development of HEP and the invention of the electric furnace in 1920. Main metals produced are (i) Steel mainly at Mo-i-Rana using local Rana iron ore and local HEP from Rossaaga Falls. (ii) Aluminium at Sogne Fjord and Sunnsdalsora. (iii) Ferro-alloys at many plants, especially at Notodden, Larvik, Kristiansand and Drammen. (iv) zinc near Kristiansand. Very high quality products are made.

Electro-chemical industry

Based mainly on the production of artificial fertilisers from nitrogen; other chemicals produced include ammonia, sulphur acid and calcium carbide. Main centres for nitrates are at Notodden, Rjukan and Porsgrunn: calcium carbide at Sarpsborg and Odda.

Fig.75 Production of selected materials

75a Which product has shown the most marked increase?

75b Find out total world production figures for all the materials shown and compare Norway's output.

75 PRODUCTION OF SELECTED MATERIALS

STEEL — ALUMINIUM — NITRATES
100 000´s metric tons
(812) (600) 1963 RY — (512) (225) 1963 RY — (459) (300) 1963 RY

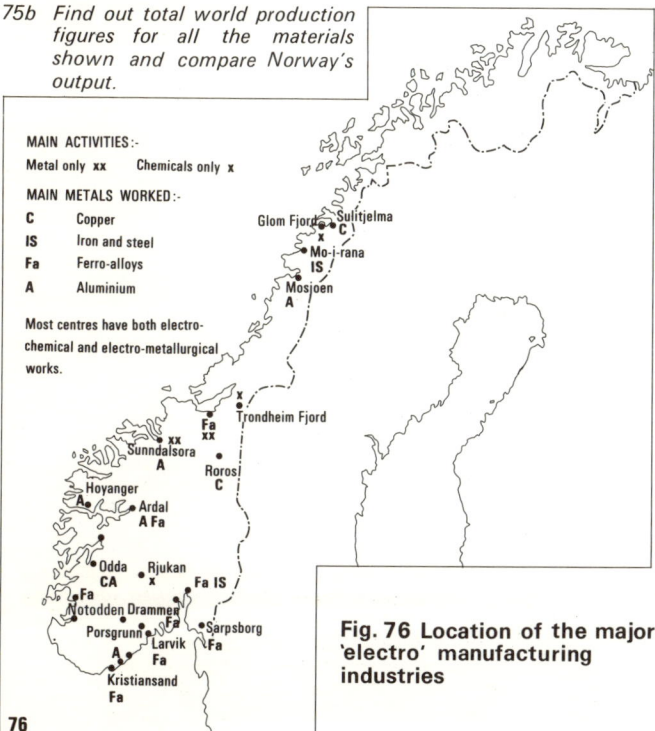

MAIN ACTIVITIES:-
Metal only **xx**   Chemicals only **x**

MAIN METALS WORKED:-
C Copper
IS Iron and steel
Fa Ferro-alloys
A Aluminium

Most centres have both electro-chemical and electro-metallurgical works.

Fig. 76 Location of the major 'electro' manufacturing industries

Fig.77 The tonnage of the merchant fleet

77a Why did the tonnage drop between 1938 and 1945?

77b Why have tankers increased so greatly in tonnage since the War?

77c 'Nature has made of Norway a sea-faring Nation... The land divides them but the sea unites them.' Explain these statements.

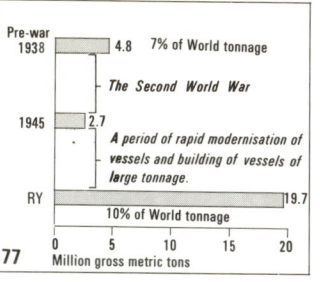

Pre-war 1938 — 4.8 — 7% of World tonnage
The Second World War
1945 — 2.7
A period of rapid modernisation of vessels and building of vessels of large tonnage.
RY — 19.7
10% of World tonnage
77 — 0 5 10 15 20 — Million gross metric tons

Fig.78 Composition of Norway's merchant fleet by tonnage

78a Maritime transport accounts for nearly 12% of Norway's G.N.P. Which type of maritime traffic would you think contributes most?

78b If Norway's total tonnage is 19·7 million, what is that (i) of the world (see fig.77), (ii) of her oil-tanker fleet?

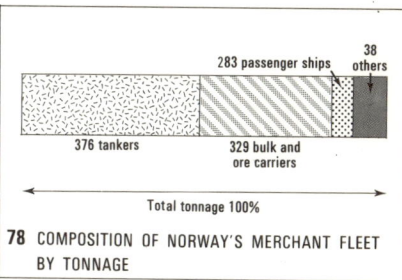

283 passenger ships — 38 others
376 tankers — 329 bulk and ore carriers
Total tonnage 100%
78 COMPOSITION OF NORWAY'S MERCHANT FLEET BY TONNAGE

Norwegian **shipbuilding** has developed from early fishing vessel days and has flourished in recent years because of the adaptiveness and inventiveness of her ship-builders, e.g. at Stord Yard island off the west coast where a 220,000 metric ton tanker was launched in 1970; until that year the largest vessel made there was under 1,000 metric tons.

Fig.79 Trade and balance of payments

79a What two items dominate foreign earnings for Norway?

Fig.80 The regions of Norway

80a Examine all the material on Norway in this book (pages 14-19). Is there any other information which we might add to the descriptions of the regions (relief, soils, climatic details, vegetation, land use, population, distribution of HEP plants, mining industry, forestry and fishing)?

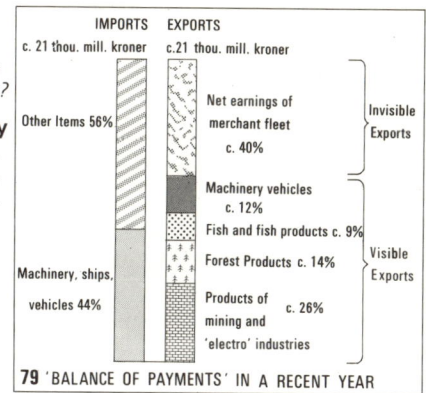

IMPORTS c. 21 thou. mill. kroner — EXPORTS c.21 thou. mill. kroner
Other Items 56% — Net earnings of merchant fleet c. 40% — Invisible Exports
Machinery, ships, vehicles 44% — Machinery vehicles c. 12% / Fish and fish products c. 9% / Forest Products c. 14% / Products of mining and 'electro' industries c. 26% — Visible Exports
79 'BALANCE OF PAYMENTS' IN A RECENT YEAR

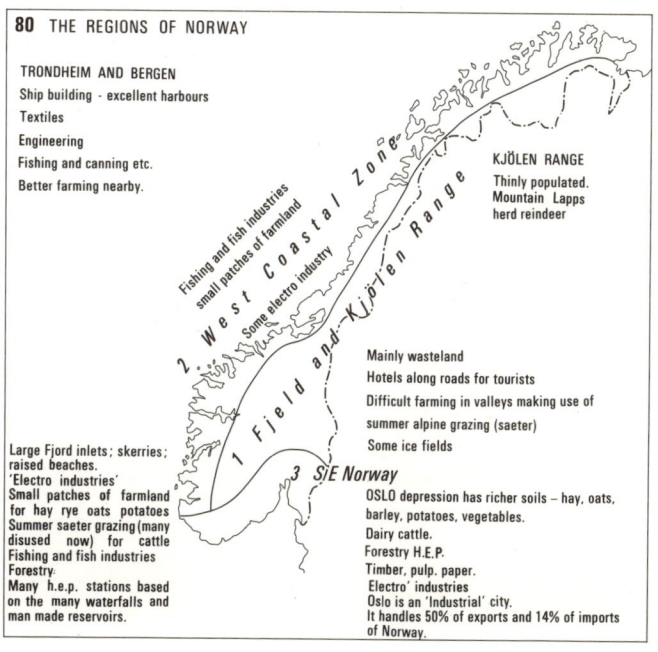

80 THE REGIONS OF NORWAY

TRONDHEIM AND BERGEN
Ship building - excellent harbours
Textiles
Engineering
Fishing and canning etc.
Better farming nearby.

2. West Coastal Zone
Fishing and fish industries small patches of farmland
Some electro industry

KJÖLEN RANGE
Thinly populated. Mountain Lapps herd reindeer

1 Fjeld and Kjölen Range
Mainly wasteland
Hotels along roads for tourists
Difficult farming in valleys making use of summer alpine grazing (saeter)
Some ice fields

Large Fjord inlets; skerries; raised beaches.
'Electro industries'
Small patches of farmland for hay rye oats potatoes
Summer saeter grazing (many disused now) for cattle
Fishing and fish industries
Forestry
Many h.e.p. stations based on the many waterfalls and man made reservoirs.

3 S/E Norway
OSLO depression has richer soils – hay, oats, barley, potatoes, vegetables.
Dairy cattle.
Forestry H.E.P.
Timber, pulp. paper.
'Electro' industries
Oslo is an 'Industrial' city.
It handles 50% of exports and 14% of imports of Norway.

Fig. 81 Basic facts of area, etc., main international roadways, main areas of industry and iron ore.

81a Describe the location of (i) iron ore areas, (ii) wood industry, (iii) glass industry, (iv) textile industry.

81b What do you notice about the direction of flow of the main rivers? Explain it.

81c Identify (name terminal ports) three ferry routes to Denmark, one to Finland, and one to Germany.

81d Name one town in the western world (outside Scandinavia) which is on roughly the same latitude as Stockholm.

81e How many European highways join Sweden to Norway?

81f Which is the only highway which joins the east coast of Sweden with the west coast of Norway?

81g Why is the population density figure very misleading?

Fig. 83 Physical Divisions of Sweden

A **The Caledonian mountain area** forms the Kiolen Ranges (Keel Ridges). These uplands have been reduced to an average of about 3000', 915 metres but some peaks rise to nearly double this figure. The surface is typical fjeld—bare rock, tundra and small ice caps.

B(i) **The Baltic Shield area of the Norrland terrain** slopes away to the East, and where it abuts the Caledonian mountains there exists a glint line zone of lakes. More long narrow lakes occur lower down the slopes to the east, where ice-gouged hollows in the river valleys have filled with water and been blocked downstream by morainic deposits. Rivers flow over rapids or falls. Better soils than those afforded by the general smearing of boulder clay are found in 'Jämtland depression' and this low pass in the Kiolen range is followed by a main highway; Foraskeel (E 75).

(ii) **The Baltic plains** are low-lying and covered with silts laid down when the sea extended over them, and with river deposits. The drop from the Norrland Shield to the coastal plains is marked by waterfalls.

C **Central Lowlands** is a faulted zone containing fault-formed lakes. Depression beneath postglacial inland seas has given rich and varied soils, which today form very rich farmlands. Uneven glacial deposits give undulating lowland.

D **Smaland** is an ancient and eroded plateau, made of granites and gneiss. Infertile boggy moorland. Forests.

E **Scania**: Glacial and post-glacial inland sea deposits cover the surface. Rich fertile farmland.

83a Name the main lakes of the Central Lowlands.

83b Contrast the winter temperatures of G (Gothenburg) with those of S (Stockholm): try to account for the difference.

83c Why does the West coast of Sweden receive much more rain than east?

83d What is the temperature range at (i) Haparanda, (ii) Gothenburg? Give two reasons to explain the difference between them.

83e Scania is not only covered with fertile soils, it is also the most southerly part of Sweden. Why should this latter point be important?

83f Most of the winter precipitation is snow. Are the seas, rivers, and lakes frozen in winter?

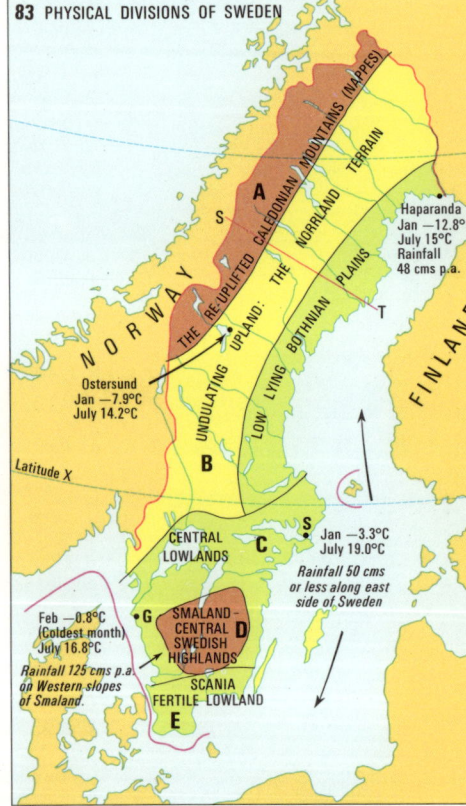

81 SWEDEN
- Iron Ore
- Wood Industry
- Glass Industry
- Textile Industry
- European Highway
- B Bergslagen District
- □ Millionaire Towns (Stockholm 1·28 million)

AREA 449793 sq kms (173654 sq mls)
LENGTH 1574 km (972 mls)
POPULATION 7·9 million
POPULATION DENSITY 19 per sq km (46 per sq ml)

83 PHYSICAL DIVISIONS OF SWEDEN

Haparanda
Jan −12.8°C
July 15°C
Rainfall 48 cms p.a.

Ostersund
Jan −7.9°C
July 14.2°C

Latitude X

Jan −3.3°C
July 19.0°C

Rainfall 50 cms or less along east side of Sweden

Feb −0.8°C (Coldest month) July 16.8°C

Rainfall 125 cms p.a. on Western slopes of Smaland

CENTRAL LOWLANDS

SMALAND-CENTRAL SWEDISH HIGHLANDS

SCANIA FERTILE LOWLAND

Note: Three diagrams in this book give details of Sweden's land use. In each case the proportions given for various uses of the land differ—though not too greatly. It should be remembered that all such figures are estimates and that different authorities interpret the use of land differently e.g. what exactly is forest or waste? These are particularly difficult to define. Also, the proportions change continuously.

82a The forest land lies mainly north of 60°N. About what fraction of Sweden is forested?

82b A little under 9% of Sweden is under some form of agricultural use (1% is pasture). 9% of Sweden is about 3·6 million hectares. 3% of Norway is about 1 million hectares. What is the significance of 3% for Norway in this question?

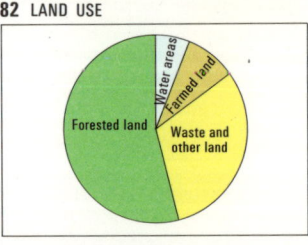

82 LAND USE

Forested land
Water areas
Farmed land
Waste and other land

Fig. 84 Transect along S - T on fig. 83

84a Describe the changes from west to east under the following headings: relief, denudation, vegetation

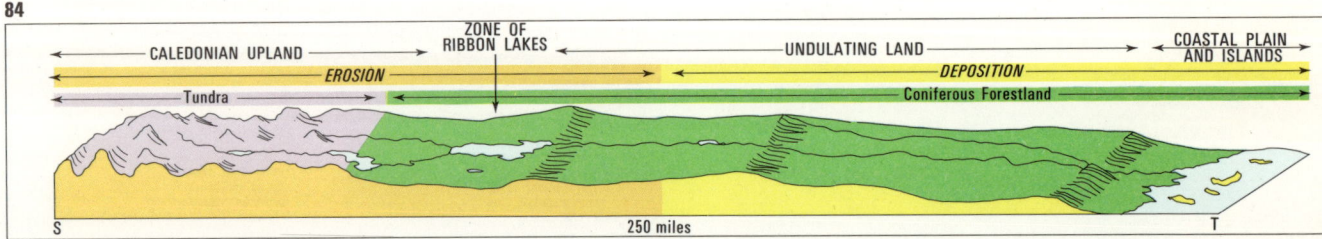

84

CALEDONIAN UPLAND — ZONE OF RIBBON LAKES — UNDULATING LAND — COASTAL PLAIN AND ISLANDS

EROSION — DEPOSITION

Tundra — Coniferous Forestland

S   250 miles   T

A relatively favourable climate, thanks to the influence of the N.A.D. and westerlies, makes farming possible in most parts of Sweden despite its northern location. However, arable land covers only about 8% of the land area, due mainly to soil conditions. Most of the arable land is located in the southern-most provinces and around the great lakes in the central part of the country. A long tradition of plant improvement and other agricultural research, together with high fertilizer consumption, have brought the average yield per acre of the main crops in line with many of the most efficient countries in Western Europe.

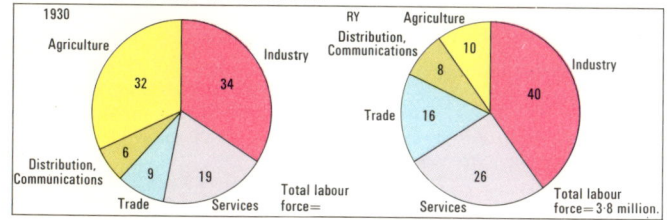

Fig. 85 Changing pattern of employment

85a Which occupations have experienced a (i) decline in percent-age, (ii) an increase in percentage?
85b Which sector has shown little change in percentage employed?

Fig. 86 Uses of cultivated land

86a Roughly what percentage of the cultivated land is used for pastures?
86b The large area devoted to pasture and fodder crops suggests that farming is much concerned with ..... What?

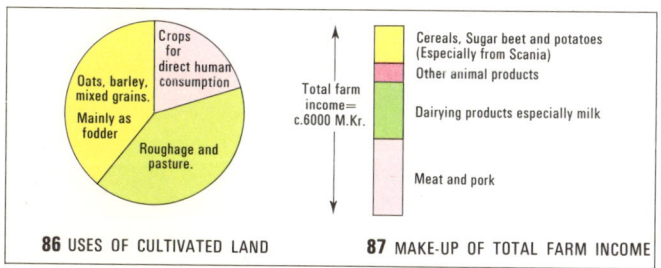

Fig. 87 Make-up of total farm income

87a What products dominate the farmers income?
87b About how valuable (in kroner) is the dairying industry to Sweden?
87c (Look also at fig. 90 (iv).) In which part of Sweden is the pork industry concentrated?

Fig. 88 Livestock and farm machinery trends
(Sheep are unimportant in Swedish farming.)
88a Although (as fig. 85 shows) employment in farming is decli-ning, the total outputs from farms do not decline. Explain this.
88b Explain the reduction in the use of the horse.
88c Milk output does not fall although total cattle (all kinds) has fallen. Try to account for this apparent paradox.

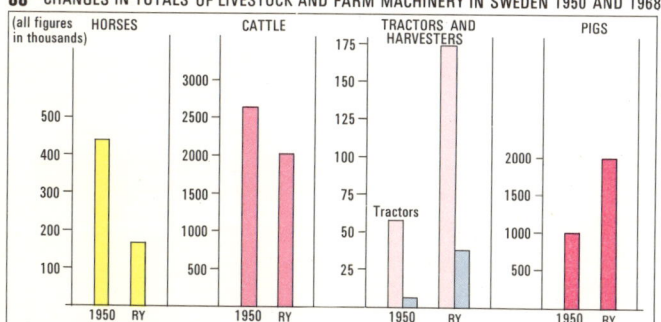

Fig. 89 Distribution of holdings and arable land

89a Which 2 size groups comprise some 52% of all Swedish farms?
89b What percentage of Swedish farms are 100 hectares or more in area?
89c Do the larger or smaller farms have the greatest percentage of Swedish arable land?
89d In general are farms larger, smaller or about the same size as in Norway?
89e Would you expect the farmers with only 2-5 hectares of land (22% of all Swedish farmers) to have secondary occu-pations? If so, suggest a possible second source of income for them.
89f The tendency is for small-holdings to be amalgamated into larger units and this is encouraged by increasing farm mech-anisation. Why?

Note: In addition to the increase in mechanisation and the reduction in manpower in farming, another feature of structural change is a trend towards increasing specialization in one or two crops and/or animal products. Growing numbers of farms are selling off their cattle. In 1970, 31% of the farms had no cattle.

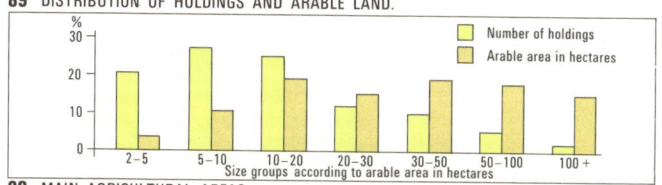
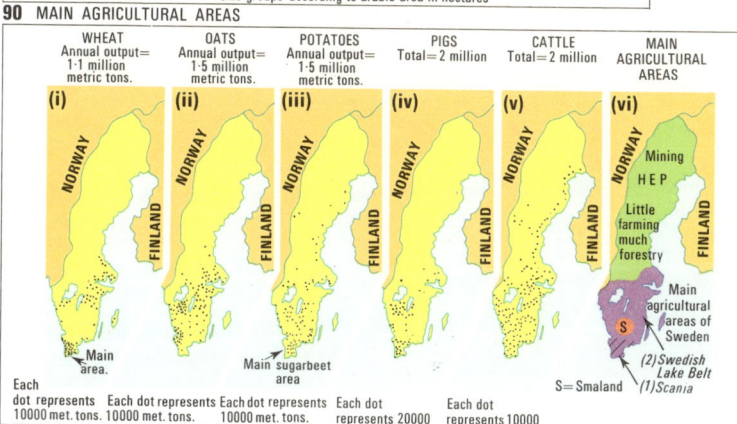

Fig. 90 (i-vi) Distribution of crops and livestock: main farming areas

90a In what area is the limited farming of the northern part of Sweden concentrated? Why?
90b Suggest reasons (climate, soil, relief, demand, transport) for the agricultural importance of Scania and the Swedish Lake Belt.
90c Suggest reasons for the limited agriculture of Smaland.
90d On which farm products does Scania concentrate?
90e Compare annual outputs and livestock totals given with those for oats, potatoes and cattle in Norway.

Farmers' Cooperation
A certain degree of cooperation between farmers in Sweden has existed for more than a century, but it was not until the 1930's that a nationwide collaboration was achieved. The cooperatives market farm products and supply farmers with equipment. They are based on voluntary membership and are intended to promote the common economic interests of the farmers. About 80% of the sales of agri-cultural products are handled by the farmers' economic associations. Through these associations the farmers own a significant part of the Swedish food industry, thus exercising an important influence on the market and also on agricultural policy. Practically all farmers producing for the market belong to one or more organizations within the agri-cultural cooperative movement organization.
From 1971 the head organization of the cooperative associations and the farmers' trade union have merged. The new organization of the Swedish farmers is called the Federation of Swedish Farmers (LRF).

The climate of Sweden allows the growth of a limited variety of trees— in the North (N of 60°N) coniferous trees dominate while South of 60°N deciduous trees are also found.

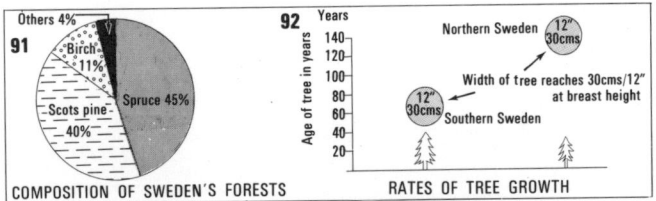

Fig. 91 The composition of Sweden's forests

Fig. 91 The composition of Sweden's forests
91a Both the main trees are suitable for sawing or the production of cellulose pulp. Are conifers hard- or soft-woods?
91b Why does variety of tree-type increase to the south of Sweden?
91c What percentage of Sweden is under forest?

Fig 92 Tree growth in North and South Sweden
92a Trees grow four times/three times/twice as fast in southern as in northern Sweden- which is correct?

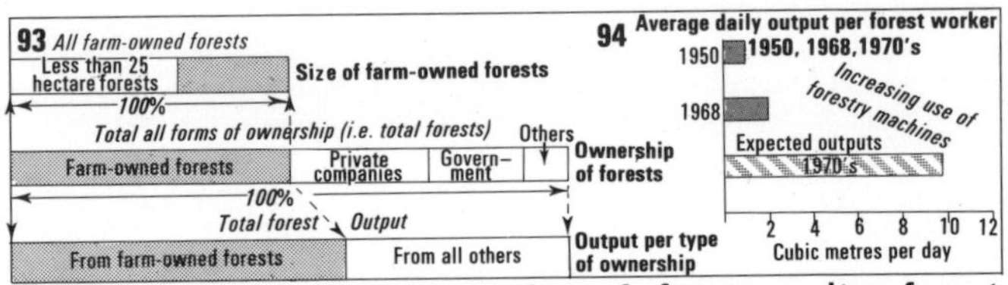

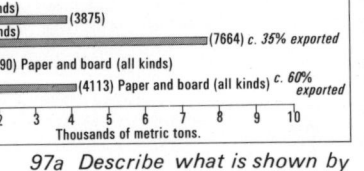

Fig 93 Forestry ownership; size of forest units: forest outputs

There are 230 000 small farmer-owners who between them own about 12 million hectares of forest. They tend to own the best forest-land, which is in the South. Because of the difficulty of mechanising small units these farmers are forming associations and working together.
93a The forest is clearly an important source of funds to the farming population. Is the same true of Norwegian farmers?
93b Read the section Integration in Forest Industries below very carefully: then explain the meaning of vertical integration using a diagram to help you.

Integration in Forest Industries
A characteristic feature of the forest industry's structure is the high degree of integration within the bigger companies, which by means of their great wood-capacity have had the possibility of bringing about a vertical integration with forests, transportation facilities, sawmills, joinery industries, pulp and paper production and by-product recovery within the framework of their organisations.

Fig.94 Average daily output per forest worker
94a What 2 main points does the figure show?

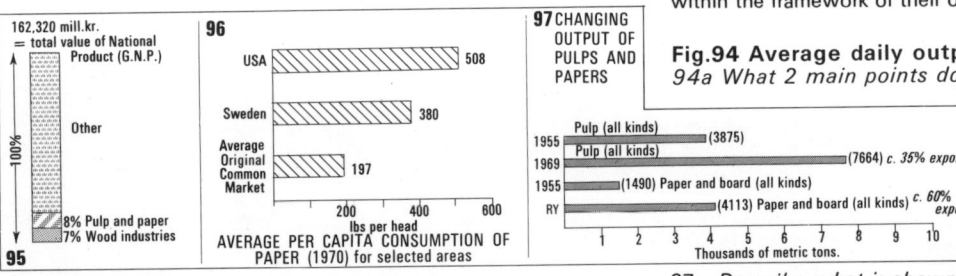

Fig.95 The place of 'wood industries' and 'pulp and paper' in Swedish economy

95a If the GNP is about 162,000 million kroner, what is the approximate value of each of these industries?

Pulp and Paper
For centuries the chief value of the forests lay in fuel woods, in charcoal, in tar and timber for export. In the 19th century the steam engine and relaxed trade regulations in UK turned saw-milling into Sweden's main export industry. Towards the end of the 19th century demand grew for wood fibre to make paper, and Swedish forest industry began to concentrate on chemical pulp for paper. Now Sweden is also engaged in making paper and cardboard for herself, and as well as continuing to export pulp she is now exporting its chief products.

Fig.96 Average per capita consumption of paper (1970) for selected areas

80% of the demand for paper comes from economically advanced countries (USA, W Europe, Australia, Japan). The developing countries therefore account for only about 20%. The USA consumes some 46 million metric tons per annum and Western Europe about 29 million metric tons. The developing countries used only 7 million metric tons in 1970. World demand is expected to be about 200 million metric tons in 1980.
At first the pulp industry was concentrated along the Bothnian coast where: (i) there was much wood (ii) water power could be harnessed (iii) logs could be floated down the parallel streams to processing sites on the coast. Recent years have seen a shift of the industry to central and southern Sweden because (i) there is ample wood in the south where' stands' are richer and faster growing (ii) road transport has taken precedence over clumsy log-floating (iii) electric power is now as cheaply available in the south as in the north.
Today there are 97 pulp mills and 69 paper plants in Sweden (most of the latter are in central Sweden).

97a Describe what is shown by fig. 97

Fig.98 Location of Swedish pulp mills

98a The majority of pulp mills are located on rivers and on the coast of Bothnia. Give reasons for this.

Fig.99 Exports of pulp, paper and board

Note: Swedish sawn timber is used to make doors, window frames. planks, plywood, wall-board. The (deciduous) aspen is used to make matches (Jönköping). The chemical pulp is used to make writing and other papers, cellulose, paints, varnish, ethyl-alcohol. Some charcoal is still made for smelting high quality steels. Pine trees are used to make telegraph poles, pit-props, railway sleepers. Mechanical pulp (timber ground up in water) is used for newsprint.

99a Which two single countries (i) import most chemical pulp (76% of all pulp is chemical i.e. cut into chips and boiled in chemicals) from Sweden (ii) import most paper and board from Sweden?

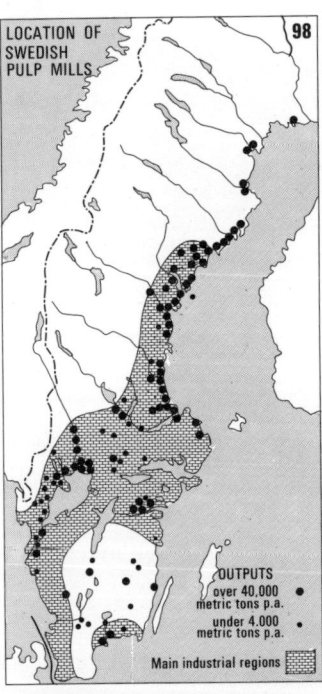

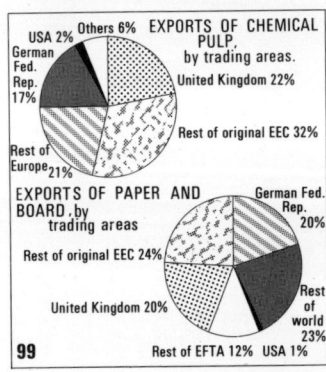

Industrial development depends upon energy. A country with no sources of energy must either import coal, oil or other power by pipe or cable, or it will not have more than domestic industry. Sweden has no coal or oil or natural gas worth mentioning. Her imports of coal are also negligible though she imports a great deal of oil (31.8 million cu. meters p.a.). However, although much oil is used for industry the bulk is for heating shops, homes, offices etc. and is used for transport. It was not and is not the basis of her industry. The relatively high precipitation, the long slopes of the valleys to the Gulf of Bothnia, the natural lakes which act as water regulators, have all led to the development of HEP in great quantity. Water flow in the northern rivers is notably uneven throughout the year e.g. average June flow is 10x the average March flow. The power load is greatest in winter and therefore regulation of flow is very necessary. Today there are over 1000 HEP stations, 180 of which have a capacity of 5000 kWh or more and 10 have a capacity of 200,000 kWh or more. The largest is Stornorrfors with a capacity of 410 000 kWh. The rivers do not generally flow over great waterfalls, and to develop their power properly underground hydro-plants are common (see fig. 105).

Fig.100 Relative importance of different sources of energy in Sweden

100a Suggest sources of the considerable oil imports.

Fig. 101 Consumption of electricity in Sweden

101a Describe what the diagram shows and relate it to the cable system, fig.106.

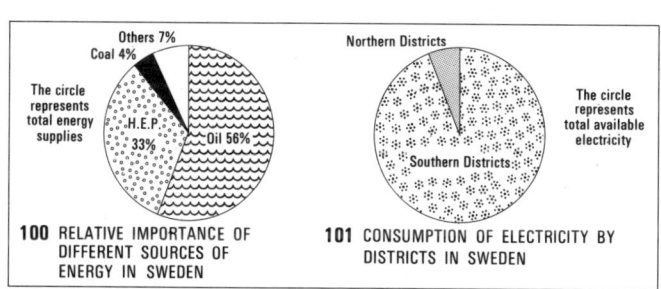

100 RELATIVE IMPORTANCE OF DIFFERENT SOURCES OF ENERGY IN SWEDEN

101 CONSUMPTION OF ELECTRICITY BY DISTRICTS IN SWEDEN

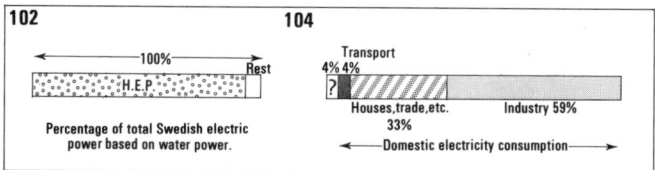

102

Percentage of total Swedish electric power based on water power.

104

Domestic electricity consumption

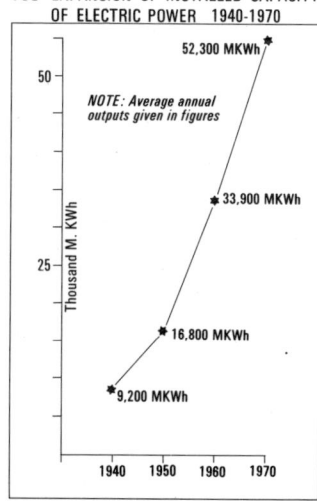

103 EXPANSION OF INSTALLED CAPACITY OF ELECTRIC POWER 1940-1970

NOTE: Average annual outputs given in figures

52,300 MKWh
33,900 MKWh
16,800 MKWh
9,200 MKWh

Fig. 102 Percentage of total Swedish electricity based on water power

102a What is another source of electrical power?

Fig. 103 Expansion of installed capacity of electric power 1940–1970
(see also fig. 26(iv))

The great increase has been paralleled by a comparable increase in electrification of the home and of industry as well as a great expansion of the latter.

Fig. 104 Domestic electricity consumption

104a Describe the diagram.
104b How much is exported?

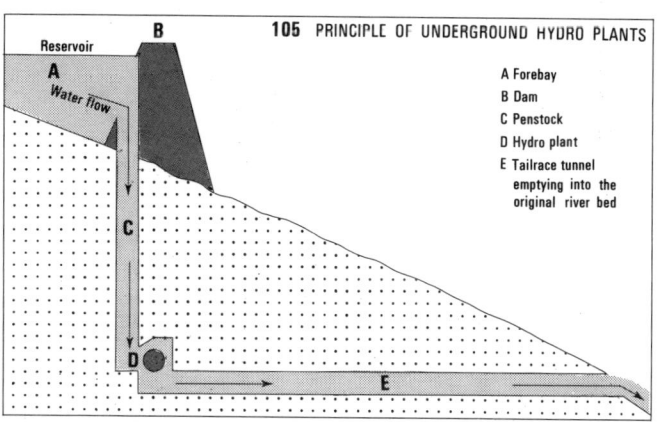

105 PRINCIPLE OF UNDERGROUND HYDRO PLANTS

A Forebay
B Dam
C Penstock
D Hydro plant
E Tailrace tunnel emptying into the original river bed

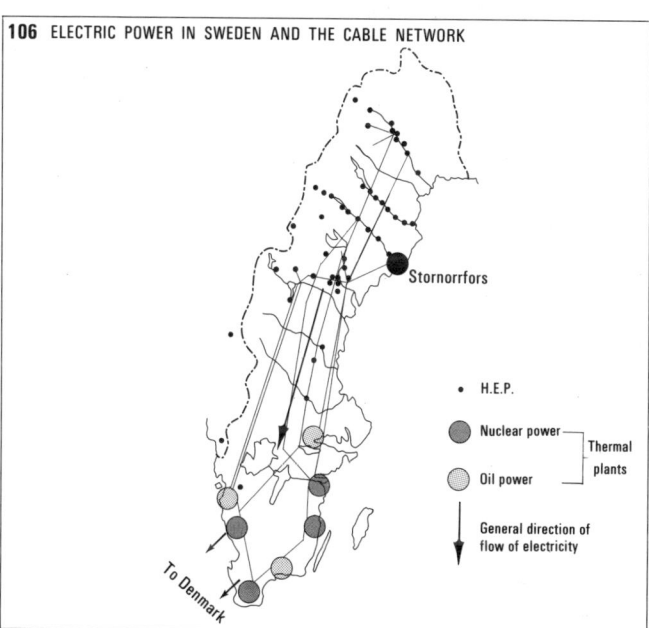

106 ELECTRIC POWER IN SWEDEN AND THE CABLE NETWORK

Stornorrfors

• H.E.P.

● Nuclear power ─┐
                 ├ Thermal plants
○ Oil power ─────┘

General direction of flow of electricity

To Denmark

Fig. 105 Principle of underground hydro-plants

105a Explain how the system works. What is a penstock?

Fig. 106 Electric power in Sweden and the cable network

106a Most industry is in the Central Lakes zone and Scania. Most HEP is made in the North. The general flow of electricity is therefore from North to South. Does any flow across into other countries?

Fig. 107 Energy supplied in percentages

107a Examine the figures very closely looking at the changes for each energy source one by one.
107b Draw bar graphs for years 1955, 1975 and 1985.
107c In which year did atomic power develop?
107d Although the percentage of total Swedish energy provided by oil products declines in 1985 this does not mean that imports of oil are expected to decline. Explain this.

107 ENERGY SUPPLIED IN PERCENTAGES %

	1955	1965	1975	1985 (forecast)
Oil products	46	64	69	54
Coal and coke	25	8	4	3
Hydro-power	14	18	13	8
Atomic power			8	31
Indigenous fuels*	15	10	6	4
(*Wood and peat) Totals	100	100	100	100

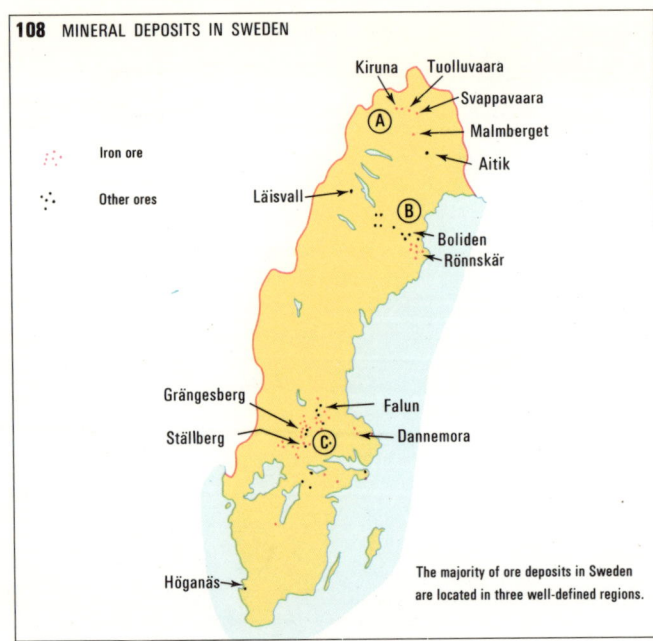

Fig. 108 Mineral deposits in Sweden

Fig. 108 Mineral deposits in Sweden

108a Suggest names for the three areas lettered A, B and C.

Fig. 109 Steel production in 1000 tons

109a Which method of production has expanded most rapidly? Try to find out how each method works.

109 STEEL PRODUCTION, IN 1,000 TONS	1960	1965
Kaldo oxygen process	126	1,028
Thomas ,,	406	373
Martin ,,	1,091	1,523
Electric ,,	1,560	1,802
Totals	3,183	4,725

Fig. 110 The mining and steel industry of N Sweden
(Look also at fig. 26(ii)).

110a Why is Narvik open for iron export all year, while Lulea is available only in summer?

110b List (i) the main copper mining centres and the copper smelting centre (ii) the main iron mining centres and the steel plant centre.

110c What would you think are two great hardships of mining and working in N Sweden?

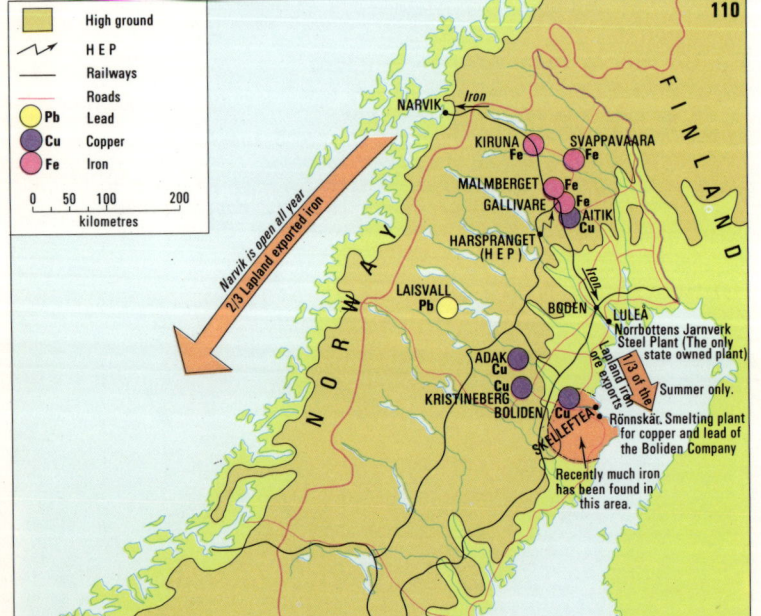

Apart of course from mining, forestry, pulp and paper, Swedish industry (which is largely privately owned) is very much concerned with the manufacture of technically advanced products. It is a country famed for its inventors and their inventions, especially in engineering industries in general.

The bases of Swedish industry are (i) a plentiful supply of iron ore (rich magnetite and haematite in the south and phosphoric ore in the North) (ii) plentiful HEP, (iii) the resourceful inventive people with a high degree of technical skill and know how. (Find out and write a note about Alfred Nobel).

There are five main sections of industry,
1 Iron and Steel

In order to combat the British iron and steel industry, the Swedish iron and steel masters have concentrated on high quality output, and production (using modern methods) has increased rapidly. The main Sheffield of Sweden is Eskilstuna (see fig. 115).
Now examine figs. 108-110 (left) and fig. 111 (below).

Fig. 111 Main importers of Swedish iron ore
111a List the main importers in order of importance.

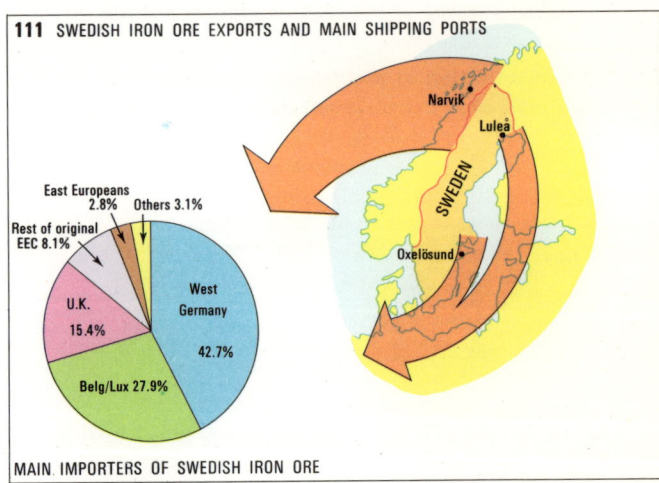

2 Engineering

Engineering comprises the largest industrial sector of Sweden employing over 40% of the labour force and accounting for some 45% of sales value of total industrial sales. Products include all kinds of mechanical and electrical goods, e.g. washing machines, electric typewriters, ball bearings, office and agricultural machinery in general, guns, cars, trucks and buses (Saab and Volvo).

Fig.112 Vehicle production

112a By how many thousand vehicles has (i) car production (ii) truck and bus production increased since 1960?

112b Find out the total output of Ford's in UK for a recent year and compare the figure with that for the Swedish car industry.

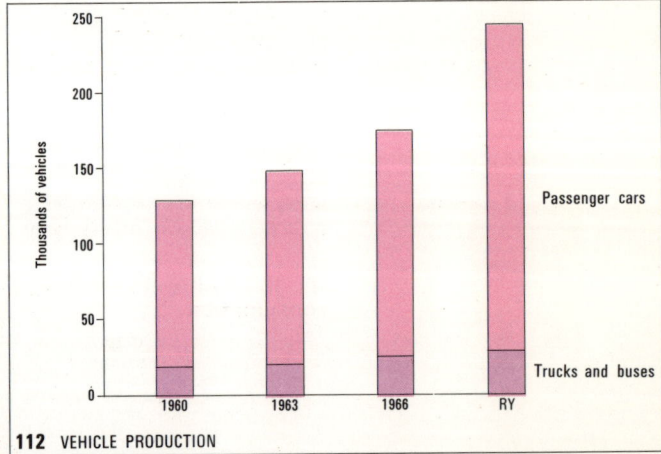

3. Textiles

Textiles are manufactured in many small establishments especially in and near Göteborg (Gothenburg). Raw materials are imported. Two main centres are Göteborg (fine cotton), Norrköping (woollens) (see fig. 115).

4. Chemicals

The chemical industry makes good use of local raw materials and HEP. Products are similar to those in Norway.

5. Ship-building

This industry has increased very greatly since World War II. It owes its development to the efficiency of its engineering industry and to the skill of the shipping producers with their determination to concentrate on modern methods, modern ships and high quality (see fig. 115).

Fig. 113 Launched tonnage by countries in recent years

113a Which country leads the industry and what is Sweden's position?

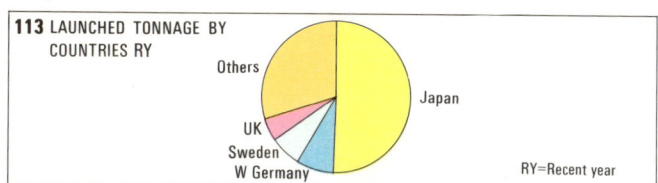

113 LAUNCHED TONNAGE BY COUNTRIES RY

Others / Japan / UK / Sweden / W Germany

RY=Recent year

Fig. 114 Ships launched in Swedish yards in recent years

114a Which two types of vessel are most important?

Of 156 giant 200 000 tons tankers ordered in 1969, Japan led with contracts to build 57, Sweden was second with 18 and France third with 16. The industry is dominated by seven main yards (which between them employ 45% of all ship-workers) all of which are on the short West coast (see fig. 115).

	Gross tons	Sweden's share of total
Tankers	390,521	6%
Bulk carriers	609,062	11%
General cargo vessels	16,138	
Misc. fishing vessels	19,692	2%
Other types	77,178	
Total	1,112,591	7%

114 (i) SHIPS LAUNCHED IN RY

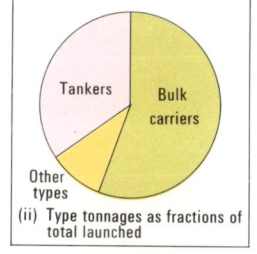

Tankers / Bulk carriers / Other types

114 (ii) Type tonnages as fractions of total launched

Fig. 116 Mining and manufacturing: sales value (total Skr 84 633 mill. recent year)

116a Which industry dominates and what are its various sections (and percentages)?
116b With what sort of items do you think the food industry is largely engaged?

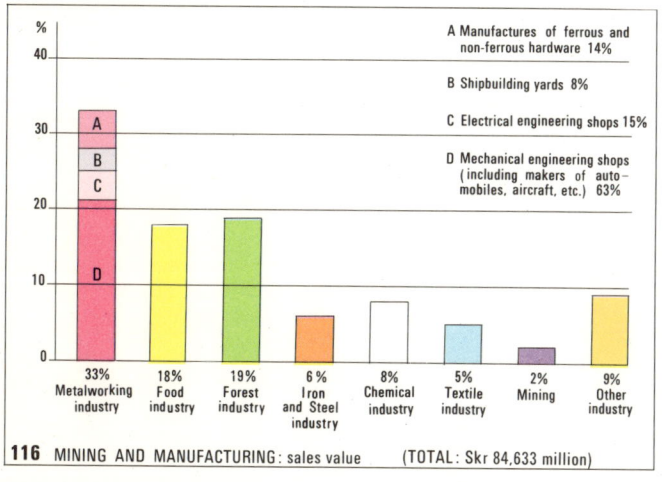

A Manufactures of ferrous and non-ferrous hardware 14%

B Shipbuilding yards 8%

C Electrical engineering shops 15%

D Mechanical engineering shops (including makers of automobiles, aircraft, etc.) 63%

33% Metalworking industry / 18% Food industry / 19% Forest industry / 6% Iron and Steel industry / 8% Chemical industry / 5% Textile industry / 2% Mining / 9% Other industry

116 MINING AND MANUFACTURING: sales value   (TOTAL: Skr 84,633 million)

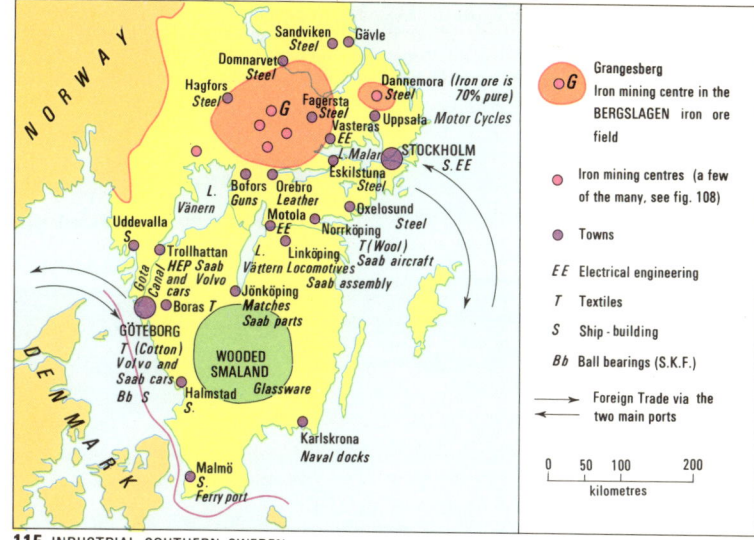

115 INDUSTRIAL SOUTHERN SWEDEN

NORWAY / DENMARK

Sandviken *Steel* / Gävle / Domnarvet *Steel* / Hagfors *Steel* / Dannemora *(Iron ore is 70% pure)* / Fagersta *Steel* / Uppsala *Motor Cycles* / Vasteras *EE* / L. Malar / STOCKHOLM *S. EE* / Eskilstuna *Steel* / Bofors *Guns* / Orebro *Leather* / Oxelosund *Steel* / Motala *EE* / Norrköping *T (Wool)* / Uddevalla *S.* / L. Vänern / Trollhattan *HEP Saab and Volvo cars* / Linköping *Locomotives Saab aircraft* / Boras *T* / L. Vättern *Matches Saab parts* / Jönköping *Saab assembly* / GÖTEBORG *T (Cotton) Volvo and Saab cars Bb S* / WOODED SMALAND / *Glassware* / Halmstad *S.* / Karlskrona *Naval docks* / Malmö *S. Ferry port*

G Grangesberg Iron mining centre in the BERGSLAGEN iron ore field

Iron mining centres (a few of the many, see fig. 108)

Towns

EE Electrical engineering
T Textiles
S Ship-building
Bb Ball bearings (S.K.F.)

Foreign Trade via the two main ports

0 50 100 200 kilometres

Fig. 115 Industrial Southern Sweden

115a Study this map very carefully, noting the concentration of iron mining and steel centres in the Central Lakes region.
115b List all named towns which (i) make steel (ii) make cars (iii) make textiles (iv) make ball bearings (v) make electrical goods (vi) make matches (vii) produce HEP (viii) make ships. Often only one main town is shown of many which engage in the industry.

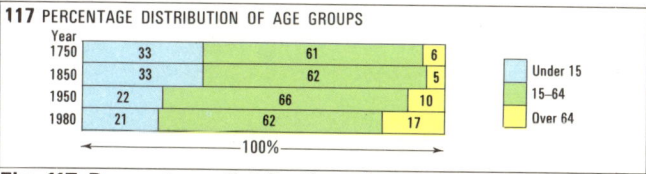

117 PERCENTAGE DISTRIBUTION OF AGE GROUPS

Year			
1750	33	61	6
1850	33	62	5
1950	22	66	10
1980	21	62	17

Under 15 / 15–64 / Over 64

—100%—

Fig. 117 Percentage distribution of age groups

117a Write a careful account of the changing pattern as illustrated by fig. 117.
117b What implications does the 1980 bar have for Sweden's economy?

TRADE: recent year

Fig. 118 (i) and (ii) : Fig. 119 (i) and (ii) : Exports and imports

118a Name (i) the three leading exports (ii) the leading import.
118b What forms the main item in fuel and power imports?
118c Make bar-graphs or pie-graphs to illustrate both sets of figures.
119a Which two blocs take most of Sweden's exports and provide most of her imports?
119b How might the difference between value of exports and value of imports be made up?

118 SWEDEN'S FOREIGN TRADE

(i) EXPORTS		%
Agricultural products		2.7
Forest products		24.5
Timber	7.0	
pulp, paper and board	17.5	
Iron ore		4.2
Basic metals		15.0
Machinery and instruments		23.6
Transport equipment		13.1
Other goods		16.9
		100.0

(ii) IMPORTS	%
Agricultural products	10.5
Fuel and power	10.5
Chemical products	8.8
Basic metal	12.4
Machinery and instruments	20.7
Transport equipment	7.3
Textiles and shoes	10.5
Other goods	19.3
	100.0

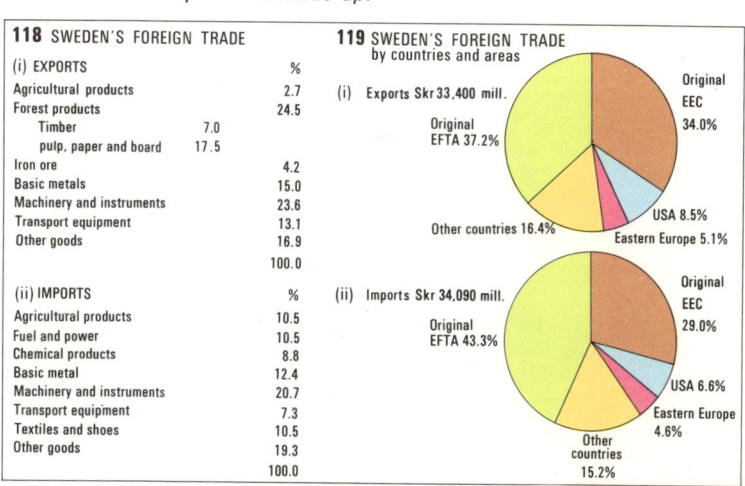

119 SWEDEN'S FOREIGN TRADE by countries and areas

(i) Exports Skr 33,400 mill.

Original EFTA 37.2% / Original EEC 34.0% / USA 8.5% / Eastern Europe 5.1% / Other countries 16.4%

(ii) Imports Skr 34,090 mill.

Original EFTA 43.3% / Original EEC 29.0% / USA 6.6% / Eastern Europe 4.6% / Other countries 15.2%

Denmark is made up of the Mainland (see fig. 120), Greenland and the Faroe Islands—wide differences exist between location, area and population totals of all three. The Faroes and Greenland have little development and very few people, and will not be dealt with here. Find them in your atlas.

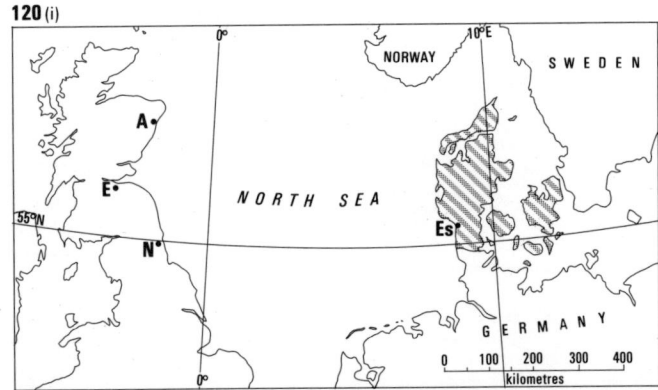

120 (i)

120 (ii)

	Population million	Area sq. km.	Density of population
Mainland	4.9	43,100	114
Faroe Islands	0.035	1,400	25
Greenland	0.04	2,176,000	–

Fig. 120(i) The position of the Mainland

120(i)a   Name places lettered E, N and Es.

120(i)b   Estimate distance between N and Es.

120(ii)   Illustrate the information provided about area and population totals by means of pie-graphs. Note population densities. The area of Scotland is 79 000 sq. km. and its population totals 5·2 million.

Surface features

The surface of Denmark is glacial and post-glacial in origin and the solid geology is almost everywhere masked by these later deposits. Bornholm is the only part which structurally belongs to Sweden.

Fig. 121 Surface deposits
Fig. 122 Terminal moraine country

121/122a   Into what two main sections may Mainland Denmark be divided?

121/122b   Briefly describe the surface features of each division.

121/122c   What is an esker, a drumlin, a terminal moraine? Describe appearance and how formed in each case.

121/122d   Where may each of these features be found in UK? Name an actual example area for each.

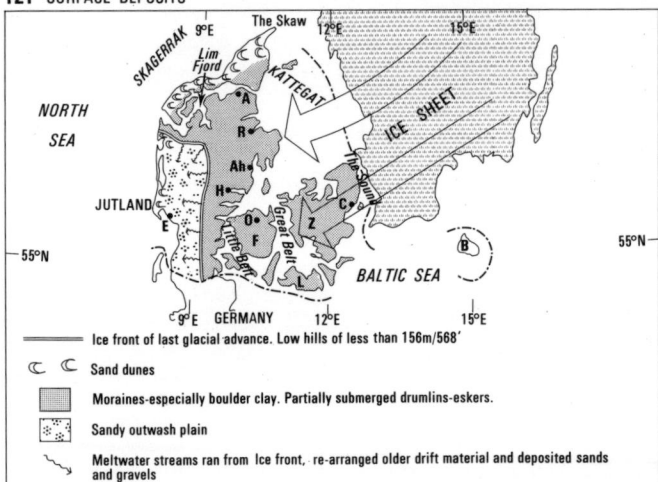

121 SURFACE DEPOSITS

Ice front of last glacial advance. Low hills of less than 156m/568'

Sand dunes

Moraines—especially boulder clay. Partially submerged drumlins-eskers.

Sandy outwash plain

Meltwater streams ran from Ice front, re-arranged older drift material and deposited sands and gravels

Fig. 123 Climate, land use and surface materials

123a   Which side of Denmark is (i) wetter (ii) warmer in winter (iii) cooler in summer?

123b   Which part has (i) conifers and marram grass (ii) grasses and mixed grains (iii) cereals, roots, vegetables (iv) cattle and pigs?

123c   Frosts occur all over Denmark in winter. Mention two ways in which frosts help cereal farmers.

Soils

Soils are largely derived from surface deposits. Those derived from glacial clays are richer than the very sandy soils (though the latter have been greatly improved by addition of artificial fertilisers). Drained peats are rich.

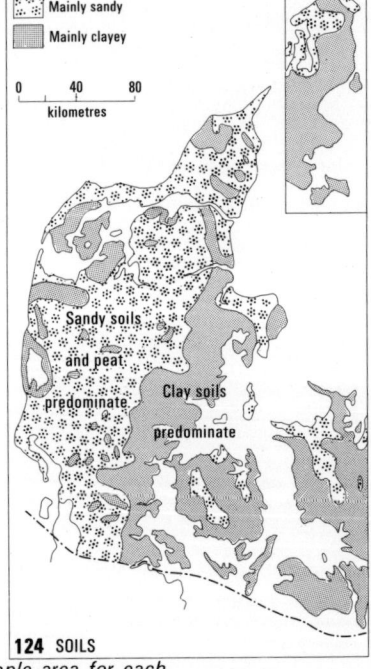

Mainly sandy

Mainly clayey

Fig. 124 Broad soil groups of Denmark

124a   To which soil group does the Danish archipelago (island group) belong?

124 SOILS

122 TYPICAL LAND SURFACE IN AREA OF GLACIAL TERMINAL MORAINE

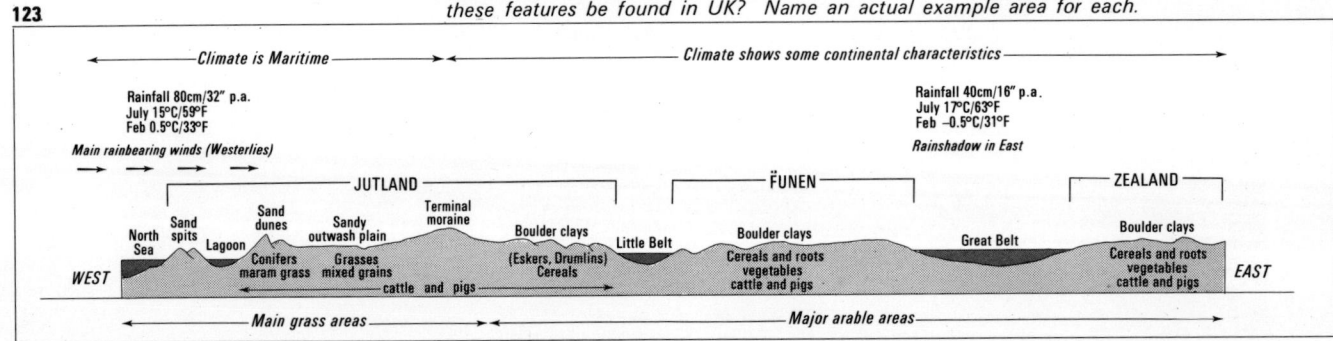

123

"Its (Denmark's) prosperity derives from its sales abroad of high-quality farm produce, notably butter, bacon, eggs and poultry . . . There is little timber and no iron-ore . . . no fuel or HEP and fisheries are less important (than Norway or Sweden)" (Western Europe, A.F.A. Mutton).

"Neither its soil nor its climate is outstandingly favourable to farming . . . its farmers co-operation in the production of quality food products is unsurpassed . . . bacon exports are the highest, the butter exports are second (and) the cheese comes third (among the world's exporters of food)" ('Denmark Farms On' F. A. Rush).

The prosperity of Danish farming has been the result of determined and continuous adjustments to meet difficulties and to seize opportunities created largely by events beyond her own borders. Today agriculture is no longer the biggest industry but is second to manufacturing in respect of total workers, value of output and export earnings.

Some important events and their results for Denmark

1 1846 Corn protection ceased in Britain and a Free Trade Policy was adopted there. One result was the beginning of the now traditional flow of butter, bacon (and then cattle and pigs) from Denmark to the northern ports of East England.

2 1850-1900 (i) Even bigger and better steamships brought greater and greater supplies of cheap corn (wheat) from the N American prairies to Europe. The Danes—previously exporters of corn but no longer able to compete—fed their home-grown cereal to their cattle and pigs and increased their sales of these animal products to the UK.

(ii) Newly established steamship services across the North Sea took even more and more butter and bacon to the growing (industrial) British market.

e.g. 1860's exports to UK were 3 000 tons of butter and 4 000 tons of bacon.

1882's exports to UK were 12 000 tons of butter and 16 000 tons of bacon.

1900's exports to UK were 78 000 tons of butter and 67 000 tons of bacon.

(iii) 1850's-1860's Folk-High Schools (inspired by Bishop Grundtvig) spread across Denmark and taught better husbandry, the need for co-operation between farmers, and the need for Credit Associations (to supply money for capital development).

(iv) 1866 The Danish Heathland Society began work (see fig. 125).

(v) 1882 The invention of a continuous cream separator made possible for the first time really important co-operation in bulk-butter production. The co-operative dairy idea was born. By 1888 there were 215 and by 1935 over 1 400 Co-operative Dairies (since reduced to 650 by mergers). Other such co-operatives soon developed in all aspects of farming, e.g. breeding, purchasing, selling, bacon-curing, quality control.

3 1950's-1960's Post-war Europe's demand for Danish farm products declined as other countries improved their own supplies of typical Danish exports e.g. value of Danish egg exports to UK in 1958= £20 mill. and in 1967 only £4 mill.

The use of subsidies and the development of self-centred economies threatened to strangle trade expansion, and to combat this the EEC and EFTA were formed. Denmark belonged to EFTA (1960) but not to EEC and therefore her exports to EEC countries declined. In May 1961 it was realised that international economic diplomacy made Government support for Danish farmers imperative, and grants are now paid each year and used particularly to improve techniques in all aspects of farming.

4 In 1967 Denmark applied for membership of EEC (along with Norway, UK and Eire). In 1973 she was accepted and a new chapter in her farming history now opens before her.

Fig 126 Agricultural statistics

Examine the statistics in fig. 126 very carefully.

126a Suggest reasons for: (i) the reduction in number of young people taking up farming, (ii) the increase in output per man, (iii) the increase in farm outputs in general in spite of the decline in farm workers, (iv) the changes in farm size since 1951 (increase in mechanisation and modern techniques requiring large capital outlay, and the higher costs of farming in general make small units unprofitable).

Translation of Danish poem which marked the formation of the first dairy co-operative.

"West Jutland peasants in common feeling,
This stone to progress consecrate;
Alone we fail, united we accomplish,
The good of all on Denmark's dear estate."

125 MAIN AREAS OF HEATHLAND IN JUTLAND 1800 AND 1960

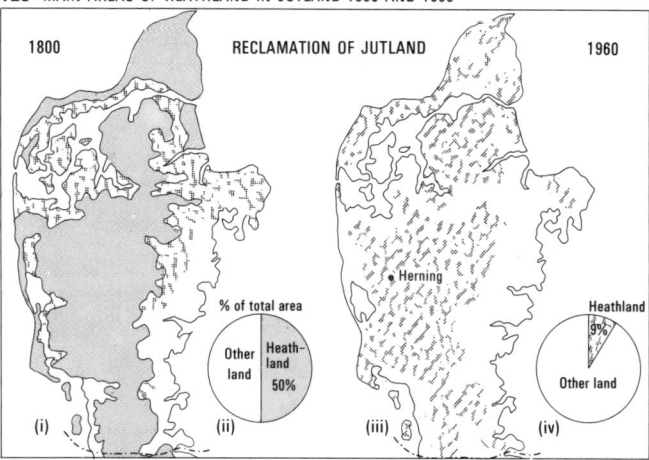

Fig. 125 Heath clearance

The Danish Heathland Society was formed in 1866 to reclaim the wastes of Jutland. New towns (e.g. Herning) grew up amid the new farmlands in what used to be desolate, worthless and unpopulated heathland.

125a Which areas had the most heath?

125b What was the main land surface material in the heathland?

125c The total area of farmland in Denmark is about 3 million hectares. How many hectares are still heath-covered?

Note: The land is heavily fertilized (three times as much in use today as 30 years ago), limed and manured as required.

126 SOME AGRICULTURAL STATISTICS FOR DENMARK

AREAS; EMPLOYMENT; MECHANISATION	UNIT OUTPUTS
(i) Numbers of farms 1946 c. 206,000 1970 c. 140,000	(v) With production index per man for 1935-39 as 100 the output per man index 1965-69 = 250
(ii) Millions of full-time farm workers 1950 c. 470,000 (21% of labour force) (including the farmer) 1970 c. 211,000 (8% of labour force)	(vi) Crop yield 1940 c. 35 c.u.* per hectare (average all crops) 1970 c. 50 c.u. * 1 crop unit (c.u.)=fodder value of 100 kg of barley
(iii) Thousands of young people entering full-time farming p.a. 1940's 14,000 1960's 5,000	(vii) Milk yields per 1900 c. 1000 kg dairy cow p.a. Total dairy cattle c. 1 million 1960's c. 3000 kg c. 1.4 million
(iv) Total number of tractors in use 1940's Not available 1960's 175,000	(viii) Butter output 1900's c. 40 Mkg p.a. 1960's c. 3000 Mkg p.a.
Total combine harvesters in use 1940's Not available 1960's 40,000	(ix) The British like streaky (lean) bacon (Danish 'land race' pig) 1956 Fat area figure for tested pigs 38.4 sq cms 1966 Fat area figure for tested pigs 27.5 sq cms

(x) CHANGES IN FARM SIZE 1951-67

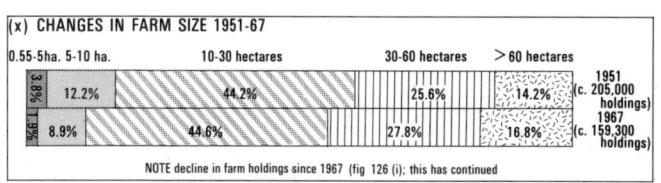

NOTE decline in farm holdings since 1967 (fig 126 (i); this has continued

127 DENMARK'S LAND USE: IN DETAIL

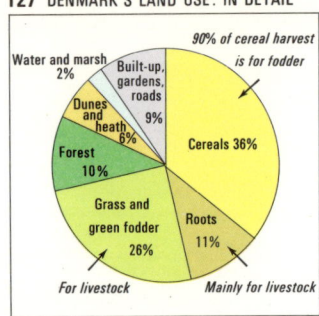

Water and marsh 2%
Built-up, gardens, roads 9%
90% of cereal harvest is for fodder
Dunes and heath 6%
Cereals 36%
Forest 10%
Roots 11%
Grass and green fodder 26%
For livestock
Mainly for livestock

128 CROP YIELDS

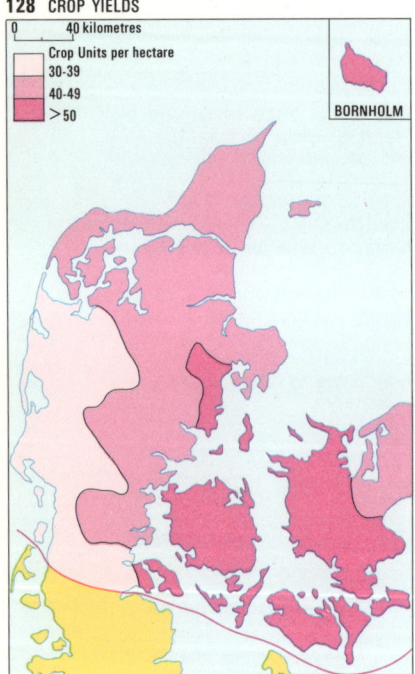

0   40 kilometres

Crop Units per hectare
30-39
40-49
>50

BORNHOLM

129 THE TWO MAIN AGRICULTURAL REGIONS

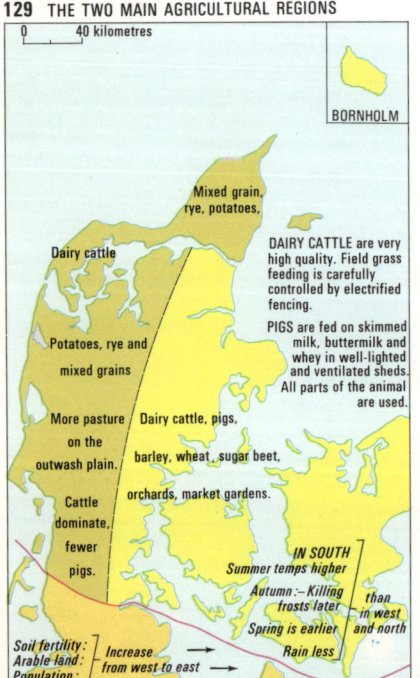

0   40 kilometres

BORNHOLM

Mixed grain, rye, potatoes.

Dairy cattle

DAIRY CATTLE are very high quality. Field grass feeding is carefully controlled by electrified fencing.

PIGS are fed on skimmed milk, buttermilk and whey in well-lighted and ventilated sheds. All parts of the animal are used.

Potatoes, rye and mixed grains

More pasture on the outwash plain.

Dairy cattle, pigs, barley, wheat, sugar beet, orchards, market gardens.

Cattle dominate, fewer pigs.

IN SOUTH
Summer temps higher
Autumn:- Killing frosts later   than in west and north
Spring is earlier
Rain less

Soil fertility:
Arable land: Increase
Population: from west to east

Fig. 127 Land use in detail

127a What percentage of the land is used to supply livestock needs?

127b Where are most of (i) the sand dunes today (ii) the water and marsh areas?

Fig. 128 Crop yields

128a Which areas (broadly) have the highest and which the lowest yields?

Fig.129 The two main agricultural regions

Note the items which increase from West to East. The more productive the land the higher the population density.

129a Try to account for the higher productivity of the islands.

129b Note carefully the main product differences between the two regions.

Ingredients for a famous Danish open sandwich—the Hans Andersen.

Put the following on a slice of rye bread: crisp fried bacon covered with alternate panels of liver paste and sliced tomato topped with horseradish and aspic.

Fig.130 Agricultural exports - make up and markets

Denmark exports about 70% of the total value of her agricultural products.

130a What is the approximate value of her butter exports?

130b Which two of the items 1-5 were most important exports to pre–1973 EFTA?

130c Which two items (1-5) were most important exports to pre–1973 EEC?

Fig. 131 Agricultural exports-markets

130 AGRICULTURAL EXPORTS

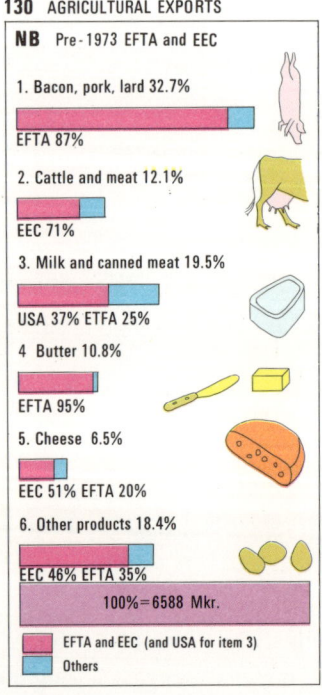

NB Pre - 1973 EFTA and EEC

1. Bacon, pork, lard 32.7%
EFTA 87%

2. Cattle and meat 12.1%
EEC 71%

3. Milk and canned meat 19.5%
USA 37% ETFA 25%

4. Butter 10.8%
EFTA 95%

5. Cheese 6.5%
EEC 51% EFTA 20%

6. Other products 18.4%
EEC 46% EFTA 35%
100%=6588 Mkr.

EFTA and EEC (and USA for item 3)
Others

132 MAIN INDUSTRIAL CENTRES

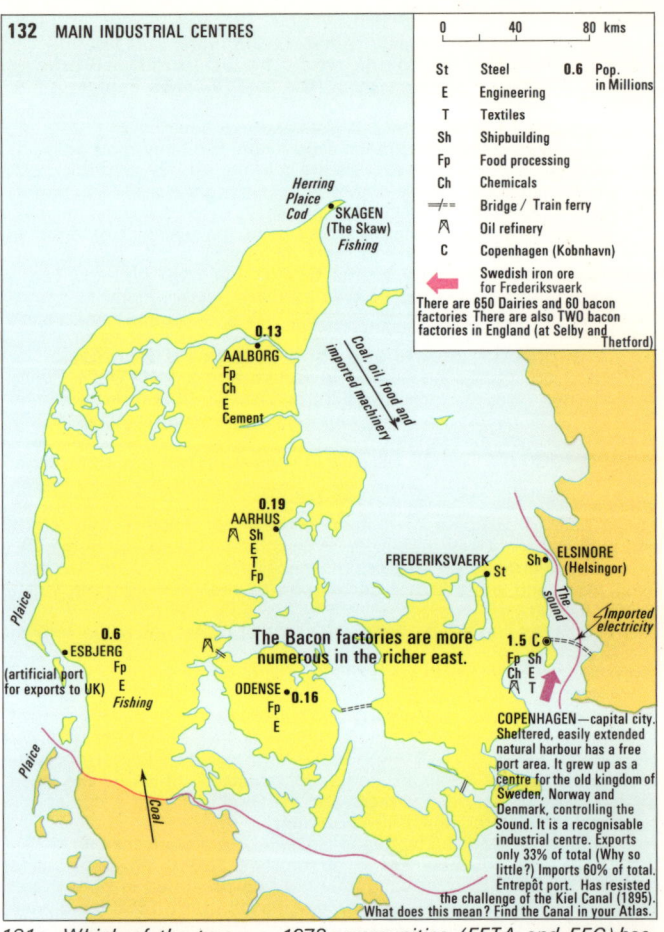

0   40   80 kms

St   Steel   0.6   Pop. in Millions
E   Engineering
T   Textiles
Sh   Shipbuilding
Fp   Food processing
Ch   Chemicals
=== Bridge / Train ferry
⋏   Oil refinery
C   Copenhagen (Kobnhavn)
→   Swedish iron ore for Frederiksvaerk

There are 650 Dairies and 60 bacon factories There are also TWO bacon factories in England (at Selby and Thetford)

Herring Plaice Cod
SKAGEN (The Skaw) Fishing

0.13
AALBORG
Fp Ch E Cement

Coal, oil, food and imported machinery

0.19
AARHUS
⋏ Sh E T Fp

FREDERIKSVAERK St

ELSINORE (Helsingor)
Sh

Plaice

0.6
ESBJERG
Fp E
(artificial port for exports to UK) Fishing

The Bacon factories are more numerous in the richer east.

The Sound
Imported electricity

1.5 C
Fp Sh
Ch E T

ODENSE   0.16
Fp E

Plaice

Coal

COPENHAGEN—capital city. Sheltered, easily extended natural harbour has a free port area. It grew up as a centre for the old kingdom of Sweden, Norway and Denmark, controlling the Sound. It is a recognisable industrial centre. Exports only 33% of total (Why so little?) Imports 60% of total. Entrepôt port. Has resisted the challenge of the Kiel Canal (1895). What does this mean? Find the Canal in your Atlas.

131a Which of the two pre–1973 communities (EFTA and EEC) has (i) increased (ii) decreased its share of Danish farm produce? Explain the latter change.

131b Which non-European country has taken a greater share of Danish exports in recent years? (Canned meat.)

Note: Agriculture produces about 9% of Gross National Product (89 400 Mkr) and about 33.5% of total exports (19 400 M kroner). Examine fig. 135. (7.5Kr =1 U.S. $.)

Industry

Fig.132 Main industrial centres

132a List the main industries, and next to each name its main centre(s)

132b Where are Selby and Thetford (UK)?

131 AGRICULTURAL EXPORTS

DISTRIBUTION ACCORDING TO MARKET (Pre-1973)	1959 %	1969 %
EFTA of which Great Britain's share	45.1	52.8
	41.0	44.5
EEC of which Western Germany's share	37.2	24.3
	27.4	13.1
USA	5.6	9.0
Eastern bloc countries	3.3	3.0
Remainder of world	8.8	10.9
TOTAL AGRICULTURAL EXPORTS	100.0	100.0
	5,262	6,588 Million Kroner

Fig. 133 Urban/rural distribution

Although agriculture is vitally important to Denmark; most people live in towns. West Jutland is a region of scattered farms, low population density and rapid growth in population. East Jutland has villages, high population and a declining rural population.

133 URBAN/RURAL DISTRIBUTION

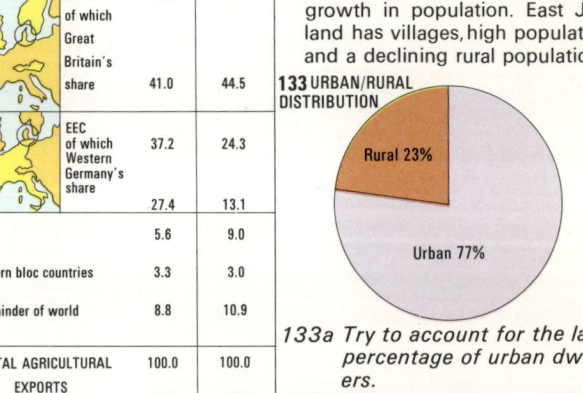

Rural 23%
Urban 77%

133a Try to account for the large percentage of urban dwellers.

133b What percentage of UK population is urban?

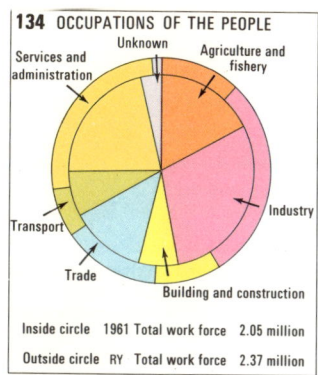

134 OCCUPATIONS OF THE PEOPLE

Services and administration · Unknown · Agriculture and fishery · Industry · Building and construction · Trade · Transport

Inside circle   1961 Total work force   2.05 million
Outside circle   RY Total work force   2.37 million

Industry, trade, population age structure

Fig. 134 Occupations of the people
134a By how many did the working population increase?

134b Which activities have increased their labour percentage and which have shown a decrease? (Make two lists.)

Fig. 135 Gross National Product
(7.5 Kroner=1 U.S. $)
135a By what percentage has industry increased its share of total gross product?
135b Which activity in particular has decreased its percentage share? Note the doubling of public services percentage.
135c Illustrate the latest GNP figures (three groups -industry, agriculture,the rest) with a pie graph

Fig. 136 Industrial employment
136a Which single industry provides work for the largest group of workers?
136b Where does Denmark obtain her iron ore?

Fig 137 Urban location of industry
137a Why do people like to live and work in towns?

135 GROSS NATIONAL PRODUCT

at factor cost according to trades	1950 %		RY %	
Industry (incl. public works)	19.5		21.1	
The trades	9.7	35.8	9.2	39.8
Building and construction work	6.6		9.5	
Agriculture	18.8		7.5	
Gardening, forestry, fishing, fur farming, etc.	2.4	21.2	1.4	8.9
Trade and commerce	19.8		16.4	
Transport	8.3		10.0	
Public services	7.3		14.7	
Other services	3.2	43.0	4.5	51.3
Use of dwelling houses	4.4		5.7	
GROSS FACTOR INCOME in millions of kroner	100.0% 21,600		100.0% 89,400	

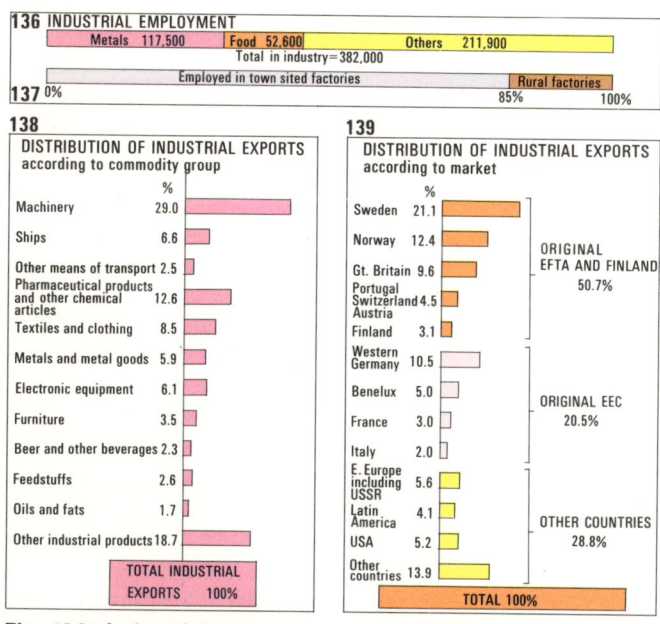

136 INDUSTRIAL EMPLOYMENT
Metals 117,500   Food 52,600   Others 211,900
Total in industry=382,000
137 0%   Employed in town sited factories   85%   Rural factories   100%

138 DISTRIBUTION OF INDUSTRIAL EXPORTS according to commodity group %
	%
Machinery	29.0
Ships	6.6
Other means of transport	2.5
Pharmaceutical products and other chemical articles	12.6
Textiles and clothing	8.5
Metals and metal goods	5.9
Electronic equipment	6.1
Furniture	3.5
Beer and other beverages	2.3
Feedstuffs	2.6
Oils and fats	1.7
Other industrial products	18.7
TOTAL INDUSTRIAL EXPORTS 100%	

139 DISTRIBUTION OF INDUSTRIAL EXPORTS according to market %
	%	
Sweden	21.1	
Norway	12.4	ORIGINAL EFTA AND FINLAND 50.7%
Gt. Britain	9.6	
Portugal	4.5	
Switzerland Austria		
Finland	3.1	
Western Germany	10.5	ORIGINAL EEC 20.5%
Benelux	5.0	
France	3.0	
Italy	2.0	
E. Europe including USSR	5.6	OTHER COUNTRIES 28.8%
Latin America	4.1	
USA	5.2	
Other countries	13.9	
TOTAL 100%		

Fig. 138 Industrial exports by commodities
138a Which commodity leads all the others?
138b Draw a bar-graph showing total exports of industry, specifically indicating machinery and chemical products. Put all the others together as 'the rest'.

Fig. 139 Industrial exports by markets
139a Which of the three markets indicated, has dominated industrial exports?
139b Which country imported most Danish industrial exports?

140 FOREIGN TRADE 1959 AND RY, distribution by market areas

	IMPORTS		EXPORTS	
	1959 %	RY %	1959 %	RY %
GREAT BRITAIN	16.5	13.9	25.8	23.1
Sweden, Norway and Finland	14.3	21.6	13.2	23.3
Switzerland, Austria and Portugal	2.4	4.2	2.0	4.1
Total original EFTA countries	33.2	39.7	41.0	50.5
Western Germany	20.5	19.2	21.4	12.1
Other original EEC countries	16.3	13.5	10.3	10.8
Total original EEC countries	36.8	32.7	31.7	22.9
Eastern Europe including USSR	4.7	4.0	4.6	4.3
USA and Canada	9.7	9.2	8.8	8.1
Other countries	15.6	14.4	13.9	14.2
TOTAL	100.0	100.0	100.0	100.0
in millions of Kr.	11,020	21,855	9.506	17,257

Foreign Trade

Fig. 140 Distribution of foreign trade by markets
140a Which market area has shown a definite increase in both imports from and exports to Denmark- and which has shown a marked decrease in trading activity?

Note: Totals have, of course, increased in both exports and imports.

140b What was the deficit in Denmark's trade balance recently ?

Note: The trade deficit is met by 'invisible earnings' (what are these?) and 'borrowing' (investments by foreigners).

141 DENMARK'S IMPORTS
	1958 %	RY %
Raw materials for Agriculture (especially fertiliser from Norway)	10	6
Raw materials for industry	24	20
Fuels, petrol, electricity	16	10
Semi-manufactures	18	21
Machinery and apparatus	10	15
Transport equipment	10	12
Finished consumer goods	5	10
Foodstuffs etc.	7	6
TOTAL IMPORTS	100	100
Million kroner	9,395	21,855

Fig. 141 Denmark's imports
141a Which imports have (i) increased their percentage share of total imports since 1958 (ii) shown a percentage share decline? (Make two lists.)
141b What were the money values of each group of imports in the two years ? Have any declined ?

142 DISTRIBUTION OF EXPORTS by commodity group
	1959 %	RY %
Agricultural products (proper)	47.8	26.3
Canned meat and milk products	7.3	7.2
Industrial products	39.6	59.8
Fish and other commodities	5.3	6.7
TOTAL	100	100
in millions of kroner	9,506	19,400

143 DISTRIBUTION BY AGE 1901 AND 1970s

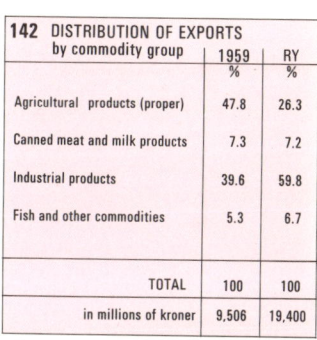

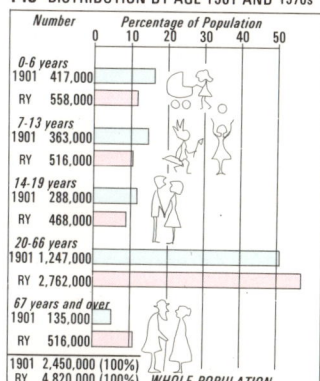

Number	Percentage of Population 0 10 20 30 40 50
0-6 years 1901 417,000	
RY 558,000	
7-13 years 1901 363,000	
RY 516,000	
14-19 years 1901 288,000	
RY 468,000	
20-66 years 1901 1,247,000	
RY 2,762,000	
67 years and over 1901 135,000	
RY 516,000	
1901 2,450,000 (100%) RY 4,820,000 (100%)	WHOLE POPULATION

Fig. 142 Exports by commodity group
142a Illustrate the two sets of figures with pie-graphs.
142b Describe and attempt to explain the changes in indicated percentage shares of total exports?
142c What were the money values of (i) agricultural and (ii) industrial exports in each illustrated year?

Fig. 143 Population - age structures 1901 and 1970s
143a Has Denmark now a greater or smaller proportion of (i) the elderly (ii) the young?
143b Why does age structure matter?

Figs 144/148 Switzerland: situation and size

144/145a How much larger is UK in area and population?
146a   Name countries 1-10.

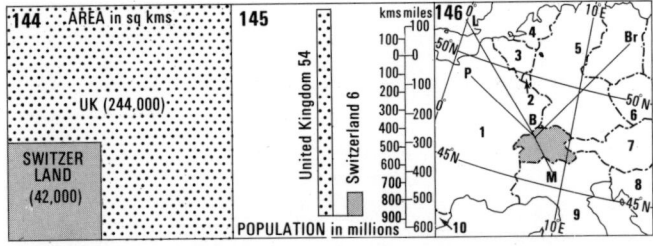

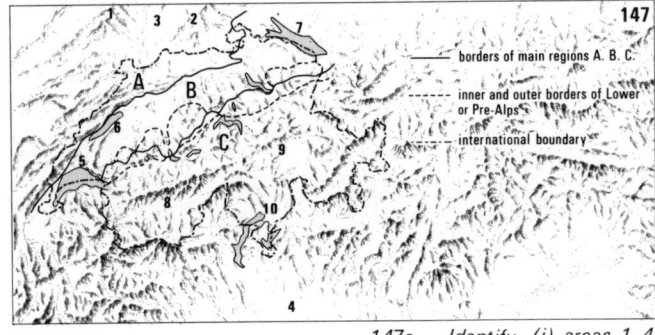

147a   Identify (i) areas 1-4, (ii) lakes 5-7,(iii) rivers 8-10.

148a   What fraction of Switzerland is made up of Area C(name the area)?

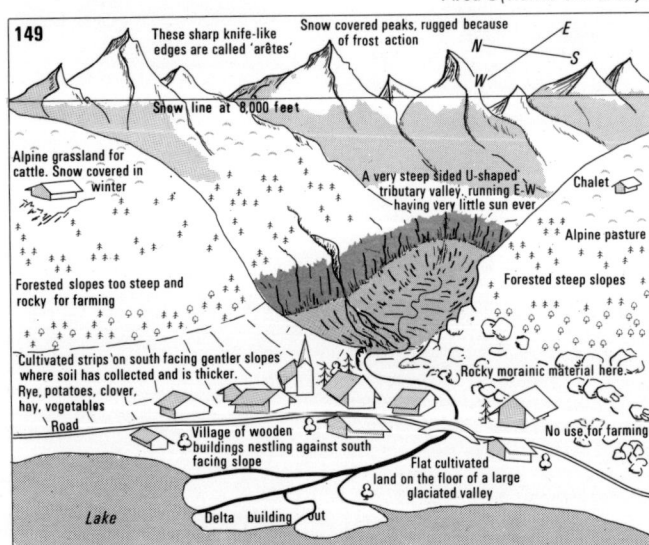

Fig. 149 An Alpine Valley

149a Make a careful examination of this drawing of an Alpine Valley and then describe(i) the relief and glaciated features (ii) the vegetation in relation to relief (iii) land use (iv) location of settlement.

The Main Regions of Switzerland

Area A Simple folded Jura and its plateau.
Mainly limestone in parallel chains of ridge and valley (anti- and synclines). Flat-topped in North. Mean height 750m. Karst features.

Area B Central Plateau.
Once an arm of the sea—then an inland sea. Sediment from Alps, Jura and Black Forest. Richest area with most people. Mean height 580m.

Area C Alpine ranges, NE-SW grain. Main granite and slate core covered with chalks, marls and other sedimentaries. Great variety of glacial forms. Difficult country—few people—tourism. Mean height 1700m.

Climate

The central position of Switzerland ensures that there is considerable variety in the air masses it experiences. This, together with the enormously varied relief makes for a variety of localised climates in valley, mountain, plateau and plain.

Westerly winds and depressions bring considerable precipitation—especially in the summer months, easterly winds in winter are cold and unpleasant, southerly winds bring the warmth of the Mediterranean.
The Jura has severe winters with snow, summers are warm (vines grow on south-facing slopes) and westerlies bring much rain.
The Swiss (Central) Plateau has chilly damp, misty winters—Berne —2°C/28°F in January; summers also damp, are warm and temperatures may rise to a July mean of 20°C/68°F.
The Alps experience a 'mountain climate' with relief dominating local conditions. Valley bottoms are 'cold pockets' in winter especially in the East (January means —5.6°C/22°F). In July temperatures average from 16.7°C/62°F to 21.1°C/70°F and decrease with height at all seasons. Precipitation varies greatly according to aspect and relief e.g. St. Gotthard massif about 250cms/100" p.a., Grisons Alps in the east about 150cms/60" p.a., Upper Rhone Valley about 60cms/24" p.a. and Rhine Valley near Lake Constance/Boden-See about 125cms/50" p.a.

150/157   Land use and population

150a What does the figure suggest is the main emphasis of farming?

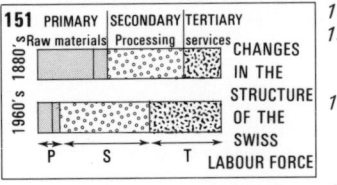

Arable and Vineyard	Feed crops	Pasture	Forest	Mountain etc.	Glaciers 4.7%	Lakes 3.3%
6.6%	19.9%	26.1%	23.8%	15.6%	Unproductive 23.6%	

150   LAND USE IN SWITZERLAND

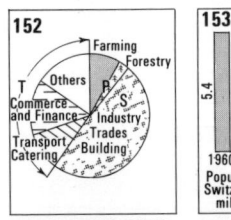

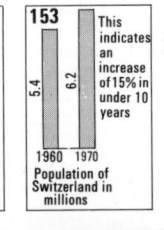

151a Describe the changes shown.
152a What occupations are included in each section, P, S and T?
153a By how many did the population increase 1960-1970 (i) in Switzerland (ii) in UK?
154a What is meant by 'dormitory area'?
154b Why is the urban population greater than that indicated?

154 RURAL/URBAN RATIO

Official figures seem to indicate that more live in the country than in the towns. However, the figures take no account of the new urban areas beyond the present town boundaries. These are expanding greatly: e.g. between 1950 and 1960 'Basle -Country' (fig.166) population increased by 38%. It is the dormitory area for Basle. Industrialisation increases the suburban at the expense of the rural area.

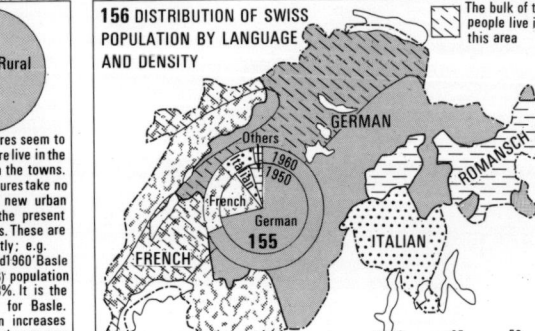

156 DISTRIBUTION OF SWISS POPULATION BY LANGUAGE AND DENSITY

155/156a Which language is increasingly spoken in Switzerland?
155/156b In which region do the bulk of the population live?
157a Try to account for the influx of Italian workers.

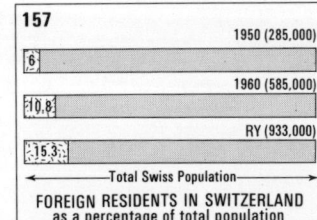

157

1950 (285,000)
1960 (585,000)
RY (933,000)

FOREIGN RESIDENTS IN SWITZERLAND as a percentage of total population

(Well over half of the foreign workers in Switzerland are Italian, most being in building)

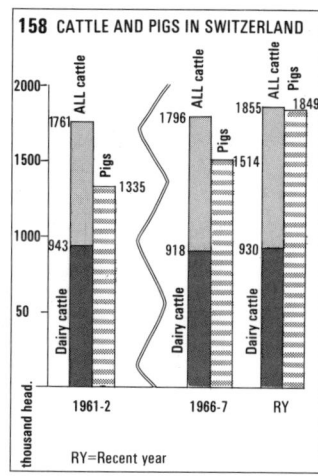

158 CATTLE AND PIGS IN SWITZERLAND

Although only a small proportion of the land can be used, the Swiss produce about 60% of all their food. Methods are intensive and scientific. Apart from the richer Central plateau natural conditions favour livestock and their feedcrops. Fewer and fewer are engaged in farming though output increases. The limited importance of foodstuffs as exports is shown by fig. 168.

Figs. 158/160 Agriculture

158a Describe what is shown.

159a Although dairy cattle numbers remain fairly constant, milk yields have risen. Try to account for this.

160a The fragmentation of cultivated strips of individual holdings has been a drawback. The plots per holding are being reduced (in 1939 the average was 10 per holding, today it is seven). What has happened to (i) total number of holdings (ii) the size of holdings?

160b Why should consolidation of holdings lead to better yields?

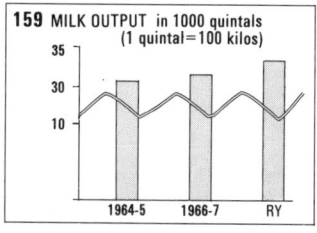

159 MILK OUTPUT in 1000 quintals (1 quintal=100 kilos)

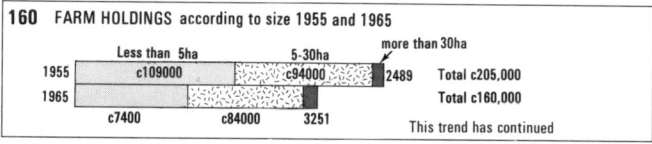

160 FARM HOLDINGS according to size 1955 and 1965

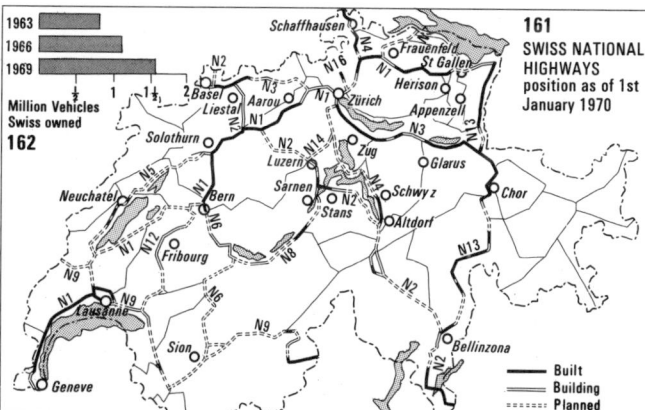

161 SWISS NATIONAL HIGHWAYS position as of 1st January 1970

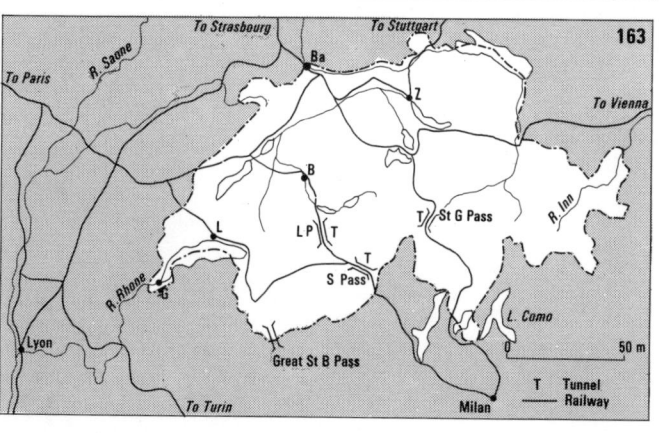

163

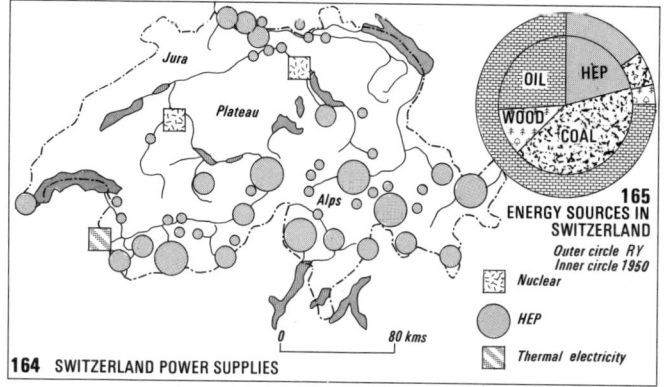

164 SWITZERLAND POWER SUPPLIES

165 ENERGY SOURCES IN SWITZERLAND
Outer circle RY
Inner circle 1950
Nuclear
HEP
Thermal electricity

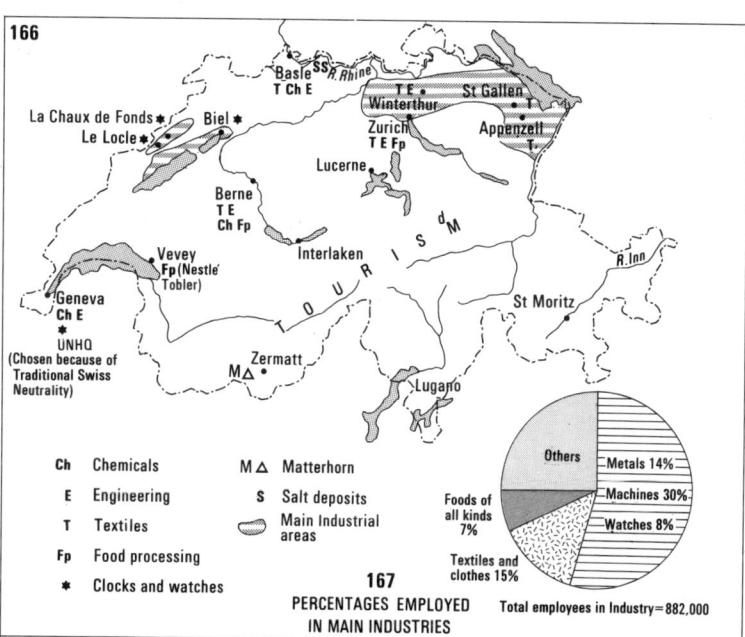

166

167 PERCENTAGES EMPLOYED IN MAIN INDUSTRIES

Ch Chemicals
E Engineering
T Textiles
Fp Food processing
* Clocks and watches
M△ Matterhorn
S Salt deposits
Main Industrial areas

Metals 14%
Machines 30%
Watches 8%
Textiles and clothes 15%
Foods of all kinds 7%
Others

Total employees in Industry=882,000

The development of industry, the specialisations of agriculture and the growth of tourism (total nights in Swiss hotels by visitors —1937=8 million, 1968=19 million) have all depended on transport developments.

Figs. 161/167 Communications and industry

161a Describe the locations of the main new highways.

163a Name Passes - Great St. B, St. G, S.Pass, L.P. Towns - G, L, B, Z, Ba.

164a In which section do most HEP stations occur and why?

165a Describe the changes in energy supplies since 1950.

166a List the main centres of (i) the clock industry (why in West and North West)? (ii) textiles.

The difficulties of (i) lack of minerals (ii) land-locked position and long supply routes (iii) small home market have been met by (i) harnessing HEP (ii) concentrating on high value, small-scale, highly finished articles (much skill) (iii) developing good transport system (iv) taking advantage of location in Europe and neutrality to develop as world finance centre.

Fig. 168 Balance of trade

168a Which four activities bring in most money on balance (i.e. income from the activity minus outgoings on that general activity)?

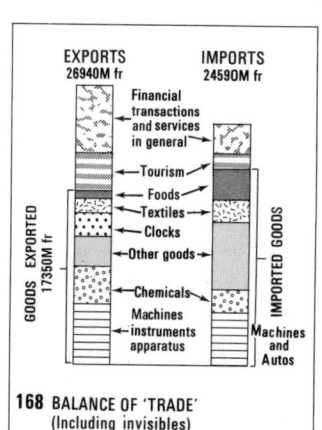

168 BALANCE OF 'TRADE' (Including invisibles)

EXPORTS 26940M fr
IMPORTS 24590M fr
Financial transactions and services in general
Tourism
Foods
Textiles
Clocks
Other goods
Chemicals
Machines instruments apparatus
Machines and Autos
GOODS EXPORTED 17350M fr
IMPORTED GOODS

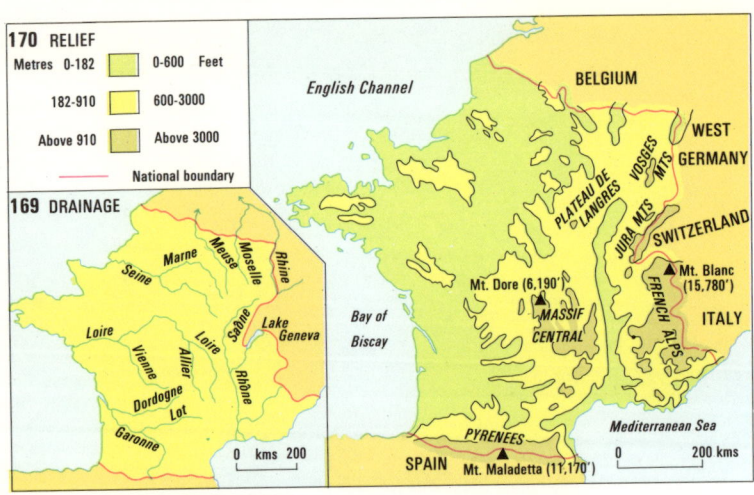

Fig. 169/170 Relief and drainage

169/170a Name and locate the main highland regions of France.
169/170b Which river(s) (i) divide the French Alps from the Massif Central (ii) rises in the Massif Central and flows West through the southern part of the Paris Basin (iii) rises in the Pyrenees and is joined by right bank tributaries from the Massif Central?

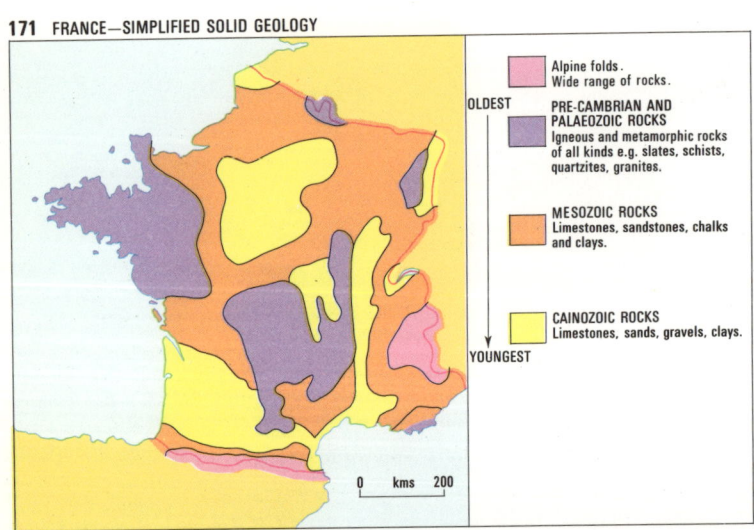

Figs 171/172 Simplified geology/main regions

171/172a (i) Name the four main regions of Pre-Cambrian and Palaeozoic rocks. (ii) Are they highland or lowland regions?
171/172b (i) Name the three main lowland regions. (ii) Are they made of young or old rocks? (iii) Quote examples.

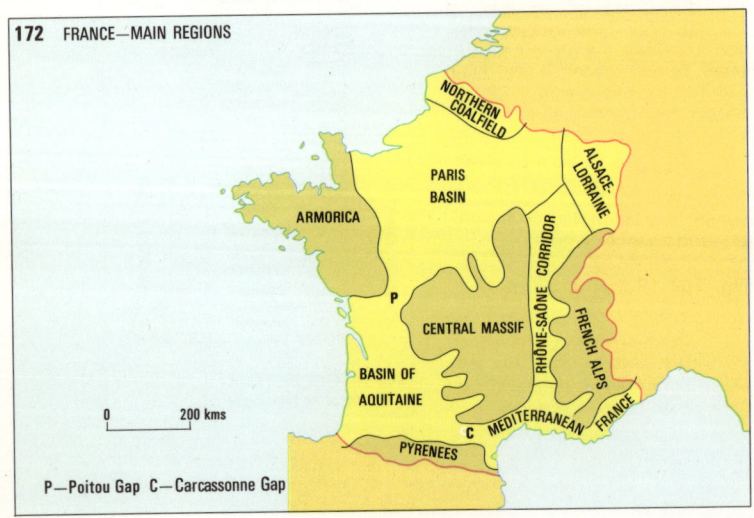

P—Poitou Gap   C—Carcassonne Gap

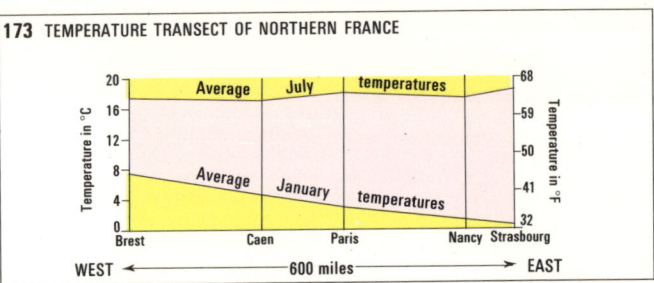

Fig. 173 Temperature transect of Northern France (for lines of transects see fig. 176)

173a Which town is warmest (i) in summer (ii) in winter?
173b (i) Compare the temperatures at Brest and Strasbourg in (a) January and (b) July. (ii) Which town has the greatest temperature range?
173c (i) In which direction do temperatures decrease (a) in winter (b) in summer? (ii) Explain why.

Fig. 174 Temperature transect of Eastern France

174a Which town is warmest all year round?
174b Compare its climate with that of Brest (see also figs. 175 and 176).
174c (i) In which direction do summer temperatures increase? (ii) Explain why.

Brest has a maritime climate, Strasbourg has a continental climate and Marseille a Mediterranean climate.

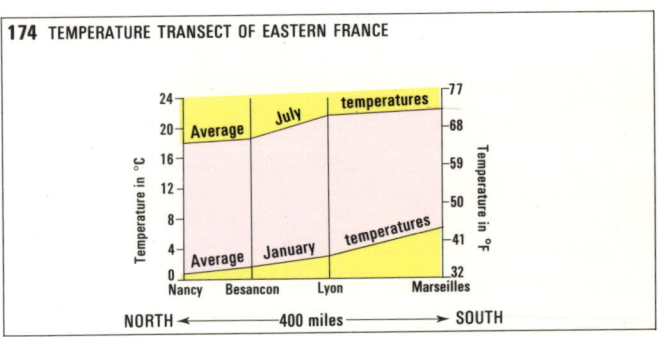

Fig. 175/176 Rainfall

175/176a Which regions of France receive (a) most rainfall (b) least rainfall? Explain why.
175/176b What type of rainfall is most common in (i) the Paris Basin (ii) Mediterranean France (iii) Armorica, and in which season is it concentrated?

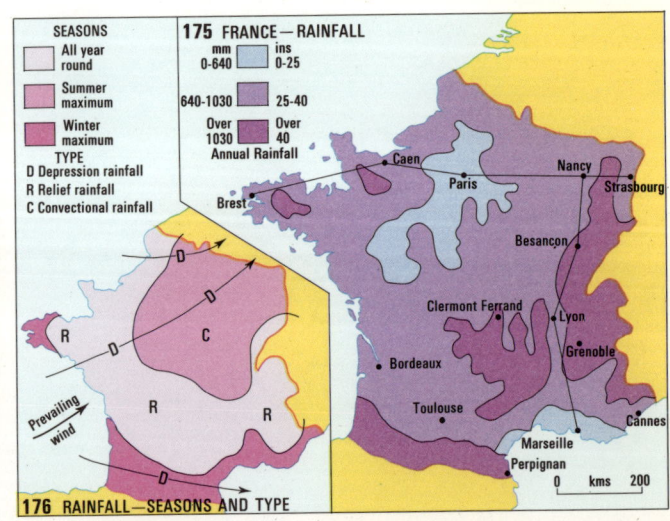

France is the foremost agricultural country in NW Europe.

177 TRADE IN AGRICULTURAL PRODUCE

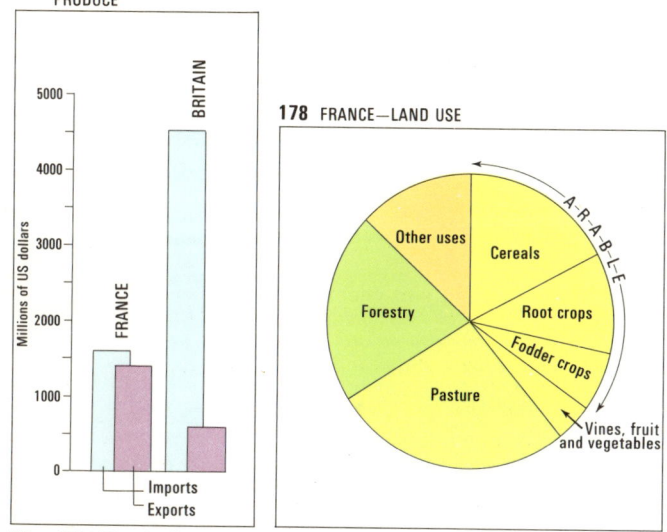

Fig. 177 Trade in agricultural produce
177a Define 'self-sufficient'.
177b Which is more self-sufficient in agricultural produce, France or Britain?

Fig. 178 Land use
178a What proportion of France is (i) farmland (ii) forested?
178b What proportion of this farmland is arable?
178c Compare land use in France and West Germany (see fig. 243)

179 FRENCH CROP PRODUCTION—as a percentage of the (pre–1973) EEC total

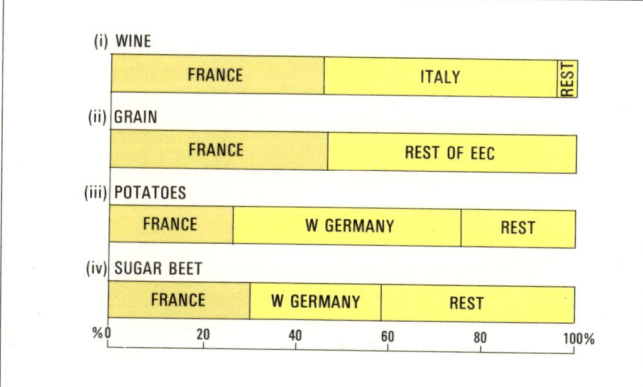

180 FRENCH LIVESTOCK—as a percentage of the (pre–1973) EEC total

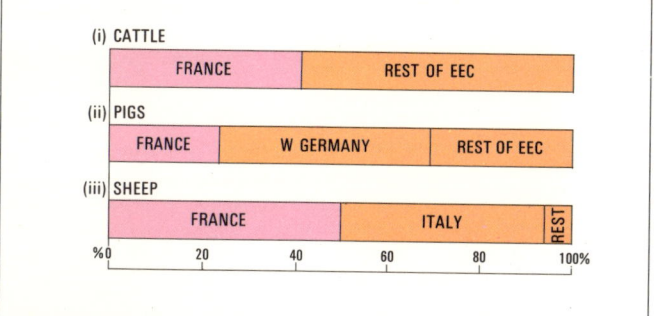

Figs 179/180 Crop production and livestock
179/180a Is France an important agricultural member of the EEC?
Quote two crop and two livestock examples to prove your answer.

Fig. 181 Percentage of farm workers

181a (i) What percentage of the working population of France is engaged in agriculture (see fig. 247)? (ii) Compare France with other EEC countries.
181b In which regions of France do farmers and farm workers exceed 45% of the total labour force?
181c What does this suggest about these regions?

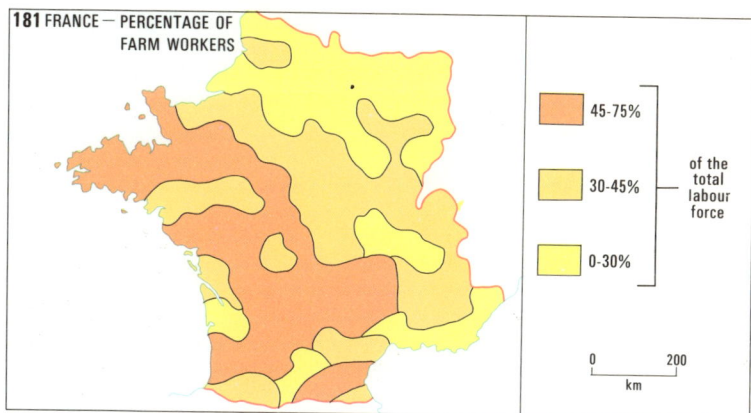

Fig. 182 Distribution of crops and livestock
182a (i) Which part of France is most important for wheat production? (ii) Is it highland or lowland? (iii) What is the climate like there? (see figs. 173—176)
182b (i) Which parts of France are important for cattle? (ii) Are they highland or lowland? (iii) Describe the common features of the climate in these parts.
182c (i) Compare the distributions of (a) wheat and maize (b) cattle and sheep. (ii) Explain the differences.

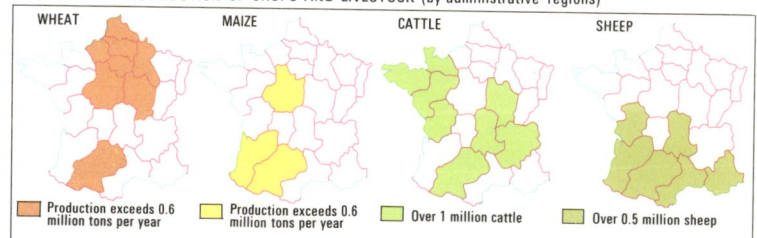

182 FRANCE—DISTRIBUTION OF CROPS AND LIVESTOCK (by administrative regions)

Fig. 183 Wine production

France is a major world producer of ordinary and quality wines. Most of the ordinary wines come from Languedoc.
183a (i) Where is Languedoc? (ii) In what way is it favoured for vine growing?
183b (i) Name the five river valleys associated with the remainder of wine (see also fig. 169) (ii) What advantages have these river valleys for vine growing?

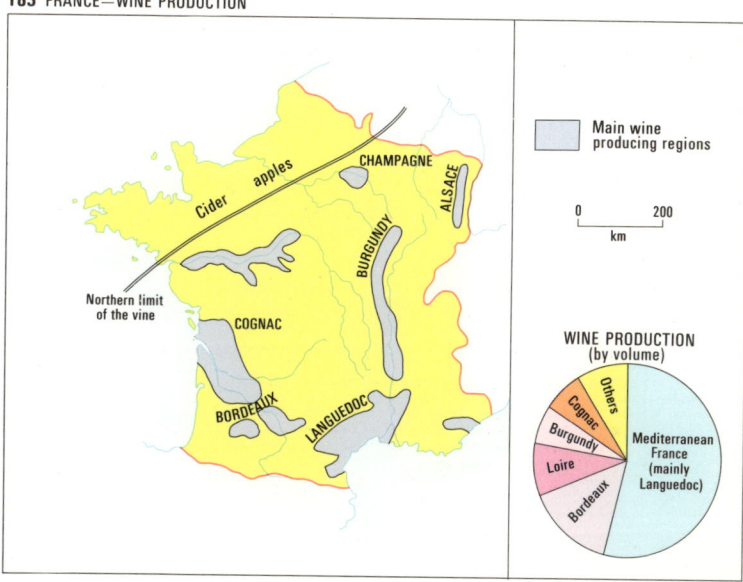

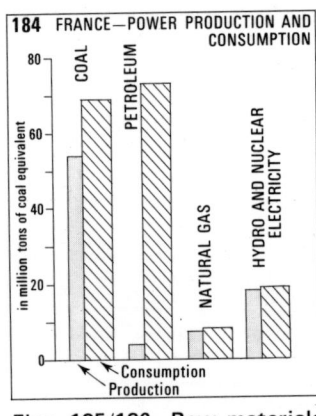

France is a major world industrial power. This position is based on good supplies of raw materials and ample power resources.

Fig. 184 Power production and consumption

184a Name France's most important source of power (i.e. power consumed).

184b Is most of it produced in France? If not, how is it obtained?

184c What is France's most important domestic source of power?

Figs. 185/186 Raw materials and power resources

185/186a (i) Name and locate the two main French coalfields. (ii) What proportion of total French coal production comes from these two fields? (iii) Is French coal production rising or falling?

185/186b (i) In which part of France is natural gas and petroleum produced? (ii) When did production begin?

(iii) Is natural gas production rising or falling?

185/186c (i) Name and locate the main iron ore field in France. (ii) What proportion of total French iron ore production comes from this field?

185/186d Compare France with other European producers of (i) iron ore (ii) crude steel.

Fig. 187 Iron and steel and associated industries

187a Name the three main iron and steel regions of France in their order of importance.

187b Indicate the sources of raw materials for the main region.

187c Name and locate three industries dependent on the steel industry.

Fig. 188 Oil refining and chemical industries

188a (i) Name the four main oil refining districts. (ii) Indicate those that have coastal locations and explain why.

188b The modern chemical industry is closely associated with oil and natural gas supplies. Locate and explain the exceptions.

Fig. 189 Textile industry

189a Name and locate the two main French textile regions.

189b In which textiles do they specialise?

189c What factors have favoured the location of this industry in these regions (think of raw materials, power, transport, etc.).

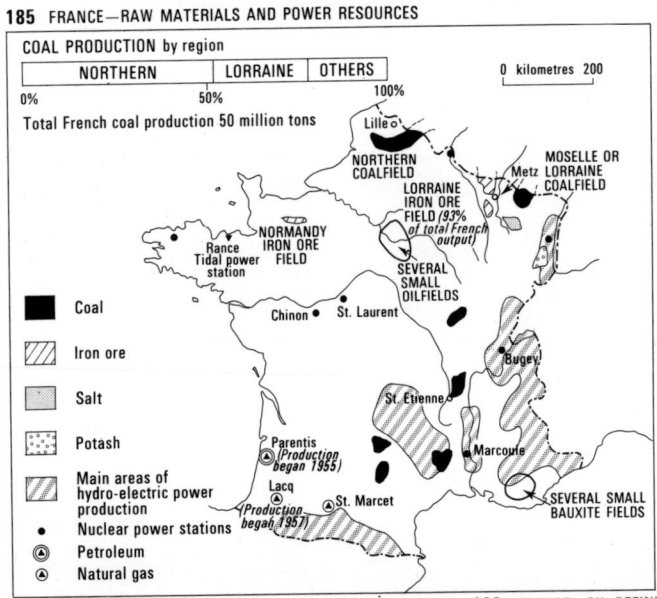

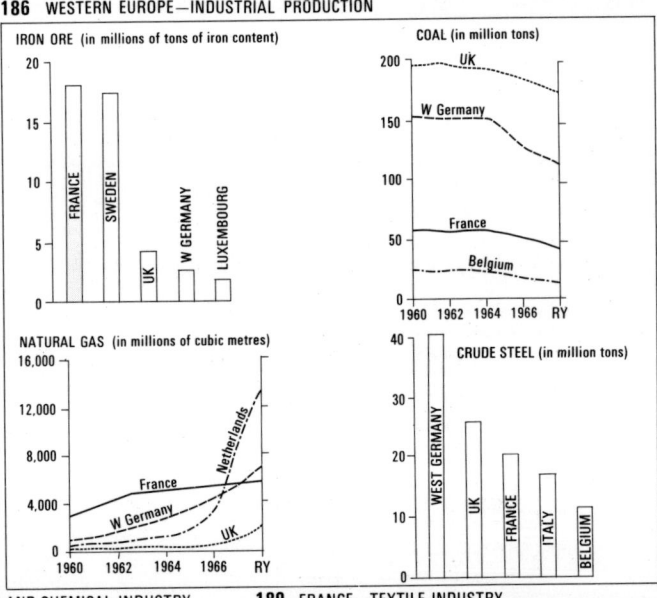

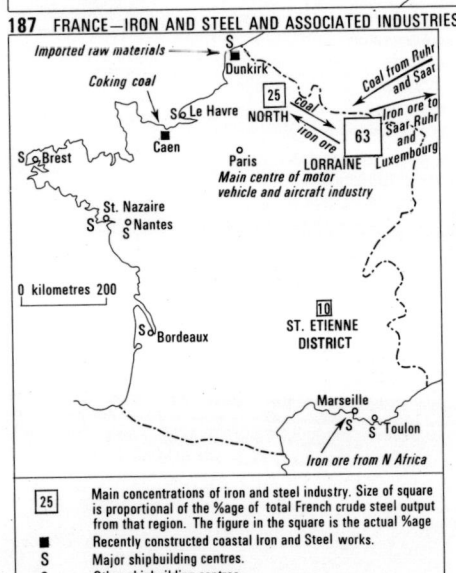

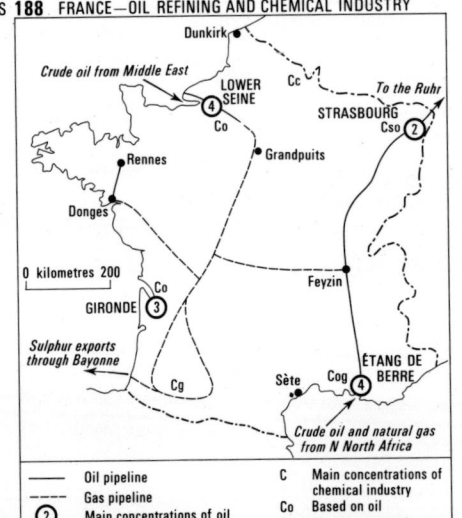

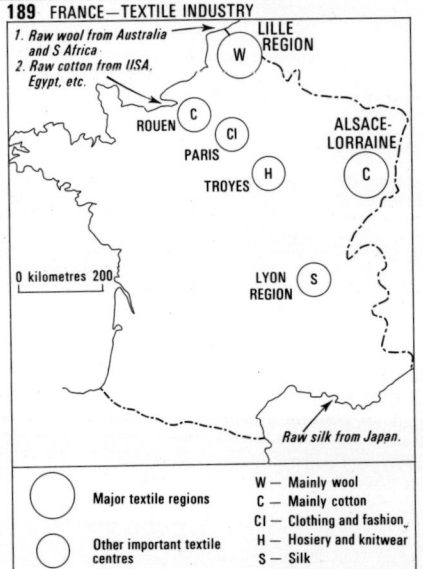

Fig. 190 Population of main French cities
190a What is the population of Greater Paris?
190b How many times bigger than Marseille (France's second city) is Paris?

Fig. 191 The site of Paris

Paris derives its name from the Parisii tribe who first inhabited the islands in the River Seine where Paris now stands.

191a (i) Name the largest island   (ii) What does it mean?
191b What advantages did these islands provide for (i) defence (ii) bridging the Seine?
191c Which important Roman road crossed the River Seine at this point?

Fig. 193 Main routeways
193a Describe the position of Paris in relation to (i) the Paris Basin (ii) France's transport network.
193b Which other European cities are linked directly with Paris?

As well as being a land route centre, Paris is an important international air transport centre (Orly and Le Bourget airports handle five million passengers each year) and inland port (15 million tons per year).

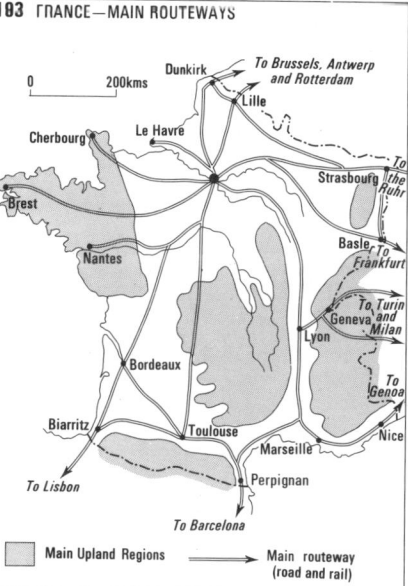

Fig. 194 Paris - employment
194a What proportion of the working population of Paris is engaged in (i) manufacturing (ii) service industries?
194b List the six main manufacturing industries in order of importance.

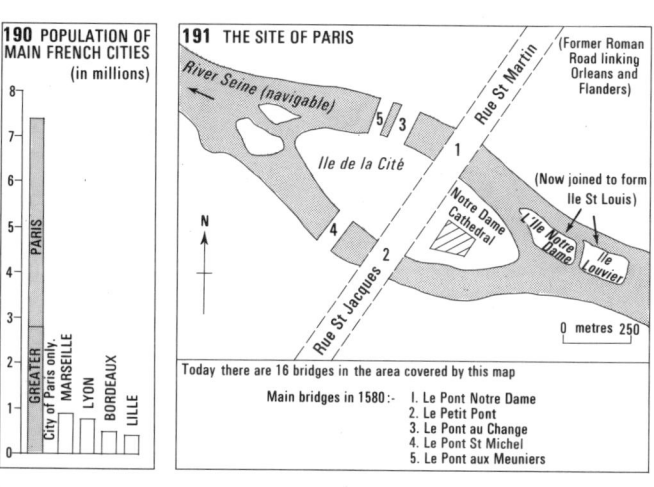

190 POPULATION OF MAIN FRENCH CITIES (in millions)

191 THE SITE OF PARIS

River Seine (navigable)
(Former Roman Road linking Orleans and Flanders)
Rue St Martin
Ile de la Cité
5 3
1
Notre Dame Cathedral
(Now joined to form Ile St Louis)
Ile Notre Dame
Ile Louvier
N
4
2
Rue St Jacques
0 metres 250

Today there are 16 bridges in the area covered by this map

Main bridges in 1580 :-
1. Le Pont Notre Dame
2. Le Petit Pont
3. Le Pont au Change
4. Le Pont St Michel
5. Le Pont aux Meuniers

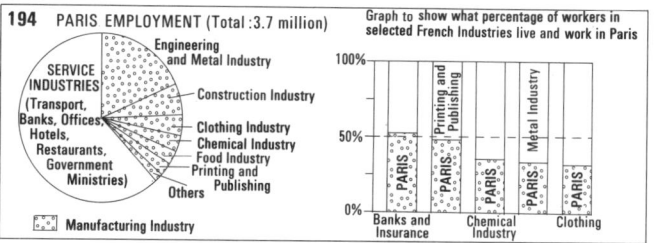

194 PARIS EMPLOYMENT (Total : 3.7 million)

SERVICE INDUSTRIES (Transport, Banks, Offices, Hotels, Restaurants, Government Ministries)

Engineering and Metal Industry
Construction Industry
Clothing Industry
Chemical Industry
Food Industry
Printing and Publishing
Others

Graph to show what percentage of workers in selected French industries live and work in Paris

Manufacturing Industry

Fig. 195 Paris - industry and wholesale markets
195a (i) Define 'wholesale market'. (ii) Why are France's main wholesale markets located in Paris?
195b Name the important industrial districts of Paris.
195c What form of transport have these districts in common?
195d (i) What proportion of the French motor industry is located in Paris? (ii) Name the main firms in order of output.
195e Paris is a major world city with a multitude of functions. In addition to those indicated above ((i) name them), Paris has important administrative, commercial and financial functions. (ii) Locate (a) the financial district, (b) the French parliament buildings (see fig. 192), (iii) What makes Paris a tourist attraction? (See fig. 192.)

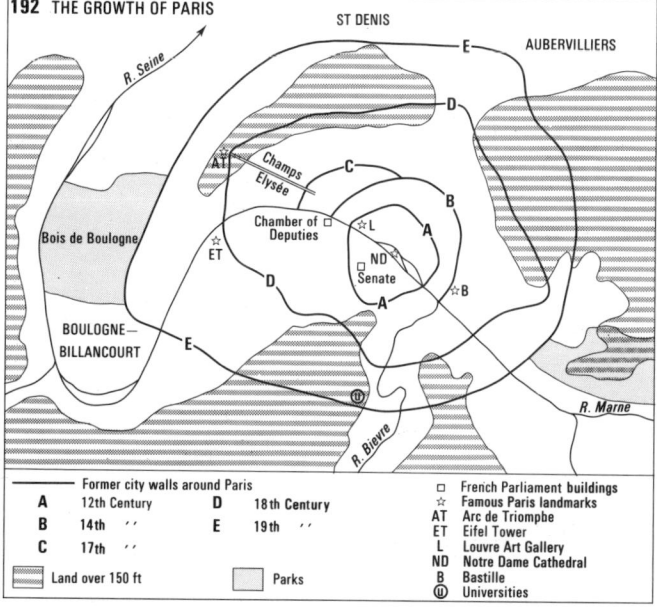

192 THE GROWTH OF PARIS

ST DENIS
AUBERVILLIERS
R. Seine
E
D
C
B
A
Champs Elysée
AT
Chamber of Deputies
L
ET
ND
Senate
B
Bois de Boulogne
D
A
E
BOULOGNE—BILLANCOURT
R. Bievre
R. Marne

Former city walls around Paris
A 12th Century   D 18th Century
B 14th "   E 19th "
C 17th "
French Parliament buildings
Famous Paris landmarks
AT Arc de Triomphe
ET Eifel Tower
L   Louvre Art Gallery
ND Notre Dame Cathedral
B   Bastille
Universities
Land over 150 ft
Parks

Fig. 192 The growth of Paris

192a The City of Paris expanded rapidly after the fourteenth century. What constructions marked each period of expansion?
192b Since World War 2, large numbers of young people have left their homes in the backward, rural parts of France and come to live in Paris. Try to explain the reasons for, and consequences of this migration.

The continual growth of Paris has created many problems. The French Government is attempting to restrict industrial and office development and encourage it elsewhere in France. However, Paris continues to expand and plans for new "towns", a third airport and a new wholesale food market have been introduced. The future growth of Paris is being directed along the Seine valley towards Le Havre.

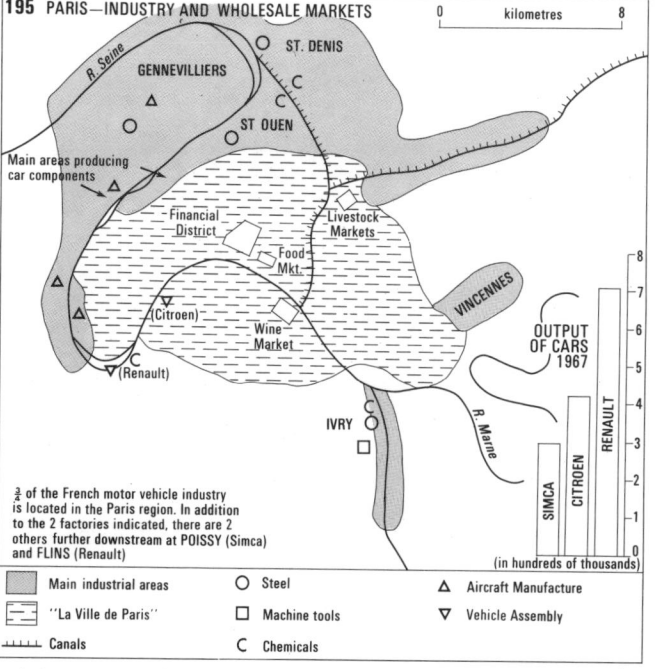

195 PARIS—INDUSTRY AND WHOLESALE MARKETS

0 kilometres 8

R. Seine
GENNEVILLIERS
ST. DENIS
ST OUEN
C
C
Main areas producing car components
Financial District
Livestock Markets
Food Mkt.
(Citroen)
Wine Market
VINCENNES
(Renault)
C
IVRY
R. Marne

OUTPUT OF CARS 1967
SIMCA
CITROEN
RENAULT
(in hundreds of thousands)

⅔ of the French motor vehicle industry is located in the Paris region. In addition to the 2 factories indicated, there are 2 others further downstream at POISSY (Simca) and FLINS (Renault)

Main industrial areas
"La Ville de Paris"
Canals
Steel
Machine tools
Chemicals
Aircraft Manufacture
Vehicle Assembly

103 FRANCE—MAIN ROUTEWAYS
0 200kms
Dunkirk
To Brussels, Antwerp and Rotterdam
Lille
Cherbourg
Le Havre
Brest
Strasbourg To the Ruhr
Nantes
Basle To Frankfurt
To Turin and Milan
Geneva
Lyon
Bordeaux
To Genoa
Biarritz
Toulouse
Marseille
Nice
To Lisbon
Perpignan
To Barcelona
Main Upland Regions
Main routeway (road and rail)

Fig. 196 Paris Basin - geology

196a Name the four Hercynian uplands surrounding the Paris Basin.

196b How wide is the Paris Basin from West to East?

196c Name and locate the youngest rocks in the Paris Basin.

196d What regions occupy the chalklands of the Paris Basin?

196e Name the three main rivers that drain the Paris Basin (see fig.169).

196f Describe and account for the relief of the Paris Basin (see also figs. 197 and 199).

Fig. 197 Agricultural transect of the Paris Basin

197a Beauce and Brie are very prosperous farming regions. Describe and account for the nature of farming in these two regions (see also p.32).

197b Explain why market gardening and dairying are important near Paris.

197c (i) Compare farming in Dry and Wet Champagne and explain the differences. (ii) How close to the northern limit of vine-growing is the Champagne district? (see fig. 183). Does this mean conditions are ideal or not?

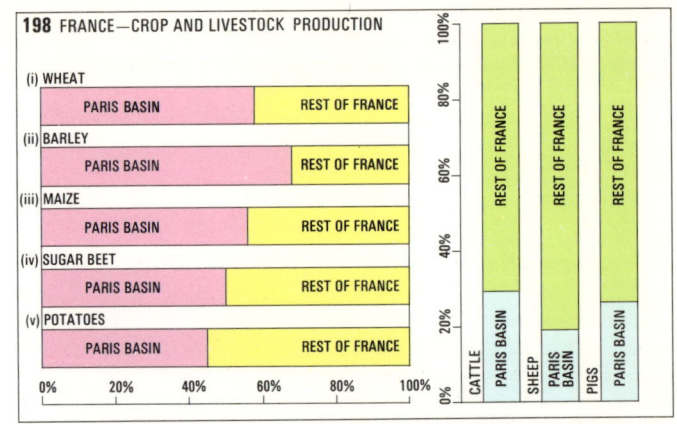

Fig. 198 French - crop and livestock production

198a How important is the Paris Basin as a producer of (i) cereals (ii) potatoes and sugar beet?

198b Is the Paris Basin an important livestock region? (Quote one example to prove your answer.)

The unique conditions in the Falaise (scarp slope) of the Ile de France produce the famous sparkling wine called Champagne. Only small quantities are produced each year and the fermentation processes are a closely guarded secret.

Figs.199/200 Alsace-Lorraine- geology and agriculture

199/200a What are climatic conditions like in Alsace-Lorraine? (see p. 32.)

199/200b Write out the following, filling in the missing words.

"Western Lorraine is composed of alternating limestone and . . . The limestone form . . . often covered with . . . while the clay forms vales where the emphasis is on . . . . . . are important on the east-facing scarp slopes. . . farming predominates on the Plateau of Lorraine while in the Uplands forests again occur. The Plain of Alsace, occupying the valley of the River . . . , is an area of varied farming depending on . . . conditions."

199/200c Suggest why the Cotes de Moselle, Cotes de Meuse and Vosges are forested.

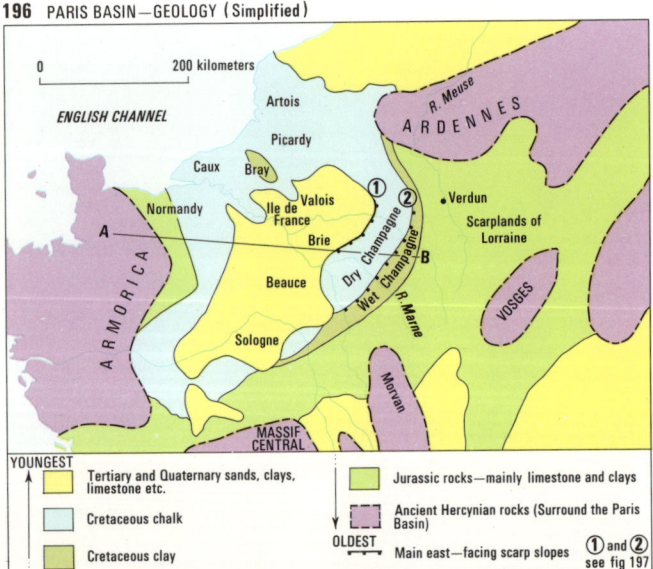

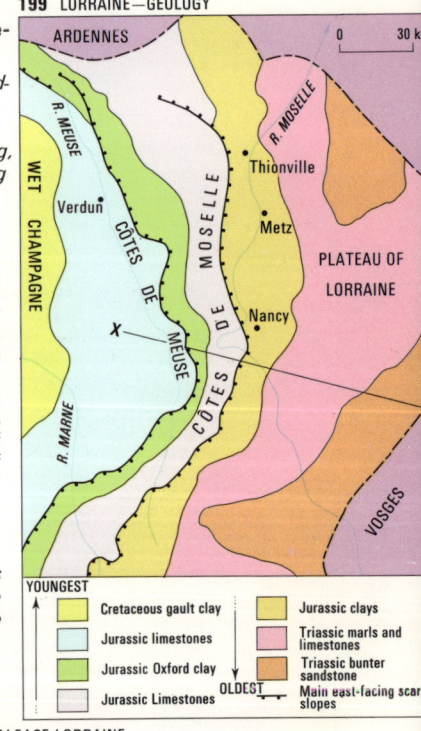

199 LORRAINE—GEOLOGY

0 30 km

YOUNGEST		
Cretaceous gault clay		Jurassic clays
Jurassic limestones		Triassic marls and limestones
Jurassic Oxford clay		Triassic bunter sandstone
Jurassic Limestones	OLDEST	Main east-facing scarp slopes

196 PARIS BASIN—GEOLOGY (Simplified)

0 200 kilometers

YOUNGEST		
Tertiary and Quaternary sands, clays, limestone etc.		Jurassic rocks—mainly limestone and clays
Cretaceous chalk		Ancient Hercynian rocks (Surround the Paris Basin)
Cretaceous clay	OLDEST	Main east—facing scarp slopes ① and ② see fig 197

197 AGRICULTURAL TRANSECT OF THE PARIS BASIN

	NORMANDY AND MAINE	BEAUCE	BRIE	DRY CH.	WET CH.
Main Towns	Caen Le Mans	Chartres, Orleans Étampes	Provins, Melun	Rheims Epernay	
AGRICULTURE	Small, hedged fields under pasture (called 'bocage') Dairying (for cheese as well as milk) and apple orchards (for cider) predominate.	A flat, open hedgeless landscape—large farms (500-1000a) highly mechanised; high yields; the most prosperous arable regions in France. Wheat and maize (especially in Beauce), barley, sugar-beet, potatoes and pasture (especially in Brie) similar to Picardy and Artois to the north. Dairying and market gardening important near Paris (also in the Valois and Ile de France regions).		Wheat, also some sheep. Vines on slopes of Falaise (produce Champagne)	Pasture predominates for both dairy and beef cattle.
SOIL	Clay with flints	Fertile limon (loam) (decreases in thickness and extent to the west).		Thin chalk soils (heavily fertilised)	Clay soils

A
Hills of Perche
R. Seine
Falaise (scarp) of the Ile de France ① ②
B
ARMORICA
Limestone
Limestones, sands and clays
Chalk Clay Limestone
WEST   CH. = CHAMPAGNE   EAST

200 AGRICULTURAL TRANSECT ACROSS ALSACE-LORRAINE

CÔTES DE MEUSE	WOËVRE	CÔTES DE MOSELLE	MOSELLE VALLEY	PLATEAU OF LORRAINE	VOSGES UPLANDS	PLAIN OF ALSACE
FORESTED—Vines on lower slopes of scarp	PASTURE with an emphasis on dairying	FOREST AND ARABLE Vines on lower slopes of scarp	INDUSTRIALISED	MIXED FARMING Emphasis on livestock — cattle (dairying); pigs and poultry.	FORESTRY AND PERMANENT PASTURE Vines on lower east-facing slopes.	Farming varies according to soils—ranges from marshy pasture to rich arable (cereals, sugar-beet, hops and tobacco)

X
R. Meuse
R. Moselle
Y
R. Rhine
WEST   EAST

Fig. 201 France - industrial production

201a Which region is the most important producer of (i) cast iron (ii) crude steel?

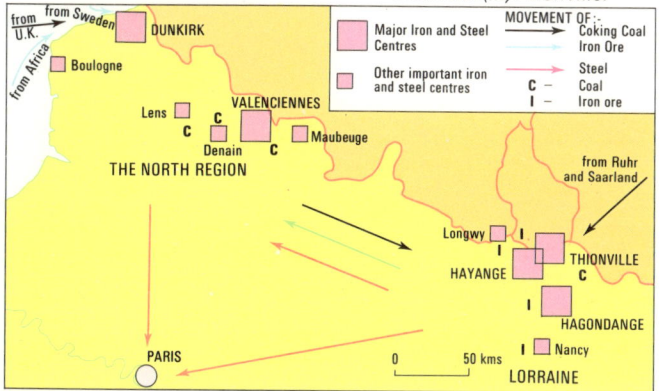

201 FRANCE: INDUSTRIAL PRODUCTION

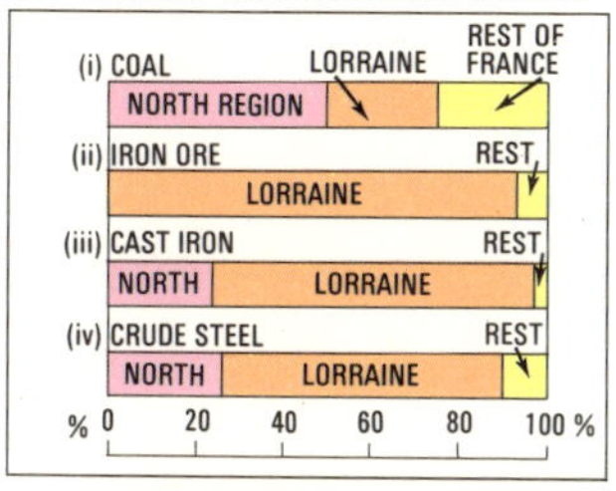

201b What proportions of French coal and iron ore production are mined in (i) the North Region (ii)Lorraine?

Fig. 202 North Region and Lorraine - iron and steel industry

202a Locate the following iron and steel centres and indicate where they obtain their basic raw materials (coking coal and iron ore).(i) Dunkirk (ii) Valenciennes (iii) Thionville.

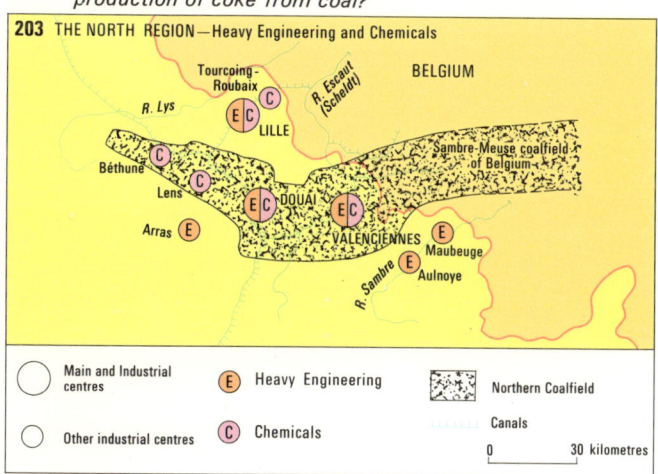

202 THE NORTH REGION AND LORRAINE—Iron and Steel Industry

202b What other factors favour the location of an iron and steel industry?

Fig.203 North Region - heavy engineering and chemicals

203a Give three examples of heavy engineering products.
203b Name the three main centres for heavy engineering and chemical industries.
203c In what way is (i) heavy engineering related to the iron and steel industry (ii) the chemical industry related to the production of coke from coal?

203 THE NORTH REGION—Heavy Engineering and Chemicals

203d Name the four main industries in the North Region.

Fig.204 France - textile production

204a (i) Draw an outline map of North and North-east France (ii) mark and label the main textile centres, using a separate symbol for each textile.
204b Which is the most important region for the following textiles? (i) wool (ii) cotton (iii)linen. Synthetic fibres and clothing are also manufactured in the North Region.

204 FRANCE : TEXTILE PRODUCTION

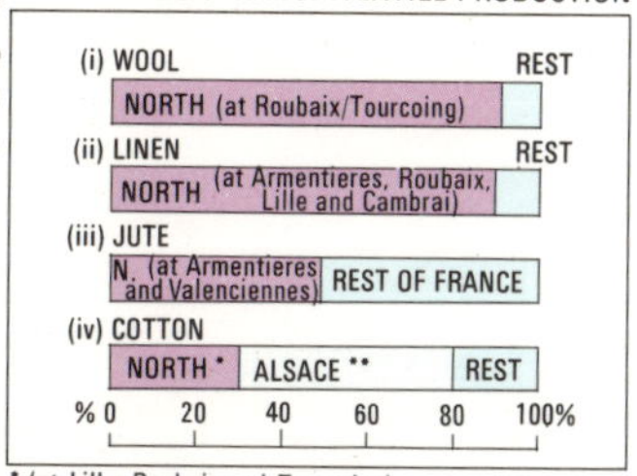

* (at Lille, Roubaix and Tourcoing)
** (at Epinal, Belfort, Colmar and Mulhouse)

205 ALSACE-LORRAINE :- Raw Materials and Industry

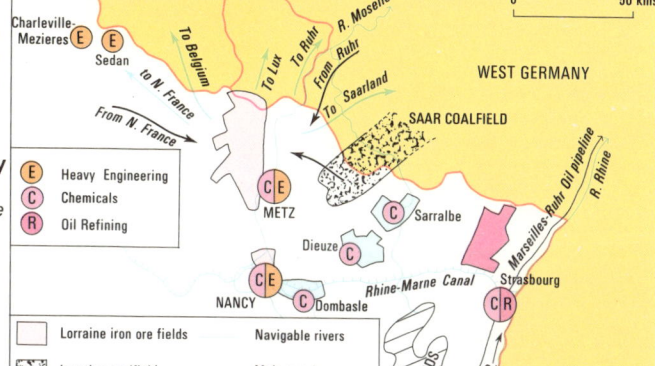

Fig. 205 Alsace-Lorraine - raw materials and industry

205a (i) Name the main basic industry in Lorraine (see fig.202). (ii) Why is it located there?
205b Lorraine is the main source of iron ore in the EEC. What other parts of (i) France (ii) the EEC receive iron ore from Lorraine?
205c (i) Name the two main engineering centres in Lorraine. (ii) Most of the steel produced in Lorraine is distributed to engineering industries elsewhere in France. Name two regions receiving Lorraine steel (see fig.202).
205d The chemical industry in Alsace-Lorraine is based on a variety of local raw materials. Name the main raw material used at the following centres: (i) Sarralbe (ii) Strasbourg (two sources) (iii)Mulhouse.

Fig. 206 Paris Basin - industry

206a Name the three most important industrial centres in the Paris Basin (excluding Paris and Lille).
206b What have they all in common?
206c Which is the most common industry in the Paris Basin- textiles, chemicals or metals and engineering (including automobile assembly and shipbuilding)?
206d Suggest some of the imports and exports that pass through Le Havre.

206 PARIS BASIN—INDUSTRY

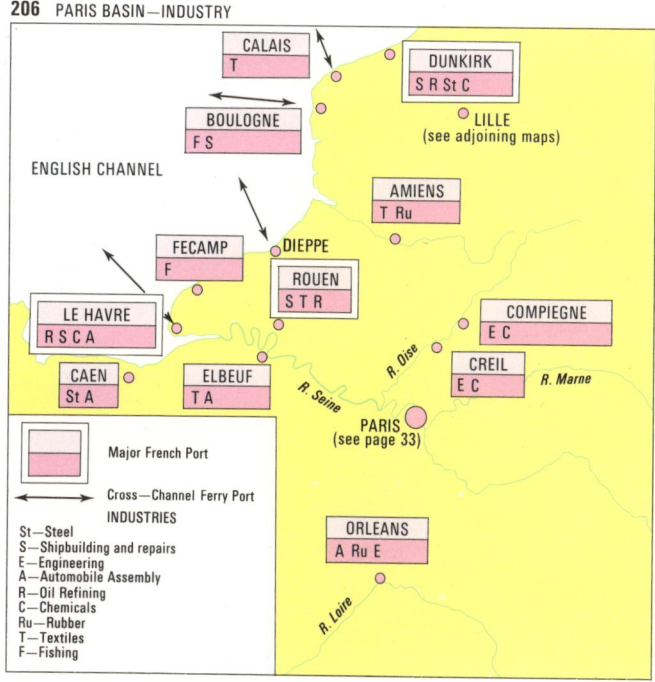

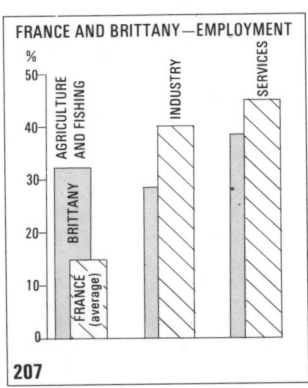

Fig. 207 France and Brittany - employment

207a Locate Brittany (see fig. 172)
207b What percentage of the working population of Brittany is engaged in agriculture and fishing?
207c Compare this with the French average.
207d What does this tell you about Brittany?

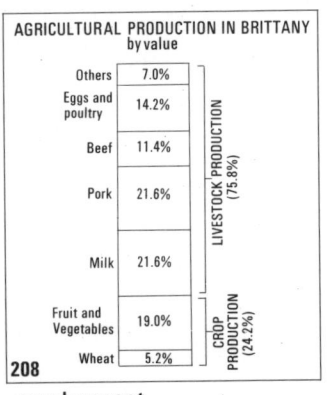

Fig. 208 Agricultural production in Brittany

208a (i) What is the most valuable sector of farming in Brittany—livestock or crop production? (ii) Quote some examples.

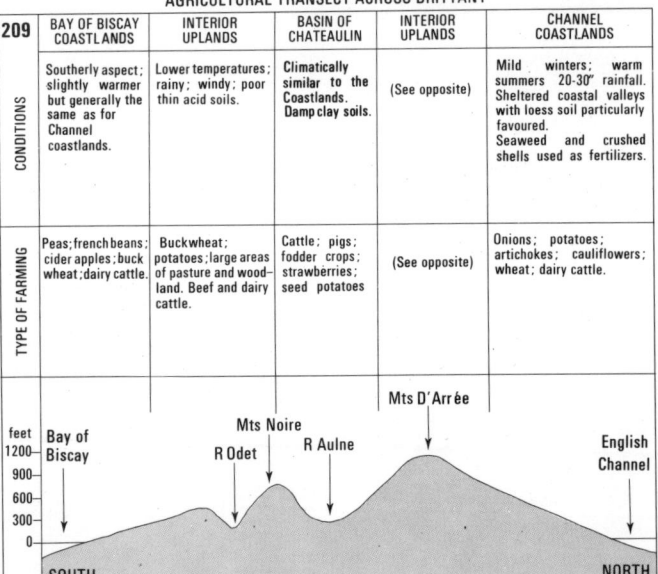

Fig. 209 Agricultural transect across Brittany

209a Describe and account for the agricultural differences between the coastlands and interior of Brittany.

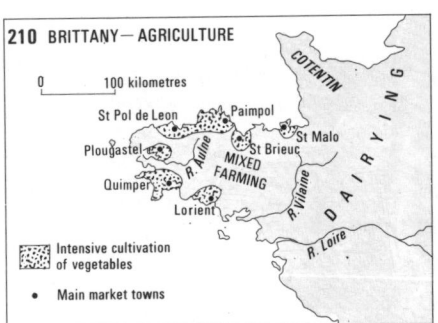

Fig. 210 Brittany - agriculture

210a In which part of Brittany is dairying most important? 70% of Cotentin is under permanent pasture and supports a greater density of cattle than any other area of France

210b Brittany is also famous for its 'primeurs' (early vegetables). (i) Name some (see fig. 209). (ii) Where are they grown? (iii) Name two market towns in these areas. (iv) Suggest how it is possible to grow some vegetables earlier here than in other regions of France (see fig. 173)

Fig. 211 Brittany - fishing

211a The term 'Armorica' means 'land of the sea'. Bretons have always been attracted to the sea - for settlement and livelihood. Suggest why.

211b (i) What percentage of the total French catch is landed in Brittany? (ii) Name the three main fishing ports.

211c Contrast the nature of deep-sea and inshore fishing.

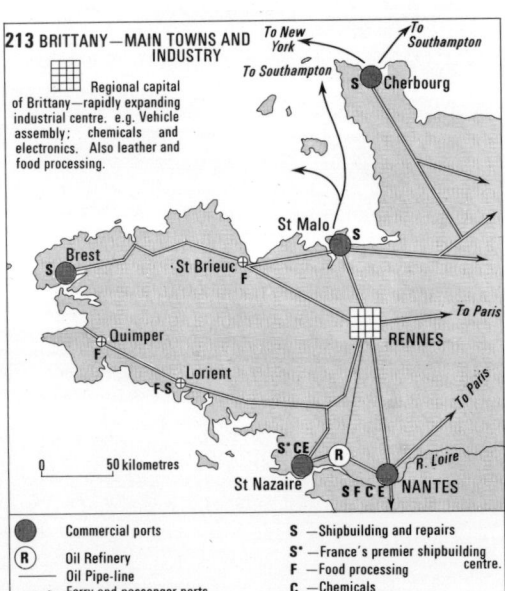

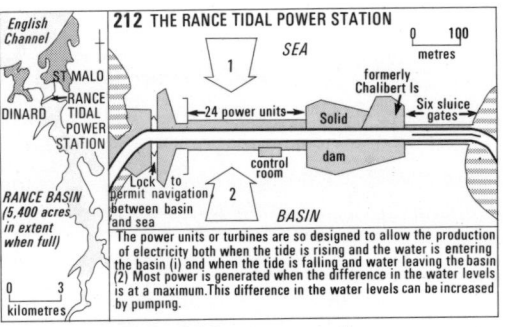

Fig. 212 Rance tidal power station

Brittany possesses few raw materials and sources of power. A unique modern development has been the construction of a tidal power station.

212a Describe the position of the Rance tidal power station.

212b Give two reasons for its location (one is an exceptionally high tidal range).

212c Explain how a tidal power station works.

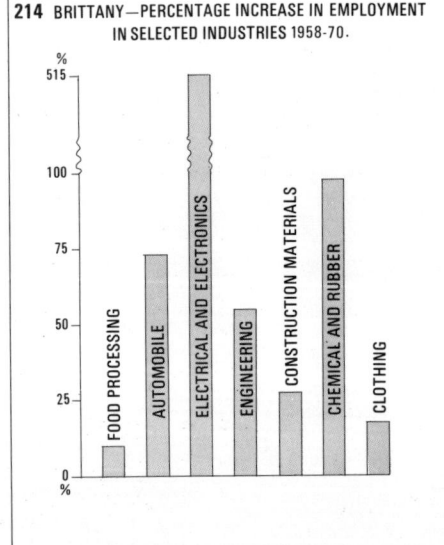

Fig. 214 Brittany - percentage increase in employment in selected industries

In Brittany industry is underdeveloped, yet in recent years new industry has been attracted as a result of government encouragement.

214a (i) Which industries have undergone most growth? (ii) What sort of industries are they?

214b Suggest one other important 'industry' likely to experience regular growth in a region so similar to Devon and Cornwall in Britain, (e.g. long varied coastline, pleasant climate, quaint fishing villages, etc.).

Fig. 213 Brittany - main towns and industry

213a Name the only major Breton town not located on the coast.

213b Why has it become the 'capital' and main regional centre of Brittany?

213c Name its main industries.

213d The Loire Estuary is an important industrial region. (i) Name the two ports (ii) indicate their main industries (iii) are they typical port industries?

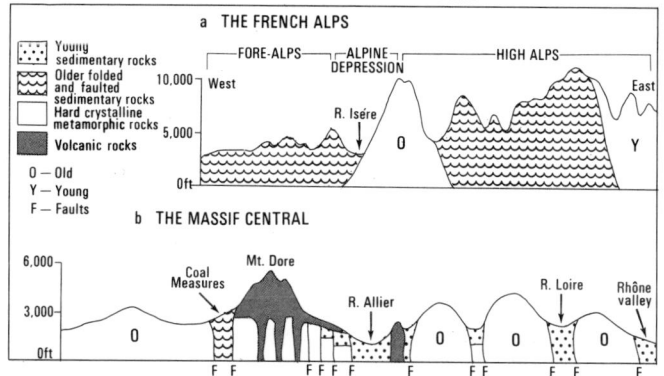

215 SECTIONS ACROSS THE FRENCH ALPS AND MASSIF CENTRAL

Fig. 215 Sections across the French Alps and Massif Central

215a (i) What proportion of France is over 3,000 ft,(914 metres)? (see fig. 170).(ii) Which highland region has most land over 3,000 ft,(914 metres)? (see fig. 170).

215b (i) Describe the main differences between the geology of the Alps and Massif Central. (ii) What type of mountain is Mt. Dore?

The mountainous country around Le Puy is famous for its relics of former volcanoes.

Fig. 216 Farming in a typical Alpine Valley

216a Describe and account for the nature of farming in the French Alps (see p. 30).

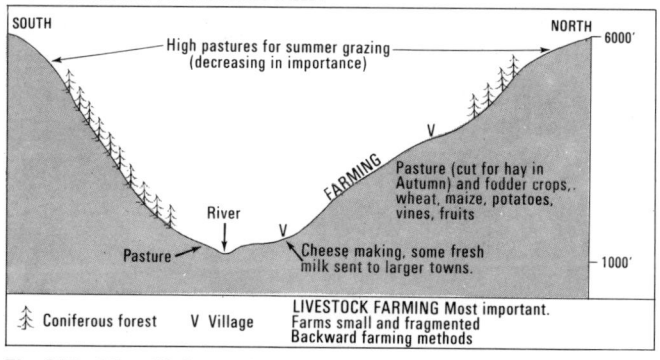

216 FARMING IN A TYPICAL ALPINE VALLEY

Fig 217 Massif Central - agriculture

217a What is the main type of farming in the Massif Central - arable or livestock?

217b Name one important region for each of the following: (i) sheep (ii) beef cattle (iii) dairy cattle (iv) arable farming.

217c Explain why arable farming is uncommon (see also p. 32).

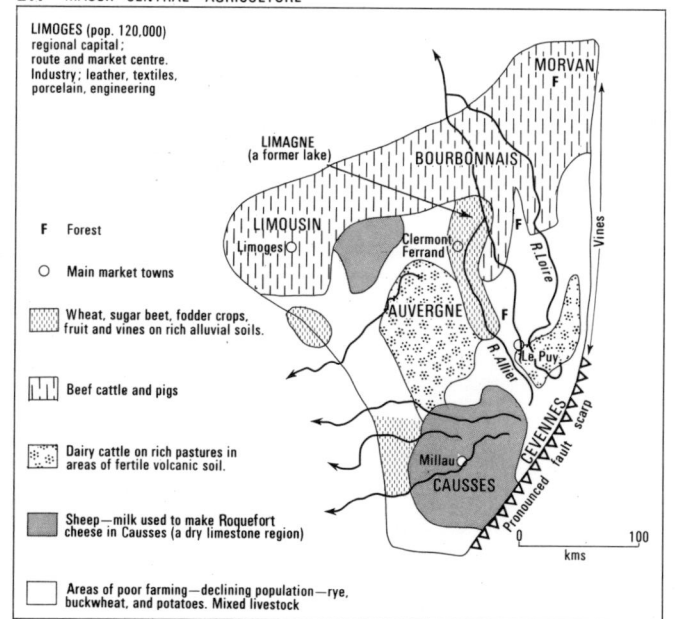

217 MASSIF CENTRAL—AGRICULTURE

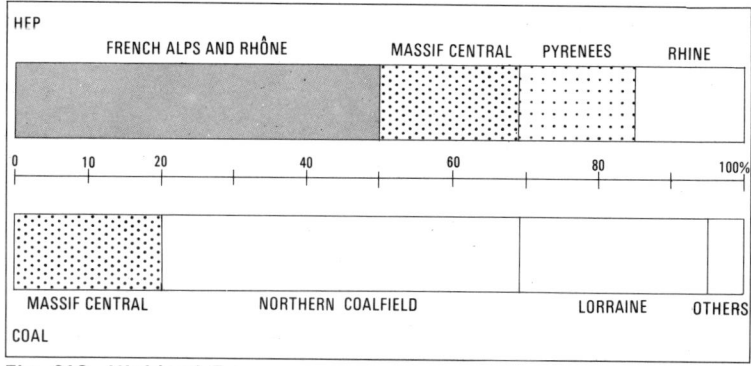

Fig. 218 Highland France - power resources

218a Which highland region possesses the only significant coal resources?

218b (i) What proportion of total French HEP production is derived from these three highland regions? (ii) Which is the most important producer of HEP? (iii) What conditions make these regions suitable for HEP production?

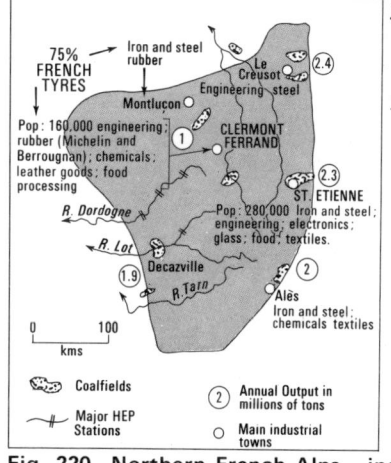

219 MASSIF CENTRAL—INDUSTRY

Fig. 219 Massif Central - industry

219a (i) Which two rivers have been harnessed for HEP? (ii) Name and locate one other source of power.

219b Name the two main industrial centres in the Massif Central and compare their industries.

Fig. 220 Northern French Alps - industry

220a Name (i) the four valleys where most industry is concentrated (ii) the two main towns and their industries.

220b The chemical and metal smelting industries predominate. Which of the following factors has not favoured their development - local supplies of HEP, local raw materials, expanding industrial labour force, good communications?

The French Alps and Massif Central are also important tourist regions, the former with an emphasis on winter sports.

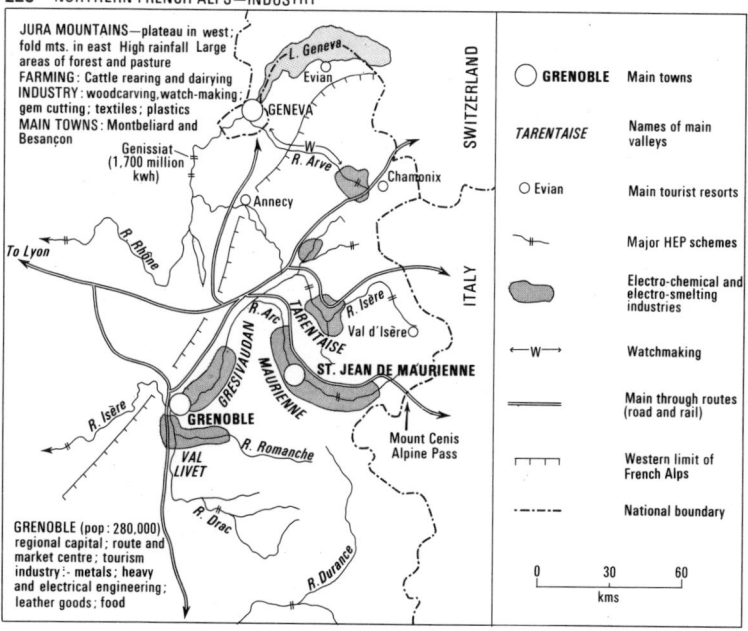

220 NORTHERN FRENCH ALPS—INDUSTRY

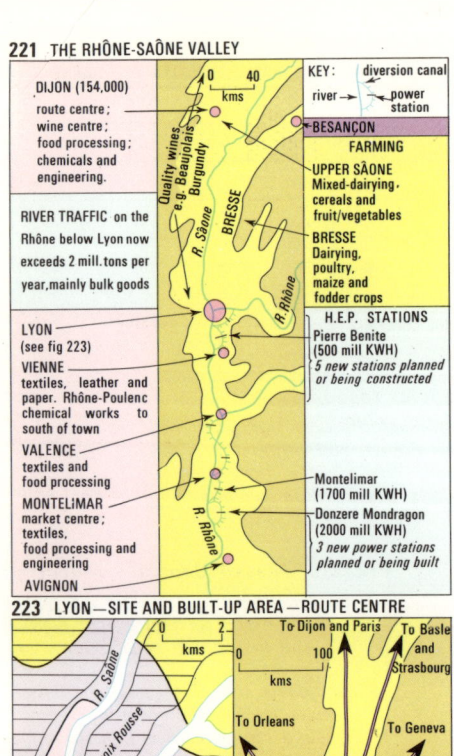

221 THE RHÔNE-SAÔNE VALLEY

KEY: diversion canal; river; power station

DIJON (154,000) route centre; wine centre; food processing; chemicals and engineering.

RIVER TRAFFIC on the Rhône below Lyon now exceeds 2 mill. tons per year, mainly bulk goods

LYON (see fig 223)

VIENNE textiles, leather and paper. Rhône-Poulenc chemical works to south of town

VALENCE textiles and food processing

MONTELIMAR market centre; textiles, food processing and engineering

AVIGNON

Quality wines e.g. Beaujolais, Burgundy

R. Saône
BRESSE
R. Rhône

BESANÇON

FARMING
UPPER SAÔNE Mixed-dairying, cereals and fruit/vegetables
BRESSE Dairying, poultry, maize and fodder crops

H.E.P. STATIONS
Pierre Bénite (500 mill KWH) 5 new stations planned or being constructed

Montélimar (1700 mill KWH)
Donzère Mondragon (2000 mill KWH)
3 new power stations planned or being built

222 AGRICULTURAL TRANSECT ACROSS THE RHÔNE VALLEY

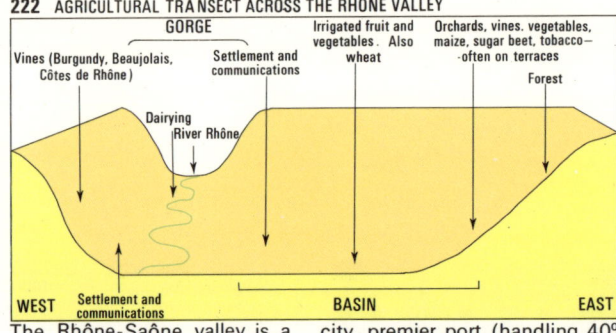

GORGE

Vines (Burgundy, Beaujolais, Côtes de Rhône)
Dairying River Rhône
Settlement and communications
Irrigated fruit and vegetables. Also wheat
Orchards, vines. vegetables, maize, sugar beet, tobacco— often on terraces
Forest

WEST — Settlement and communications — BASIN — EAST

The Rhône-Saône valley is a structural depression consisting of a series of gorges and basins.

Figs. 221/222 Rhône-Saône valley

221/222a Name the two highland regions that flank the Rhône-Saône valley.

221/222b Explain why the Rhône-Saône valley is sometimes called a 'corridor' (see fig. 172).

221/222c Make a detailed comparison of farming in the (i) Saône valley (ii) Rhône valley (iii) Mediterranean France (see also fig. 224).

221/222d (i) Compare the positions and climates of Besançon, Lyon and Marseille (see also p.30) (ii) explain the farming differences observed in question 221/222c.

221/222e How is the River Rhône harnessed for HEP? Give two examples.

223 LYON—SITE AND BUILT-UP AREA—ROUTE CENTRE

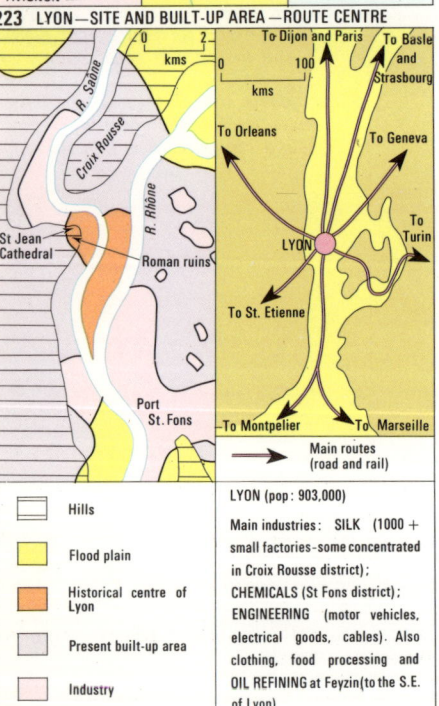

To Dijon and Paris
To Basle and Strasbourg
To Orleans
To Geneva
R. Saône
Croix Rousse
R. Rhône
St Jean Cathedral
Roman ruins
LYON
To Turin
To St. Etienne
Port St. Fons
To Montpelier
To Marseille

Main routes (road and rail)

Hills
Flood plain
Historical centre of Lyon
Present built-up area
Industry

LYON (pop. 903,000)

Main industries: SILK (1000 + small factories-some concentrated in Croix Rousse district); CHEMICALS (St Fons district); ENGINEERING (motor vehicles, electrical goods, cables). Also clothing, food processing and OIL REFINING at Feyzin (to the S.E. of Lyon)

Fig. 223 Lyon

223a Describe the site and position of Lyon.
223b In what way is Lyon a route centre?
223c Name Lyon's four main industries.
223d Do they compare with industry in the other towns of the Rhône valley? (see fig. 221). Give examples.

Fig. 224 Mediterranean France - agriculture

224a Name some common Mediterranean fruit and vegetables.
224b Describe the agricultural changes in Languedoc resulting from the introduction of extensive irrigation.
224c Suggest the main sources of irrigation water and the principal means of distribution.

Fig. 225 Mediterranean France - tourism

225a (i) Locate and explain 'Côte d'Azur'. (ii) What is its alternative name?
225b Name the two main resorts there.
225c Why has Languedoc - Roussillon been an unimportant tourist region until recently?
225d What plans are in hand to change this situation?

Fig. 226 Marseille Region - port development and industry

Marseille is France's second largest city, premier port (handling 40% total French sea-trade) and a major industrial and commercial centre.

226a The port of Marseille is composed of three separate units. Name and locate them.
226b Imports form 88% of the total traffic of the port of Marseille. Compare the import traffic of the 'Old Port' and the Etang de Berre.
226c (i) Name the two main industries located around the Etang de Berre. (ii) In what way are they related?
226d Marseille itself has three main industries:(i)food processing (sugar, flour, margarine) (ii) light, heavy and electrical engineering (including shipbuilding and marine engineering) and (iii) chemicals (soaps, paints, etc.). Which of these are connected with Marseille's function as a port?

225 MEDITERRANEAN FRANCE—TOURISM

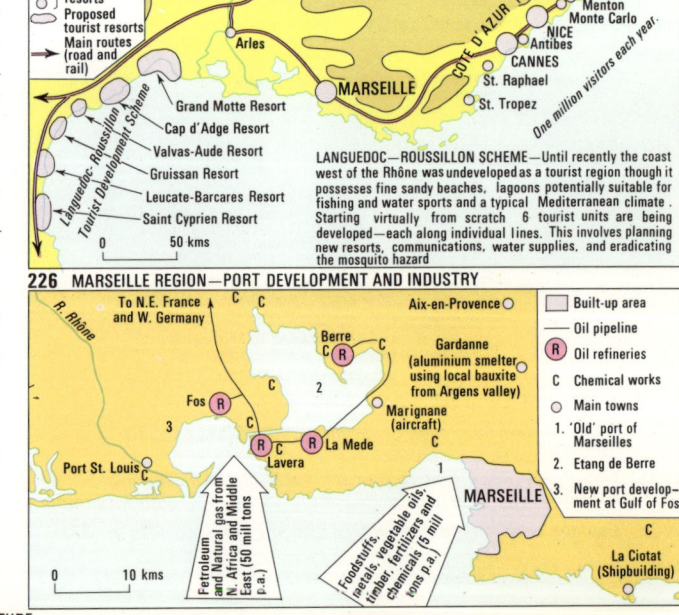

Main tourist resorts
Proposed tourist resorts
Main routes (road and rail)

Avignon
Good road and rail links with N. Europe
Arles
MARSEILLE
CÔTE D'AZUR (RIVIERA)
Menton
Monte Carlo
NICE
Antibes
CANNES
St. Raphael
St. Tropez
One million visitors each year.

Grand Motte Resort
Cap d'Agde Resort
Valvas-Aude Resort
Gruissan Resort
Leucate-Barcares Resort
Saint Cyprien Resort
Languedoc - Roussillon Tourist Development Scheme

LANGUEDOC—ROUSSILLON SCHEME—Until recently the coast west of the Rhône was undeveloped as a tourist region though it possesses fine sandy beaches, lagoons potentially suitable for fishing and water sports and a typical Mediterranean climate. Starting virtually from scratch 6 tourist units are being developed—each along individual lines. This involves planning new resorts, communications, water supplies, and eradicating the mosquito hazard

226 MARSEILLE REGION—PORT DEVELOPMENT AND INDUSTRY

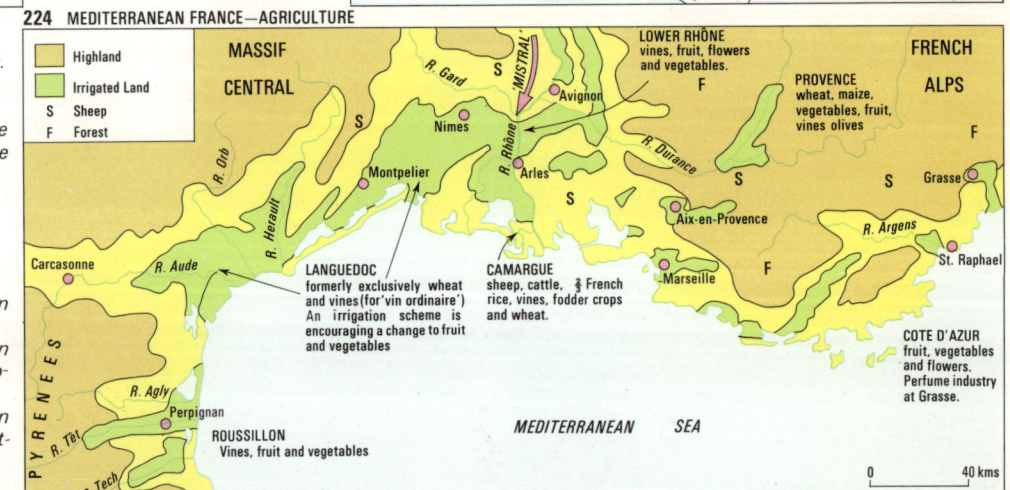

R. Rhône
To N.E. France and W. Germany
Aix-en-Provence
Berre
Fos
Gardanne (aluminium smelter using local bauxite from Argens valley)
Marignane (aircraft)
Port St. Louis
La Mede
Lavera
MARSEILLE
La Ciotat (Shipbuilding)

Petroleum and Natural gas from N. Africa and Middle East (50 mill tons p.a.)
Foodstuffs, vegetable oils, timber, fertilizers and chemicals (5 mill tons p.a.)

Built-up area
Oil pipeline
R Oil refineries
C Chemical works
Main towns
1. 'Old' port of Marseilles
2. Etang de Berre
3. New port development at Gulf of Fos

224 MEDITERRANEAN FRANCE—AGRICULTURE

Highland
Irrigated Land
S Sheep
F Forest

MASSIF CENTRAL
R. Gard
LOWER RHÔNE vines, fruit, flowers and vegetables.
FRENCH ALPS
PROVENCE wheat, maize, vegetables, fruit, vines olives
R. Orb
R. Herault
Nimes
Avignon
R. Durance
Montpelier
Arles
Grasse
R. Argens
Carcassonne
R. Aude
LANGUEDOC formerly exclusively wheat and vines (for 'vin ordinaire') An irrigation scheme is encouraging a change to fruit and vegetables
CAMARGUE sheep, cattle, French rice, vines, fodder crops and wheat
Aix-en-Provence
Marseille
St. Raphael
COTE D'AZUR fruit, vegetables and flowers. Perfume industry at Grasse.
PYRENEES
R. Agly
R. Tet
Perpignan
ROUSSILLON Vines, fruit and vegetables
R. Tech
MEDITERRANEAN SEA

Fig. 227 Transect across southern Aquitaine

227a Describe a journey across Aquitaine from the Atlantic Ocean to the Massif Central.

Fig. 228 Bordeaux - climate

228a Compare the climates of Bordeaux and Paris.
228b Explain the main differences.

Fig. 229 Aquitaine - wine production

229a What percentage of (i) French wine production (ii) French wine exports come from Aquitaine? Aquitaine produces mainly high quality wines, hence the high value of exports.

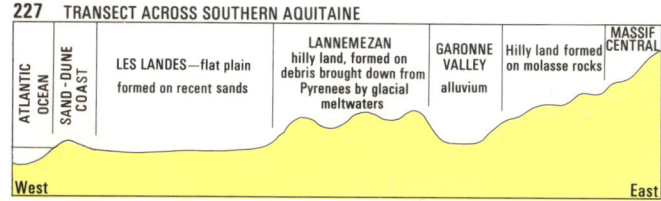

227 TRANSECT ACROSS SOUTHERN AQUITAINE

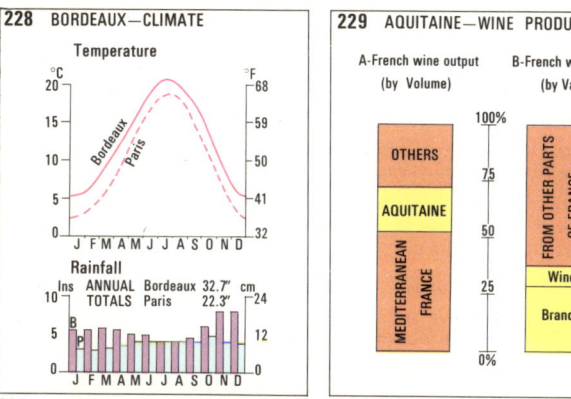

228 BORDEAUX—CLIMATE

229 AQUITAINE—WINE PRODUCTION

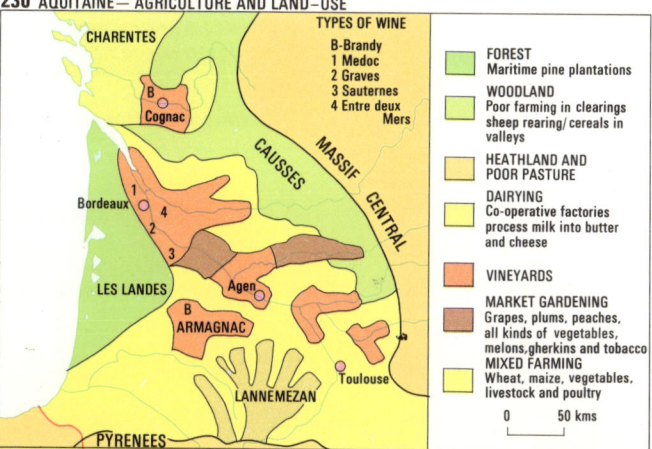

230 AQUITAINE—AGRICULTURE AND LAND-USE

Fig. 230 Aquitaine - agriculture and land use

230a Which valleys contain most of the vineyards and market gardening?(Consult an atlas)
230b What advantages have these valleys for this type of agriculture? (Climate, soil, transport, etc.)
230c (i) Compare the agriculture of the Charentes and Causses regions. (ii) Try to explain the difference.(The Causses is a limestone region.)

230d (i) Name the main forested area of Aquitaine. (ii) Is it deciduous or coniferous? (iii) Why has this area not been used for agriculture (see fig. 227). Les Landes is the largest single forest in France.

231 AQUITAINE—RAW MATERIALS, INDUSTRY AND MAIN TOWNS

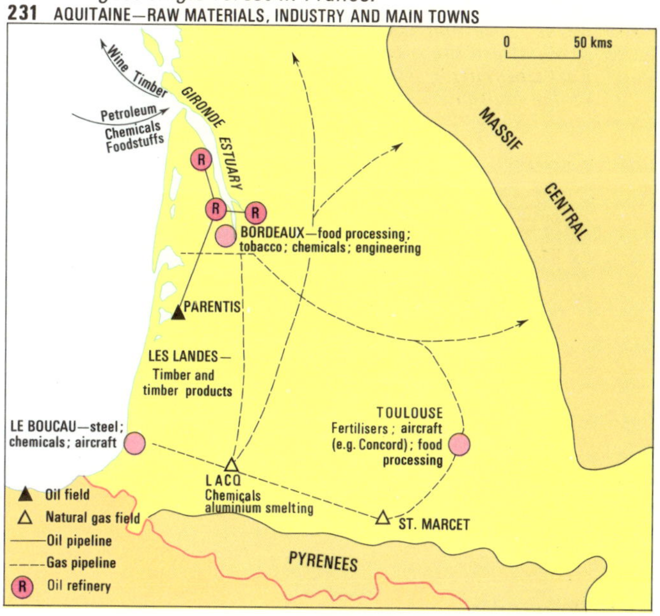

Fig. 231 Aquitaine - raw materials, industries and main towns

Industry in Aquitaine is under-developed despite the post-war discovery of important raw materials and government assistance. Most towns are market centres engaged in food processing and light engineering.

231a (i) Name and locate the two main raw materials produced in Aquitaine . (ii) What are they used for?
231b What industries have grown up in response to their development?
231c Most natural gas is piped to other parts of France. On the other hand, there is not enough local petroleum to satisfy demands. How is the extra petroleum obtained?
231d Bordeaux is the regional and commercial centre of Aquitaine and an important seaport. However , it is not an outstanding industrial centre. Describe the position of Bordeaux in relation to its function as (i) a seaport (ii) a route centre (see also fig. 193).
231e (i) Name the other main city in Aquitaine. (ii) Compare its industries with those of Bordeaux. (iii) Suggest reasons for its importance (transport, power, etc.)

Fig. 232 Pyrenees

The Pyrenees are similar to the French Alps in age, geology and scenery, although generally lower in altitude. Livestock farming predominates—particularly in the West—although crops are grown in some of the valleys.

232a Name the main source of power in the Pyrenees.
232b Compare industry in the Pyrenees with that of the French Alps (see also fig. 220).
232c What is the other main source of income for the people of the Pyrenees?

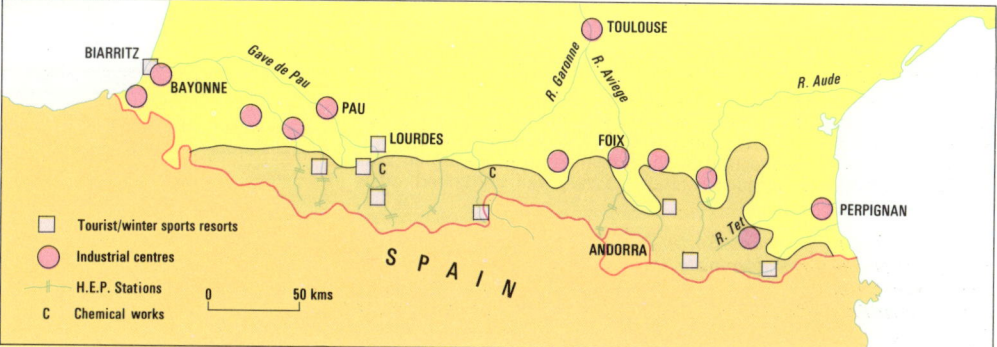

232 PYRENEES

Fig. 233 Post-war divided Germany

Germany was established as a united country in 1871 and lasted until the end of the Second World War when it was divided among four countries.

233a Name these four countries.

233b (i) What are the official names of (a) West Germany (b) East Germany? (ii) Which is the largest (in area)? (iii) Which contains Berlin?

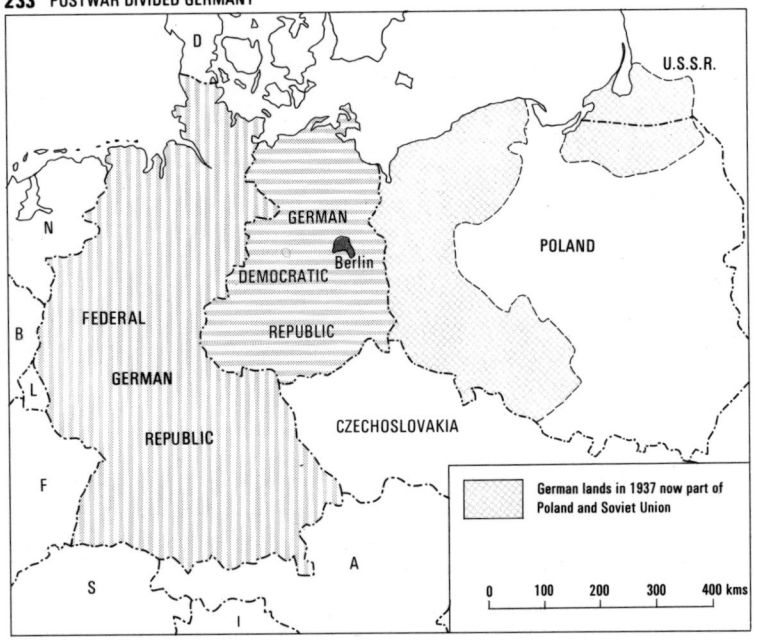

233 POSTWAR DIVIDED GERMANY

German lands in 1937 now part of Poland and Soviet Union

0 100 200 300 400 kms

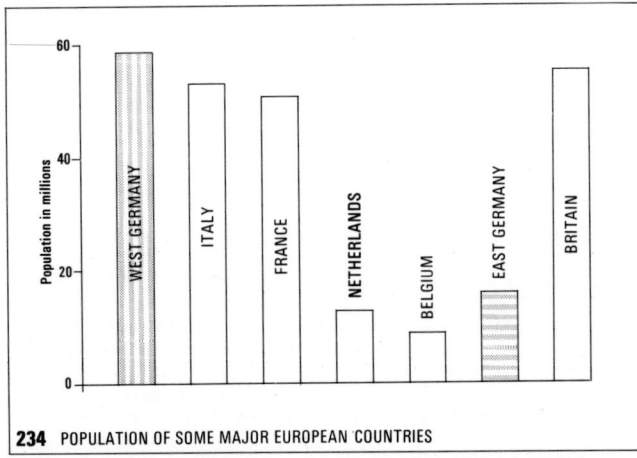

234 POPULATION OF SOME MAJOR EUROPEAN COUNTRIES

Fig. 234 Population of some major European countries

234a Compare the populations of East and West Germany.

234b Which European countries have similar populations?

Fig. 235 Berlin - divided city

Immediately after the Second World War, Berlin was divided into four military zones of occupation. In 1948 the three allied zones became West Berlin and, the Soviet zone, East Berlin. This twofold division was further emphasised by the construction of the Berlin Wall in 1961. Hence this unique situation of two self-contained cities within one.

235a The country around Berlin is flat and sandy. What two other features dominate the landscape?

235b West Berlin's population exceeds two million while East Berlin's is about one million. How do their areas compare?

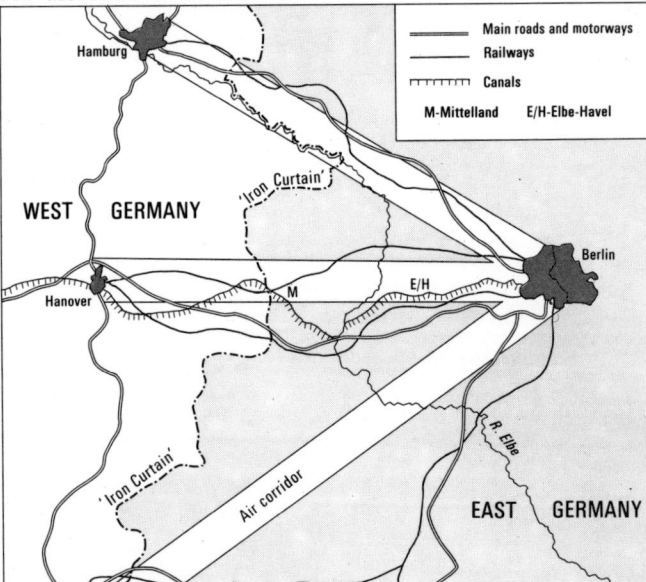

236 WEST BERLIN—LAND AND AIR LINKS

Main roads and motorways
Railways
Canals

M-Mittelland　E/H-Elbe-Havel

Fig. 236 West Berlin - land and air links

'West Berlin is a democratic island in a Communist sea.' Only restricted routeways link it with the West.

236a How many different routeways link it with the West?

236b Name the two West German Cities with which West Berlin has most direct contact.

Fig. 237 Manufacturing industry in West Berlin

In response to massive outside support and assistance, industry in West Berlin has made a dramatic recovery since the war and is now thriving.

237a Name the most important industry in West Berlin and some of the firms involved.

237b (i) Suggest some of the problems confronting industry in West Berlin and (ii) explain why industries requiring small supplies of raw materials and a high degree of skill are common.

237c Berlin has lost many of its former functions. It is no longer an administrative, financial or major route centre. Explain why.

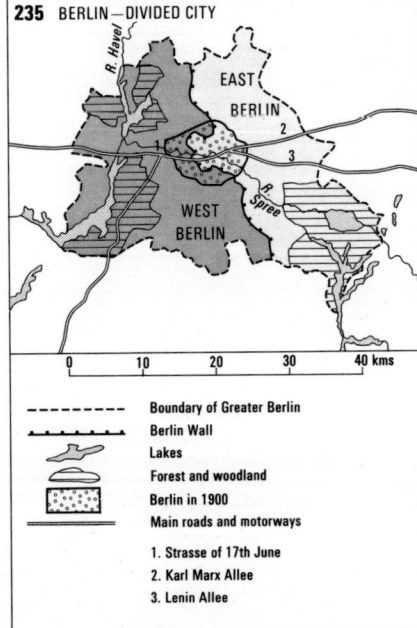

235 BERLIN—DIVIDED CITY

0 10 20 30 40 kms

Boundary of Greater Berlin
Berlin Wall
Lakes
Forest and woodland
Berlin in 1900
Main roads and motorways
1. Strasse of 17th June
2. Karl Marx Allee
3. Lenin Allee

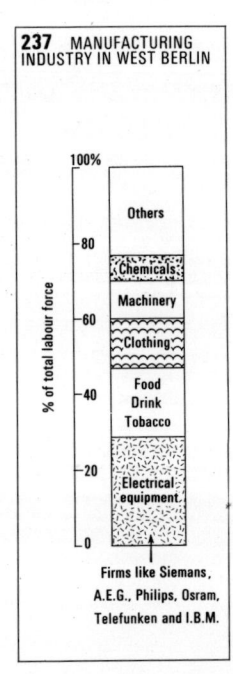

237 MANUFACTURING INDUSTRY IN WEST BERLIN

Others
Chemicals
Machinery
Clothing
Food Drink Tobacco
Electrical equipment

Firms like Siemens, A.E.G., Philips, Osram, Telefunken and I.B.M.

Fig. 238 Relief and drainage

238a (i) What proportion of West Germany is over 600ft?
(ii) Where is the highest land?
238b Using an atlas, name (i) the highland regions not indicated in the key (ii) the rivers R1 to R4.
238c Which river system dominates the drainage of West Germany?
238d Name the six main regions of West Germany.

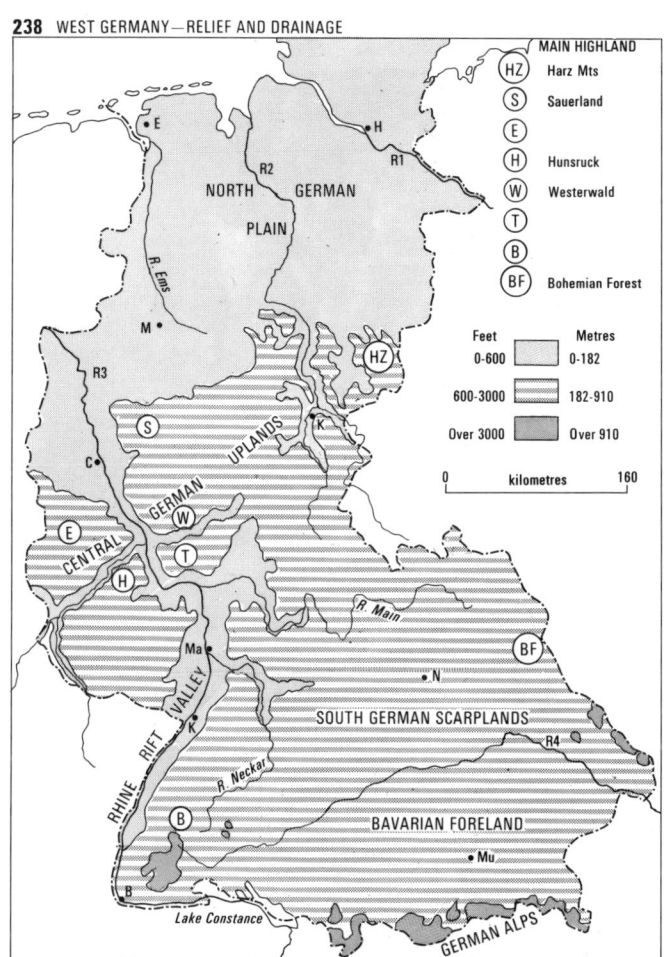

Fig. 238 WEST GERMANY—RELIEF AND DRAINAGE

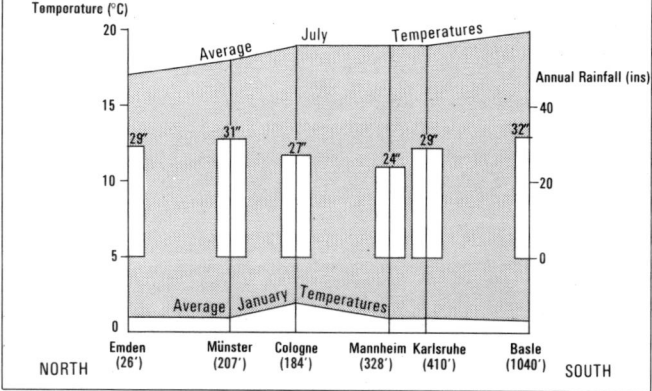

240 CLIMATIC TRANSECT ACROSS WESTERN WEST GERMANY

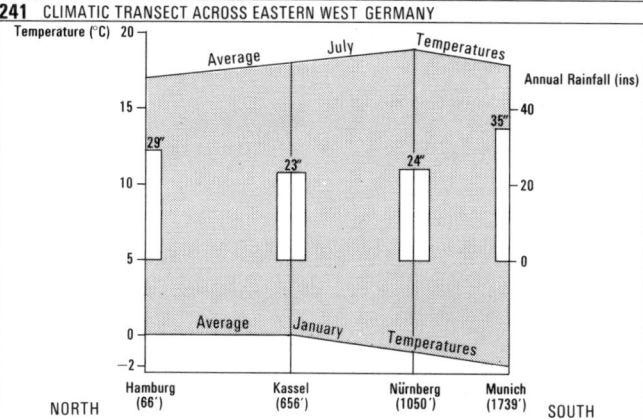

241 CLIMATIC TRANSECT ACROSS EASTERN WEST GERMANY

Figs. 240/241 Climatic transects across West Germany

(The position of the towns concerned are indicated by their initials on fig. 238).

240/241a Which towns (i) are warmest in (a) winter (b) summer (ii) are coldest in (a) winter (b) summer (iii) receive most annual rainfall? Quote figures in each case.
240/241b Describe and account for the climatic differences between the North Sea Coastlands, the Rhine Rift valley and the Bavarian Foreland.

Fig. 242 Soil quality

Loess is a fertile loamy soil. It comprises fine rock debris formed during the Ice Age and transported by the wind from Scandinavia or the Alps.

242a Where are the best soils in West Germany?

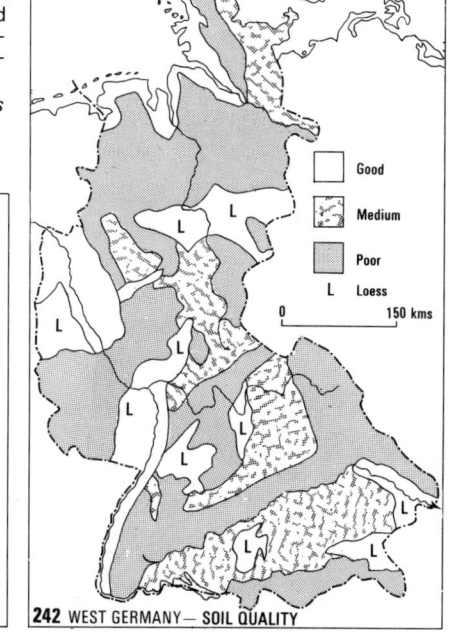

242 WEST GERMANY — SOIL QUALITY

Fig. 239 Geological transect across West Germany

239a Locate the youngest and oldest rocks in West Germany.
239b (i) What kind of rocks are they and (ii) what kind of relief do they form?

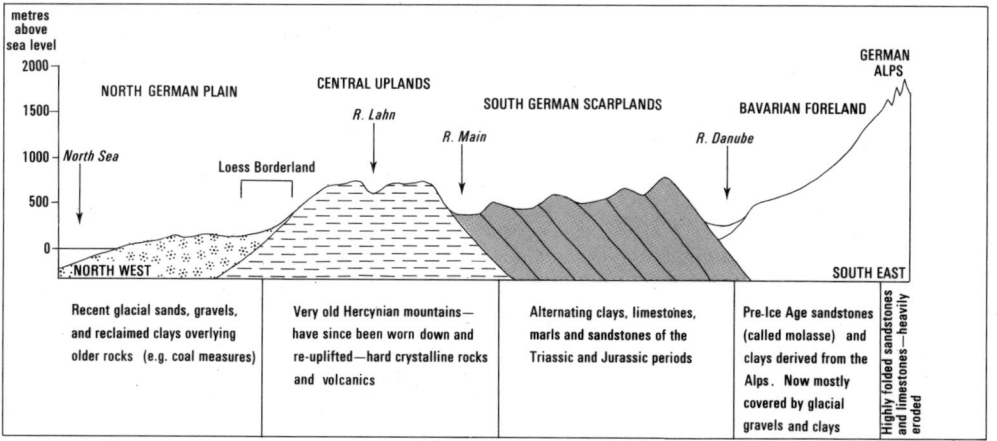

239 GEOLOGICAL TRANSECT ACROSS WEST GERMANY

Fig. 243 Land use

243a What proportion of West Germany is devoted to (i) agriculture (ii) forestry?

243b How does this compare with France? (See fig. 178).

Fig. 244 Agricultural land use

244a What proportion of agricultural land is under (i) grass (ii) grain crops?

244b How does this compare with France? (see fig. 178).

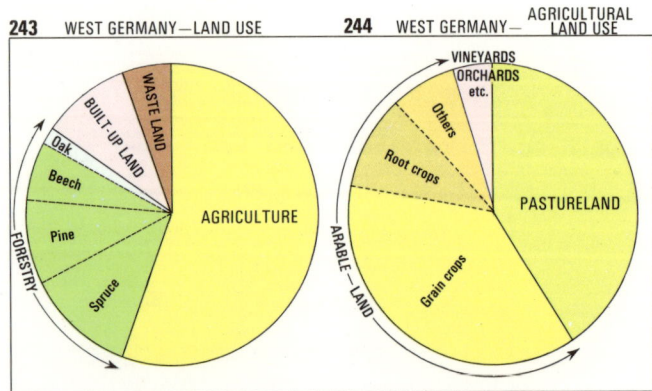

Fig. 245 West Germany/original EEC farm output

245a Name West Germany's most important (i) arable crop, (ii) livestock product.

245b Is West Germany more important as a livestock or crop producer?

245c Which is the only other EEC country to compare with West Germany as an agricultural producer?

Fig. 246 Agricultural labour force in original EEC countries

246a What is the EEC average for people working in agriculture?

246b (i) Name the countries with less than average percentage. (ii) Is West Germany one of them?

246c What do these percentages tell us?

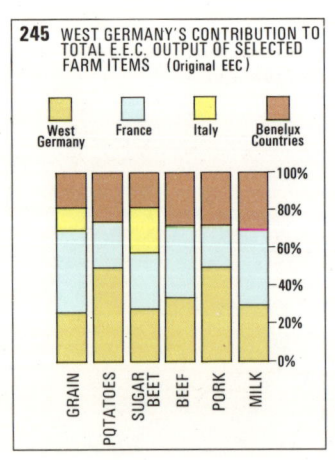

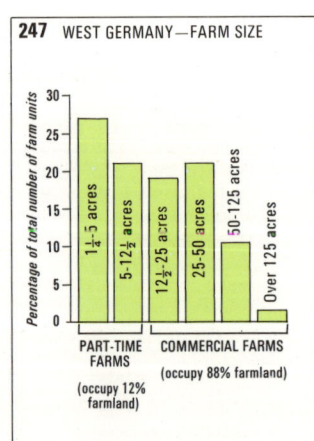

Fig. 247 Farm size

The average farm size in the EEC is 27.5 acres.

247a What percentage of West Germany's farms exceed 25 acres?

247b Are most farms in West Germany large or small?

247c (i) What is the minimum size of a commercial farm? (ii) What percentage of the total farmland do they occupy?

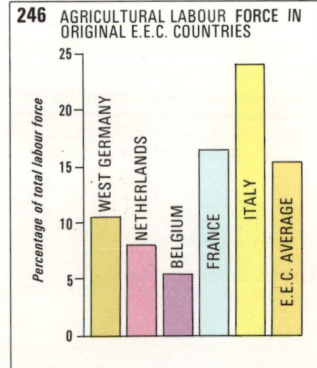

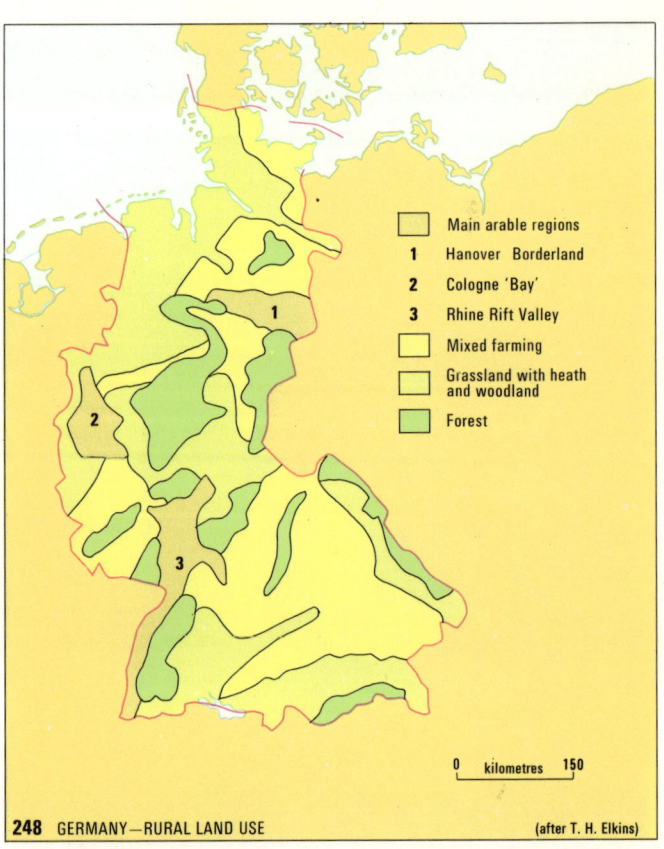

248 GERMANY—RURAL LAND USE   (after T. H. Elkins)

Fig. 248 Rural land use

248a Name the main arable regions in West Germany.

248b In what way are they related to soil quality (see fig. 242). Quote one example.

248c (i) Where are the main forested regions? (ii) What sort of country do they occupy (see figs 238, 239 and 242)?

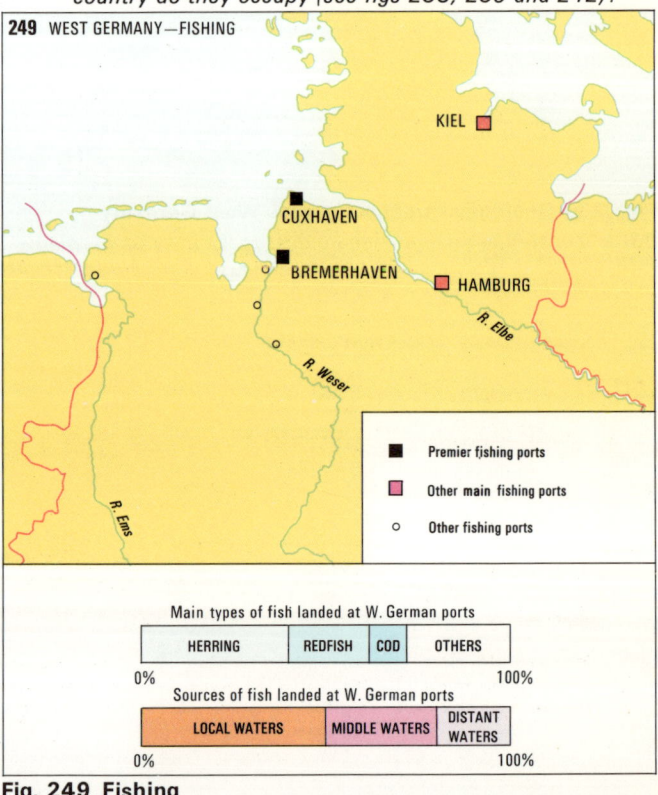

Fig. 249 Fishing

249a Name and locate the 2 main West German fishing ports.

249b What is the main type of fish landed and where is it caught?

West Germany is one of the world's major industrial powers.

Fig. 250   Raw materials and power

250a   (i) Name the four main coalfields in West Germany. (ii) Which is the biggest?

250b   What other raw materials does West Germany possess?   List them under the following three headings: fuels, metals, chemicals.

Fig. 251   Sources of petroleum

251a   What proportion of West German petroleum is imported and from where?

251b   Name five ports receiving petroleum destined for West Germany and indicate their nationality. (See fig. 250.)

Fig. 252   World output of lignite

252a   (i) What is lignite?   (ii) What is it used for?

252b   The main lignite field is in the Rhine valley. Name the major town nearby.

252c   What proportion of world output is produced in West Germany?

Fig. 255   West Germany - industrial regions

255a   (i) How many major industrial regions are there in West Germany?   (ii) Name them.

255b   Are they   (i) related to supplies of raw materials and fuels (see fig. 250) or   (ii)   well served by transport routes (see fig. 256)?

255c   Name four other industrial centres.

Fig. 256   Transport routes

256a   The River Rhine and its tributaries form the most important waterway in West Germany.   By what means is (i) Hanover (ii) the River Danube linked to the Rhine?

256b   (i) Name the three main route centres in West Germany. (ii) Explain why they are so important (see also fig 238).

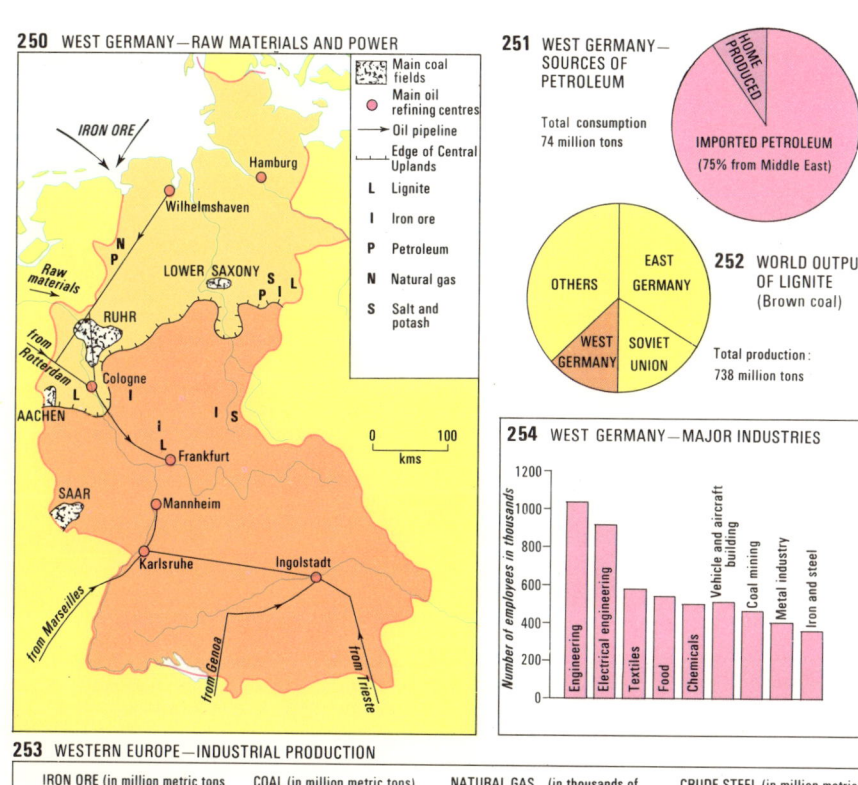

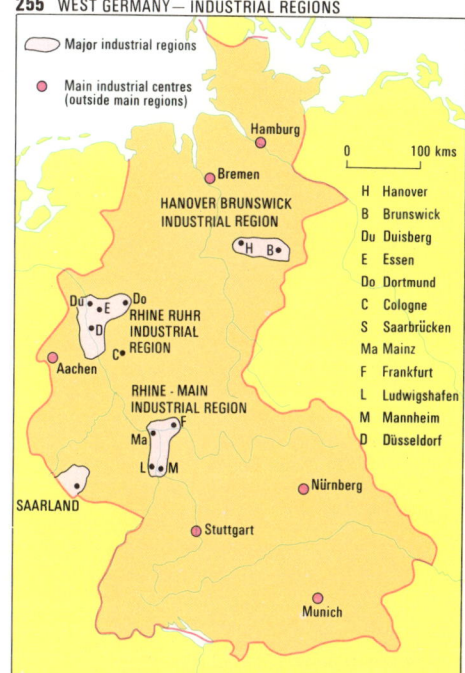

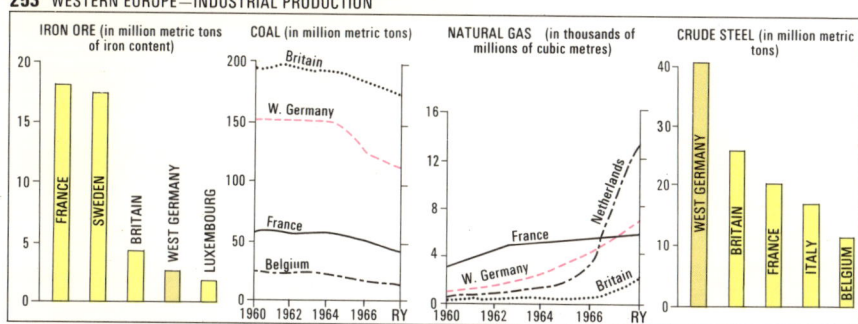

Fig. 253   Industrial production

253a   Compare West Germany's industrial production with the other countries of Western Europe.

Fig. 254   Major industries

254a   List the six main industries in West Germany.

254b   Of all the industries represented on the graph, which is the odd one out and why?

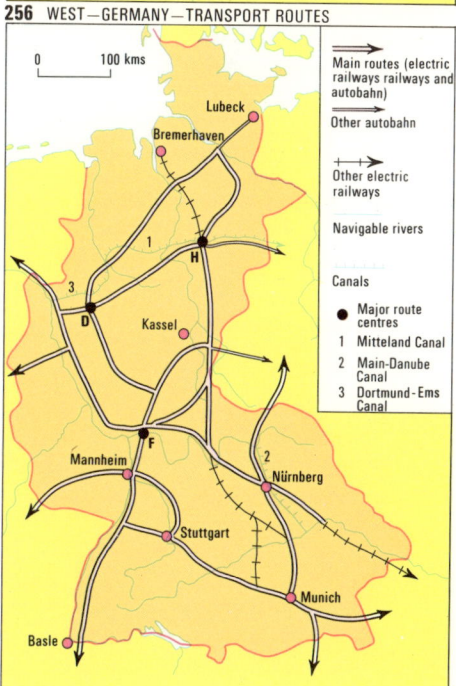

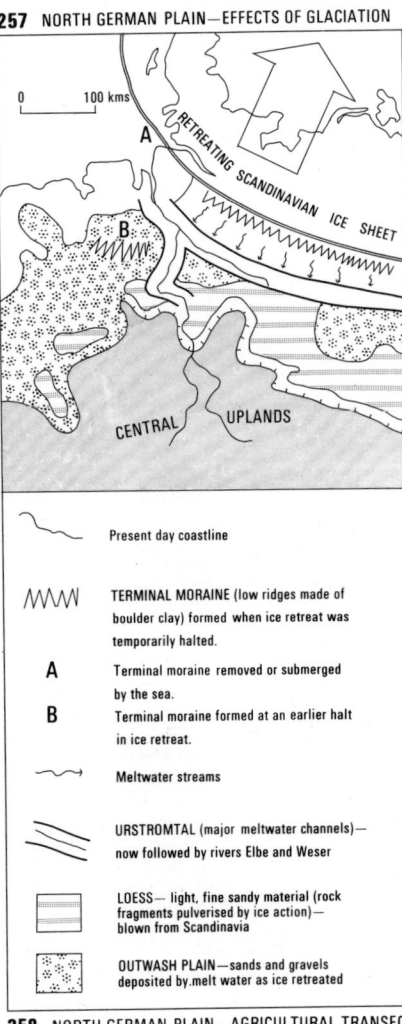

257 NORTH GERMAN PLAIN—EFFECTS OF GLACIATION

The North German Plain is part of a vast lowland plain which stretches across Europe from the Netherlands to the Soviet Union. Most of the surface features of this region are the result of glacial deposition.

Fig. 257 Effects of glaciation

257a Locate, describe and account for the following: (i) terminal moraines (ii) urstromtal (iii) outwash plain.

257b What is loess and why does it occur on the North German Plain?

257c Precisely where it is found?

257d What sort of soil does it produce (see fig. 258)?

Legend:

~~ Present day coastline

MMM TERMINAL MORAINE (low ridges made of boulder clay) formed when ice retreat was temporarily halted.

A Terminal moraine removed or submerged by the sea.

B Terminal moraine formed at an earlier halt in ice retreat.

~ Meltwater streams

≡ URSTROMTAL (major meltwater channels)— now followed by rivers Elbe and Weser

▤ LOESS — light, fine sandy material (rock fragments pulverised by ice action)— blown from Scandinavia

▨ OUTWASH PLAIN—sands and gravels deposited by melt water as ice retreated

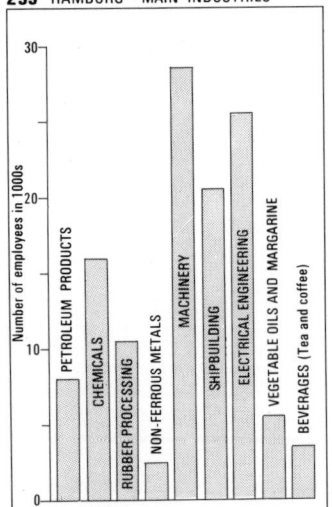

259 HAMBURG—MAIN INDUSTRIES

Number of employees in 1000s

Industries (bars): PETROLEUM PRODUCTS, CHEMICALS, RUBBER PROCESSING, NON-FERROUS METALS, MACHINERY, SHIPBUILDING, ELECTRICAL ENGINEERING, VEGETABLE OILS AND MARGARINE, BEVERAGES (Tea and coffee)

Figs. 259/260 Industry

259/260a Name the three main industrial centres on the North coast of West Germany.

259/260b What industries have they in common?

259/260c Name the main imports entering Hamburg and indicate the industries that process them.

259/260d The port of Hamburg was formerly more important than it is today. In recent years Rotterdam has cornered a lot of its trade. In addition it has lost contact with much of its former hinterland in Eastern Europe. Explain why (see fig. 233).

259/260e Hamburg stands astride the narrow channel of the River Elbe, 50 miles from the open sea. What problem does this create and how is Hamburg planning to solve it?

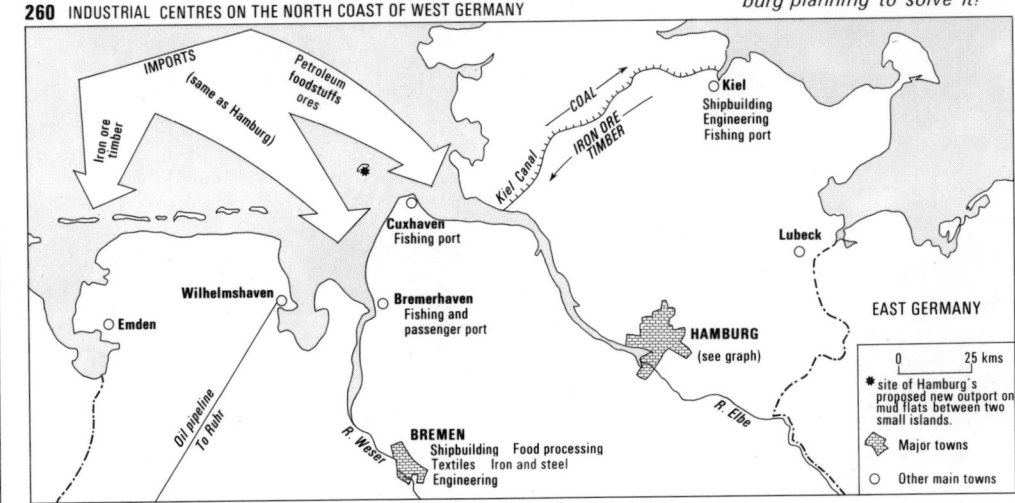

260 INDUSTRIAL CENTRES ON THE NORTH COAST OF WEST GERMANY

Kiel — Shipbuilding, Engineering, Fishing port

Cuxhaven — Fishing port

Wilhelmshaven

Emden

Bremerhaven — Fishing and passenger port

Lübeck

HAMBURG (see graph)

* site of Hamburg's proposed new outport on mud flats between two small islands.

■ Major towns

○ Other main towns

BREMEN — Shipbuilding, Textiles, Engineering, Food processing, Iron and steel

IMPORTS — Iron ore, timber, (same as Hamburg)

Petroleum, foodstuffs, ores

Kiel Canal, COAL, IRON ORE, TIMBER

Oil pipeline To Ruhr

R. Weser, R. Elbe

EAST GERMANY

258 NORTH GERMAN PLAIN—AGRICULTURAL TRANSECT FROM NORTH TO SOUTH

MARSCHEN	LÜNEBURG HEATH	URSTROMTAL	LOESS BORDERLAND	
Reclaimed river and sea marsh. Mainly PASTURE and some fodder crops. Dairying predominates.	Generally infertile—large areas uncultivated (some used for military training) 300 sq. miles now converted to CONIFEROUS FOREST. Where farming is possible RYE and POTATOES are the main crops—although the cultivation of wheat and sugar beet is possible on improved soils. Some store cattle and pigs are kept.	Mainly pastureland—forms an important transport route.	Premier West German farming region— rich fertile soil—land intensively cultivated—WHEAT, SUGAR BEET and MARKET GARDENING. Stall CATTLE are reared on sugar-beet, 'leftovers' and fodder crops.	CENTRAL UPLANDS

North Sea — Terminal moraine 570' — R. Aller (tributary of the R. Weser)
NORTH   SOUTH

Fig. 258 Agricultural transect from North to South

258a Outline the climatic conditions on the North German Plain, emphasising any differences between North and South, and East and West. (See figs. 240 and 241.)

258b Describe and account for the agricultural differences between the (i) Marschen (ii) Lüneburg Heath (iii) loess borderland.

Fig. 261 Hanover - Brunswick industrial region

261a What raw materials are obtained from this region?

261b Locate and name the industries which use these raw materials.

261c The headquarters of the Volkswagen Company is at Wolfsburg. (i) What does this company manufacture? (ii) What other towns in this region contain Volkswagen factories?

261d What advantages favour the vehicle assembly industry in this region? (Think of site, raw materials and transport.)

261e Many refugees work in this industry. Explain why?

261f Explain why food processing is important at Hanover and Brunswick (see fig. 258).

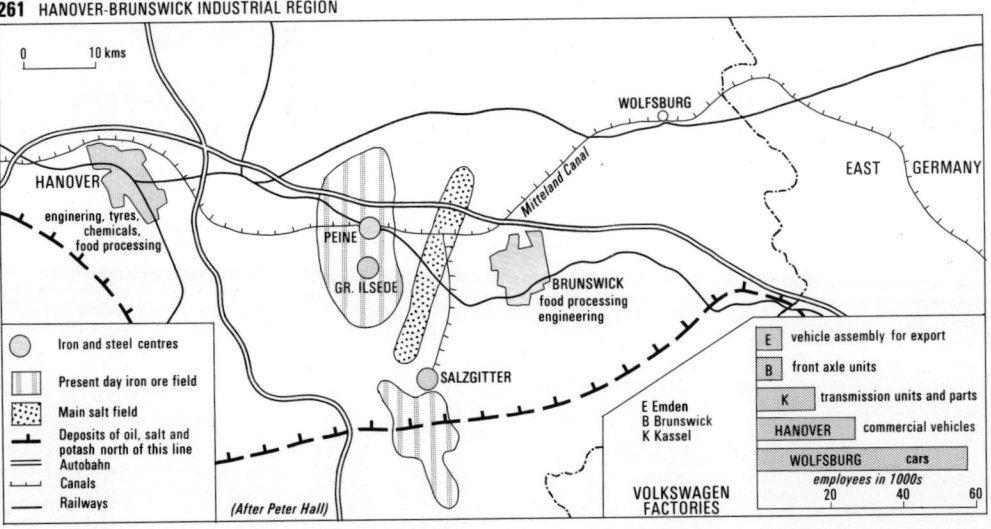

261 HANOVER-BRUNSWICK INDUSTRIAL REGION

WOLFSBURG

HANOVER — enginering, tyres, chemicals, food processing

PEINE

GR. ILSEDE

SALZGITTER

BRUNSWICK — food processing, engineering

EAST GERMANY

Legend:

● Iron and steel centres

▥ Present day iron ore field

▦ Main salt field

Deposits of oil, salt and potash north of this line

Autobahn

⊢ Canals

— Railways

(After Peter Hall)

VOLKSWAGEN FACTORIES

E vehicle assembly for export
B front axle units
K transmission units and parts
HANOVER commercial vehicles
WOLFSBURG cars

E Emden
B Brunswick
K Kassel

employees in 1000s
20   40   60

The Rhine-Ruhr region is the most important industrial region in West Germany and ranks high in the world. It occupies a basin in the North German plain which extends into the Central Highlands.

Fig. 262 West Germany - population

262a What is the population of the Rhine-Ruhr region?

262b What percentage of the West German population live in this region?

262c How does a large concentration of population favour industrial development?

Fig. 263 The Rhine-Ruhr region - main towns

263a (i) Locate precisely, and explain the main concentration of settlement (see also fig. 264). (ii) Why is this region called the Ruhr?

263b Name the three largest towns on the River Rhine.

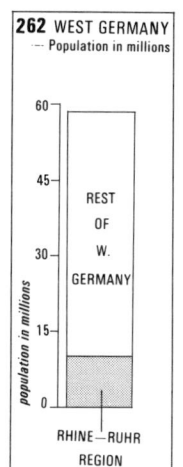

262 WEST GERMANY — Population in millions

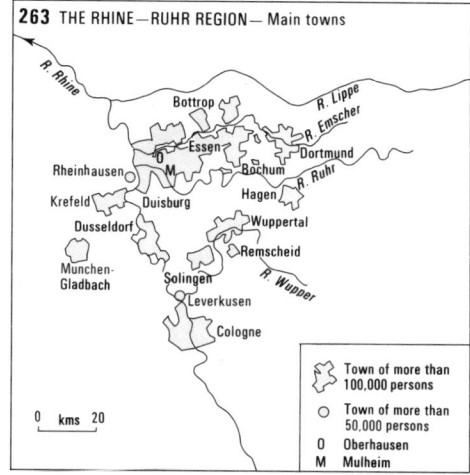

263 THE RHINE—RUHR REGION— Main towns

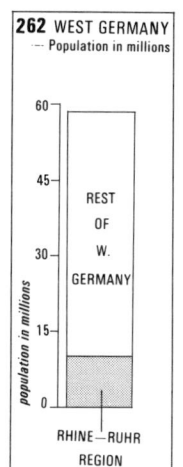

264 RHINE—RUHR REGION—coal and lignite resources

Fig.264/265 Rhine-Ruhr region- coal and lignite resources

264/265a Coal mining began in the Ruhr valley. Why? (See fig. 265)

264/265b In which valley is coal mining concentrated to-day?

264/265c The newest coal mines are located in the Lippe valley. (i) Explain why. (ii) Calculate how deep they have to be (see fig. 265).

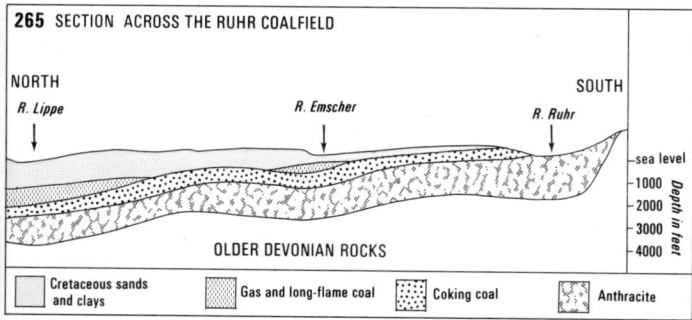

265 SECTION ACROSS THE RUHR COALFIELD

Fig. 266 West Germany - industrial production and consumption

266a (i) What percentage of West German coal production is mined in the Ruhr? (ii) How much of it is coking coal?

266b Where does West Germany obtain its iron ore?

266c How important is the Rhine-Ruhr region as a producer of (i) crude iron (ii) crude steel?

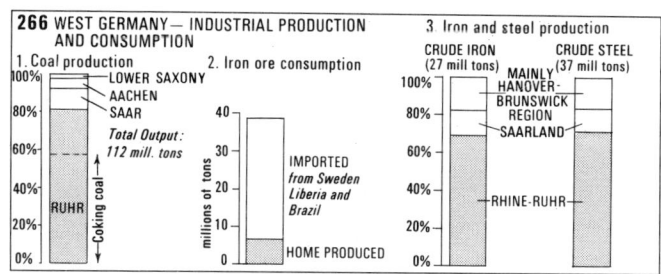

266 WEST GERMANY — INDUSTRIAL PRODUCTION AND CONSUMPTION

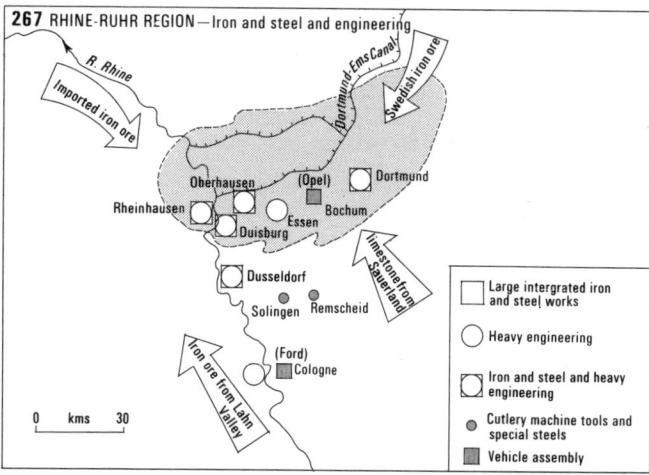

267 RHINE-RUHR REGION—Iron and steel and engineering

Fig. 267 Rhine-Ruhr region - iron and steel and engineering

267a Name the five main iron and steel and heavy engineering centres in this region.

267b Formerly, all the raw materials required for iron and steel production were obtained locally. (i) Where are the three basic raw materials obtained today? (ii) How important is water transport in supplying these materials?

267c What industries (other than heavy engineering) are closely associated with the Rhine-Ruhr iron and steel industry?

Fig. 268 Rhine-Ruhr region - chemicals and textiles

268a (i) What raw materials does the Rhine-Ruhr chemical industry use? (ii) Which raw materials are obtained outside the region? (iii) How are they transported?

268b Name five main chemical plants and indicate their location with reference to (i) the River Rhine (ii) the coalfield.

268c (i) Name and locate the three main textile centres. (ii) What factors have contributed to their location?

268d Why has Cologne become an important centre for synthetic fibres?

Many other industries exist in this region. New industries such as vehicle assembly and electrical engineering are expanding while the more traditional industries (coal, iron and steel) are contracting.

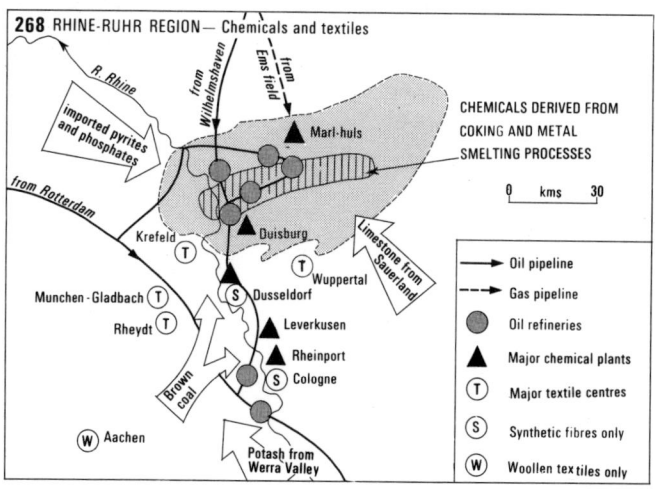

268 RHINE-RUHR REGION— Chemicals and textiles

Fig. 269 Central German Uplands

269a Name the regions North and South of the Central German Uplands (see fig. 238).

269b What height do these Uplands reach?

269c Name the five upland areas either side of the River Rhine.

The Rhine has carved a gorge through these uplands.

269d What rocks make up the Central German Uplands (see fig. 239).

The Vogelsburg and Rhön are areas of volcanic rocks.

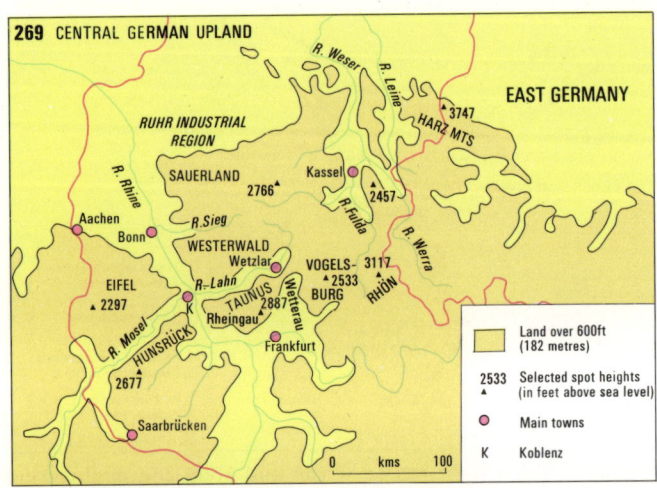

Fig. 270 Climatic Comparison - Frankfurt and Kassel

270a Compare the situations of Frankfurt and Kassel (see fig. 269).

270b Compare their climates and suggest reasons for the differences.

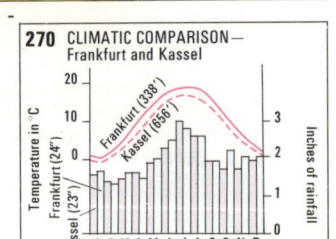

Fig. 271 The Rhine Gorge

271a The Rhine Gorge has always been a major routeway linking North and South Germany. Explain why (see fig. 269).

271b Describe (i) the nature and shape (ii) the land use of the Rhine Gorge.

271c (i) What are the problems of transport and settlement in the Rhine Gorge? (ii) How has man coped with these problems?

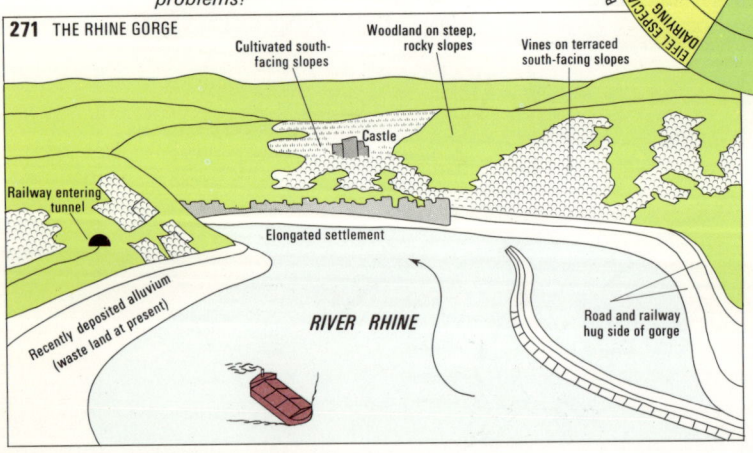

272 KOBLENZ— Major route centre in the Rhine Gorge

Fig. 272 Koblenz

272a Koblenz is the largest town in the Rhine Gorge. Suggest how its site and position favoured its development as an important route and market centre (see also fig. 269).

272b What other town in the Central Uplands is an important route centre? (See fig. 256.) Why?

Fig. 273 Central German Uplands - land use

273a (i) What proportion of these Uplands are forested? (ii) Which areas are most forested?

273b (i) Where is most of the farming land found? (ii) Name the main areas concerned.

273c Describe the nature of farming in this region (see also fig. 271).

This region is a very important producer of quality white wines—especially famous are those from the Rheingau and the Mosel valley.

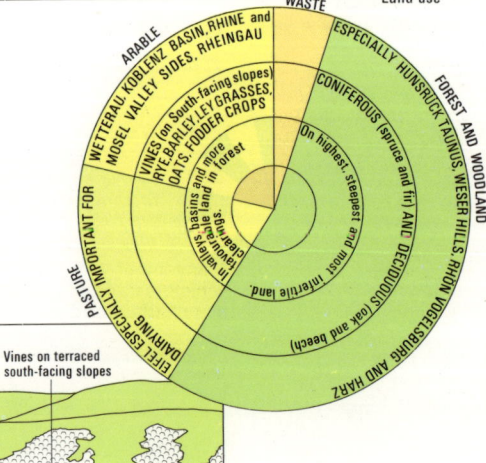

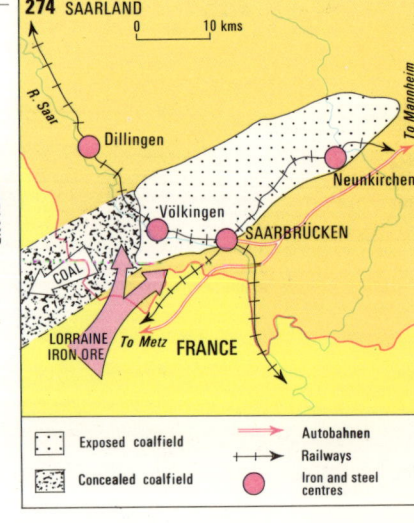

Fig. 274 Saarland

Saarland is the only significant industrial area in the Central Uplands although this region produces iron ore (Lahn valley), potash (Fulda valley), limestone and other quarry stones.

274a Suggest why Saarland is an industrial area.

274b Name the two main industries in Saarland.

274c What proportion of West Germany's annual output of (i) coal (ii) crude steel comes from Saarland? (See fig. 266.)

Saarland's coke ovens supply gas by pipeline to both Lorraine and the Rhine-Main industrial region.

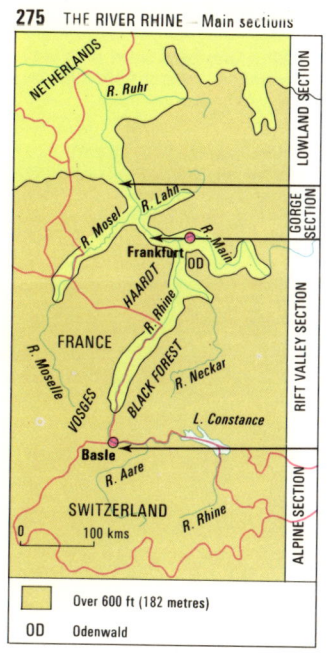

275 THE RIVER RHINE - Main sections

LOWLAND SECTION
GORGE SECTION
RIFT VALLEY SECTION
ALPINE SECTION

NETHERLANDS
R. Ruhr
R. Mosel R. Lahn
Frankfurt R. Main OD
HAARDT R. Rhine
FRANCE R. Neckar
R. Moselle L. Constance
VOSGES BLACK FOREST
Basle
R. Aare
SWITZERLAND R. Rhine
0   100 kms

☐ Over 600 ft (182 metres)
OD   Odenwald

Fig. 275 The River Rhine - main sections

275a   Name the four main sections of the River Rhine.

275b   (i) How long is the Rhine Rift valley? (ii) What proportion lies wholly within West Germany? (iii) Name the four upland areas that flank the rift valley. (iv) How high do they reach? (See fig. 276.)

275c   Name the two main rivers that enter the Rift valley from the East.

Fig. 276   Geological cross-section of the Southern Rhine Rift Valley

276a   What rocks make up (i) the Black Forest and Vosges Uplands (ii) the valley in-between?

276b   (i) How was the Rift Valley formed? (ii) In what way was the Kaiserstuhl part of this formation?

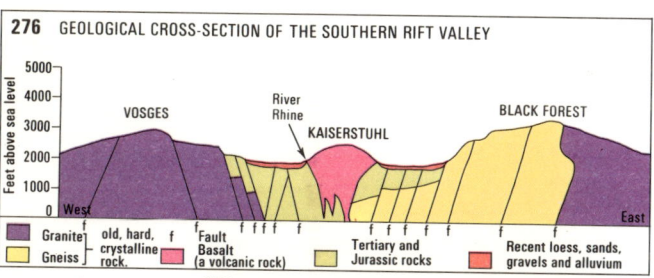

276 GEOLOGICAL CROSS-SECTION OF THE SOUTHERN RIFT VALLEY

Feet above sea level
5000
4000
3000
2000
1000
0

VOSGES   River Rhine   KAISERSTUHL   BLACK FOREST
West   East

☐ Granite } old, hard, crystalline rock.   f Fault
☐ Gneiss
☐ Basalt (a volcanic rock)
☐ Tertiary and Jurassic rocks
☐ Recent loess, sands, gravels and alluvium

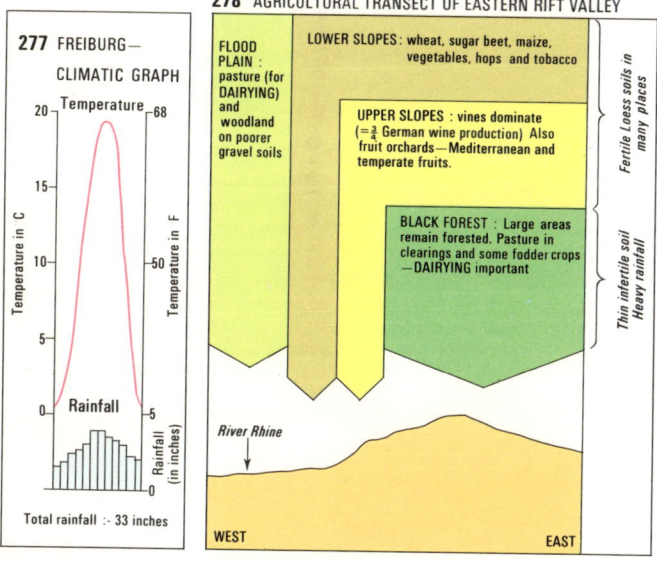

277 FREIBURG — CLIMATIC GRAPH

Temperature
20 68
15
10 50
5
0 5
Temperature in C / Temperature in F

Rainfall
Rainfall (in inches)

Total rainfall :- 33 inches

278 AGRICULTURAL TRANSECT OF EASTERN RIFT VALLEY

FLOOD PLAIN : pasture (for DAIRYING) and woodland on poorer gravel soils

LOWER SLOPES : wheat, sugar beet, maize, vegetables, hops and tobacco

UPPER SLOPES : vines dominate (= ⅔ German wine production) Also fruit orchards—Mediterranean and temperate fruits.

BLACK FOREST : Large areas remain forested. Pasture in clearings and some fodder crops —DAIRYING important

Fertile Loess soils in many places
Thin infertile soil Heavy rainfall

River Rhine

WEST   EAST

Fig. 277   Freiburg - climate graph

277a   Describe the climate of Freiburg.

277b   How does it compare with Hamburg (see fig. 241). Note: the growing season in Freiburg is much longer and spring arrives earlier.

Fig. 278   Agricultural transect of the Eastern Rift Valley

278a   Describe and account for the farming changes that occur between the River Rhine flood plain and Black Forest (see also figs. 276 and 277).

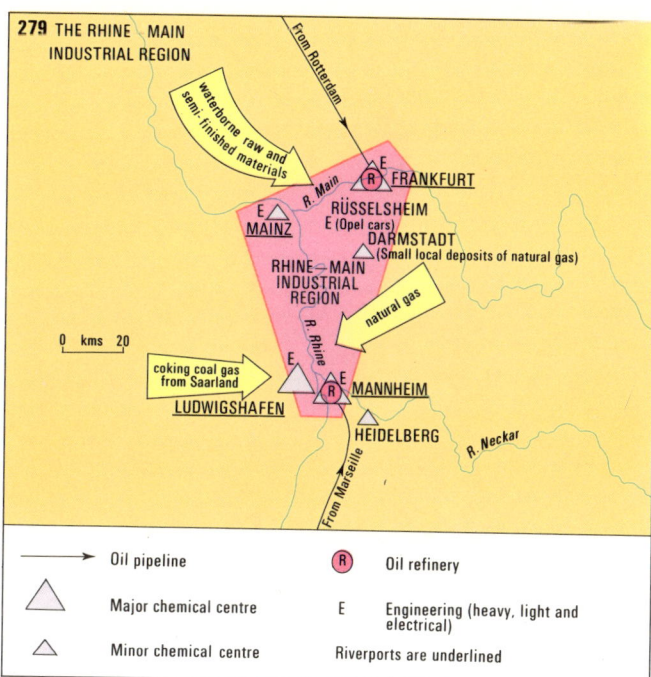

279 THE RHINE MAIN INDUSTRIAL REGION

From Rotterdam
waterborne raw and semi-finished materials
R. Main R FRANKFURT
RÜSSELSHEIM E
MAINZ E (Opel cars)
DARMSTADT (Small local deposits of natural gas)
RHINE—MAIN INDUSTRIAL REGION
R. Rhine
natural gas
coking coal gas from Saarland
LUDWIGSHAFEN E E R MANNHEIM
HEIDELBERG R. Neckar
From Marseille
0   kms   20

→ Oil pipeline   ® Oil refinery
▲ Major chemical centre   E Engineering (heavy, light and electrical)
△ Minor chemical centre   Riverports are underlined

Fig. 279   The Rhine-Main industrial region

This region contains 3½ million people, and is second only to the Rhine-Ruhr as an industrial region.

279a   What towns make up this region?

279b   Name the two main industries in this region and indicate (i) the raw and semi-finished materials they use (ii) where these materials are obtained (iii) how they are transported.

279c   What raw materials exist locally? If virtually none, suggest how this region has become so important as an industrial region (Note: find out why some towns are underlined.)

Fig. 280   Frankfurt

Frankfurt has a population of nearly ¾ million. It is the chief town of this region.

280a   With which parts of West Germany is Frankfurt linked directly by (i) autobahn (motorway) (ii) railway (iii) waterway (see also fig. 256)?

280b   Apart from being a major route centre, Frankfurt is an important commercial, financial and industrial centre. Name three of Frankfurt's industries (see fig. 279).

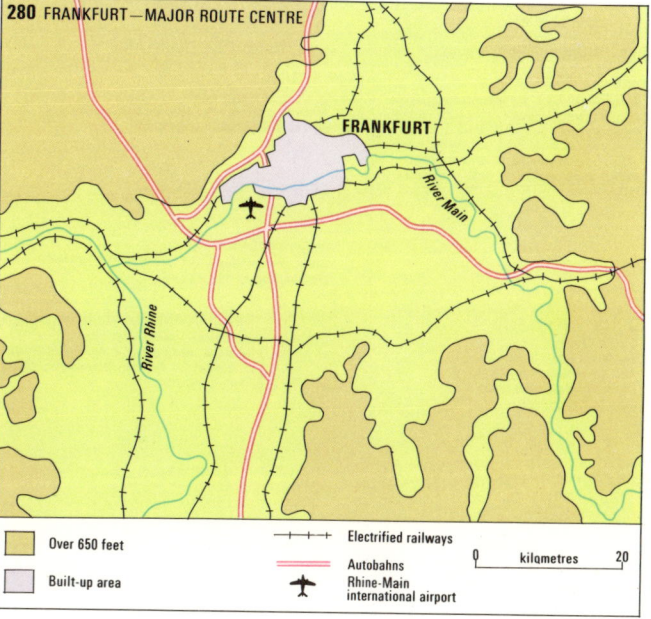

280 FRANKFURT—MAJOR ROUTE CENTRE

FRANKFURT
River Main
River Rhine

☐ Over 650 feet
☐ Built-up area
┼┼┼ Electrified railways
═══ Autobahns
✈ Rhine-Main international airport
0   kilometres   20

Fig. 281 Geology of the South German Scarplands

281a *Write out the following , filling in the missing words: 'The South German Scarplands is a basin of Triassic and Jurassic s..... rocks bounded on two sides by u..... blocks, made of o....., h..... crystalline rocks. In the basin, a succession of alternate hard and soft rocks has produced a s..... and vale landscape on a large scale. In some areas there is a covering of l..... and clays.'*

Fig. 282 Geological Section across the South German Scarplands

282a *List the succession of rocks in this region from oldest to youngest. (Note: the youngest is normally on top.)*

282b *Which rocks form (i) the most dramatic scarp slope (ii) the most extensive vale? Explain why.*

282c *(i) Name the two main rivers in this region (see fig. 281). (ii) Do they breach scarp slopes in any places or are they confined to the vales?*

Fig. 283 Agricultural transect across the South German Scarplands

Agriculture in this region is generally small scale, backward and very varied. Much of the more prosperous farming is concentrated in the river valleys, sheltered basins and on south-facing scarp slopes.

283a *Give reasons why agriculture in this region is so varied.*

283b *(i) Name the richest arable region in the South German Scarplands. (ii) Indicate the main crops grown. (iii) Why is it such a favourable region?*

283c *Summarise the rest of agriculture in the South German Scarplands.*

283d *Which areas are forested and why?*

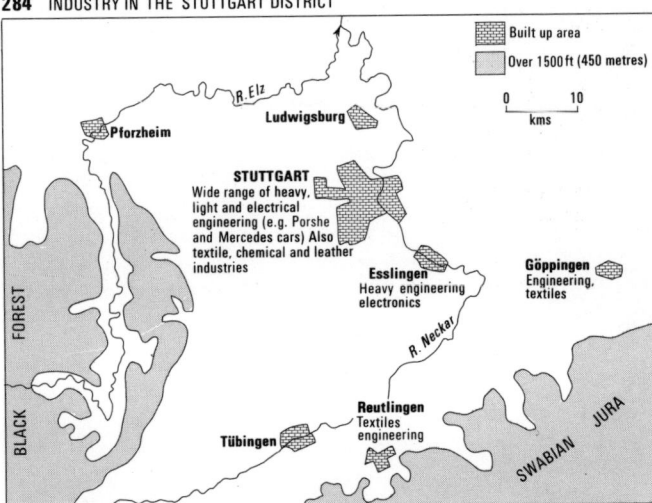

Fig. 284 Industry in the Stuttgart region

With a population of 650,000, Stuttgart is the hub of an expanding industrial region as well as being an important administrative and commercial centre.

284a *(i)What industry dominates Stuttgart and its region? (ii) Give two examples of firms involved.*

284b *Name three other important industries in Stuttgart.*

Stuttgart has no local raw materials or power resources. Its industries require small supplies of raw materials, a high degree of skill and an efficient transport network.

Fig. 285 Major transport routes in Southern Germany

285a *With what major industrial regions and centres is Stuttgart directly linked?*

285b *Name the other main route centre in the South German Scarplands. (Note: Munich is not in this region.)*

285c *What canal does it stand on? (See fig. 256.)*

Nürnberg (population ½ million) has become an important industrial centre in the same way as Stuttgart. Its industries include electrical and general engineering, glass and timber products.

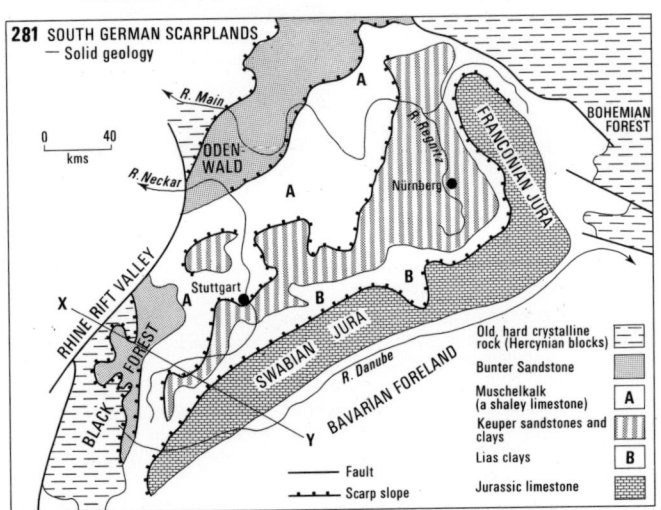

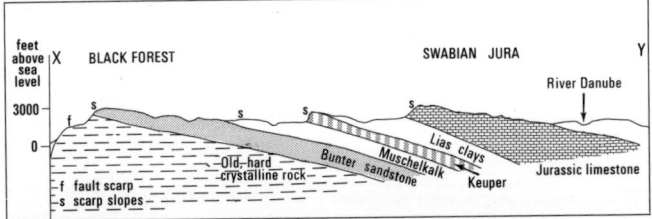

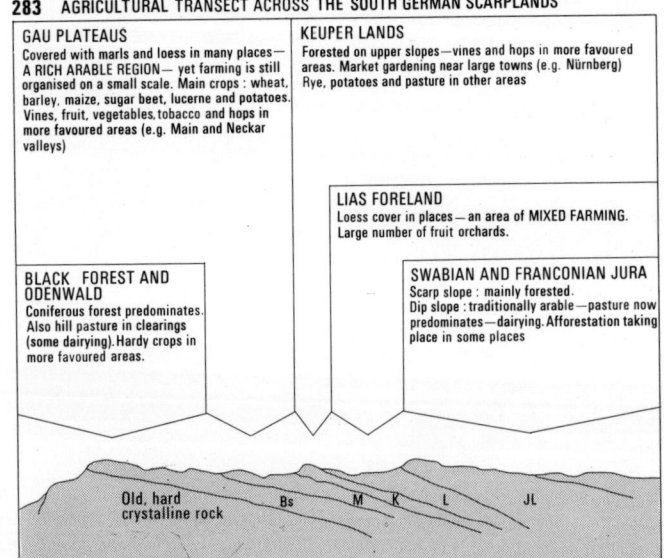

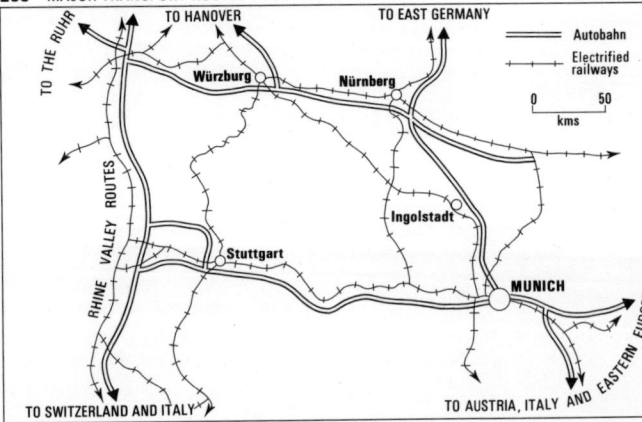

Fig. 286 Bavarian Foreland and German Alps - surface features

286a What physical features border the Bavarian Foreland in the (i) North and (ii) South?

286b Name four rivers that flow through this region to join the River Danube.

286c What changes in altitude occur between Regensburg, Munich and Zugspitze (the highest German mountain)?

286d What factor has contributed most to the nature of the land-scape of the Bavarian Foreland?

286e Name three different surface features and explain how they were formed (see also fig. 257).

Fig. 289 Power resources in Southern Germany

289a Name and locate the oil refining centre in Southern Germany where there are now five refineries.

289b (i)Where is the crude oil for these refineries obtained (ii)how is it transported?

289c What factors favour HEP production in the German Alps?

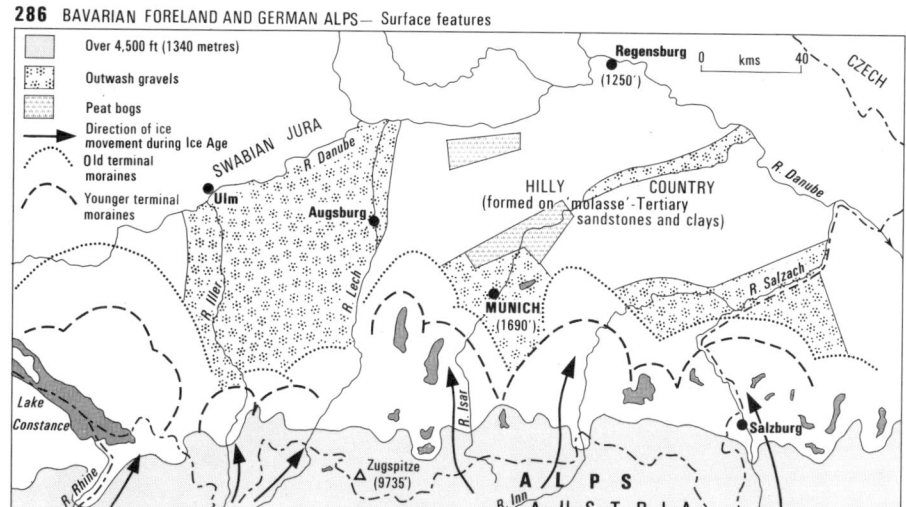

286 BAVARIAN FORELAND AND GERMAN ALPS— Surface features

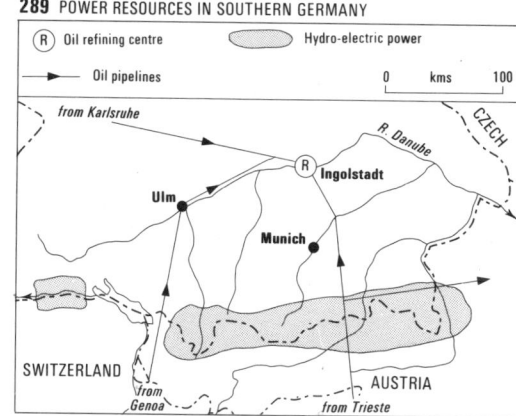

289 POWER RESOURCES IN SOUTHERN GERMANY

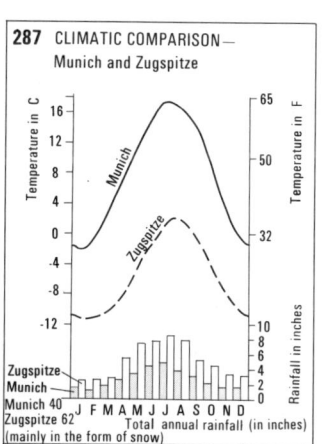

287 CLIMATIC COMPARISON— Munich and Zugspitze

Fig. 287 Climatic comparison- Munich and Zugspitze

287a Describe and explain the differences between the climates of Munich and Zugspitze.

287b How does Munich's climate compare with that of Emden (see also fig. 240).

Fig. 288 Agricultural transect across the Bavarian Foreland and German Alps

288a Describe and explain the agriculture of the Bavarian Foreland (do not forget to consider aspect and growing season).

288b In what way is it different from that of the (i) The Danube valley (ii) The German Alps?

288c Try to explain these differences.

Fig. 290 Munich - largest city in Southern Germany

290a What is the population of Munich?

290b Describe Munich's position within the Bavarian Foreland.

290c Is Munich well-served by transport routes?

290d What other factors have contributed to Munich's importance?

290e (i)What type of industry occurs in Munich?(ii)Give examples. (iii)Explain why (see notes on Stuttgart).

290f What other functions has Munich?

290g Summarise the geography of the German Alps (consult all the maps and graphs on this page).

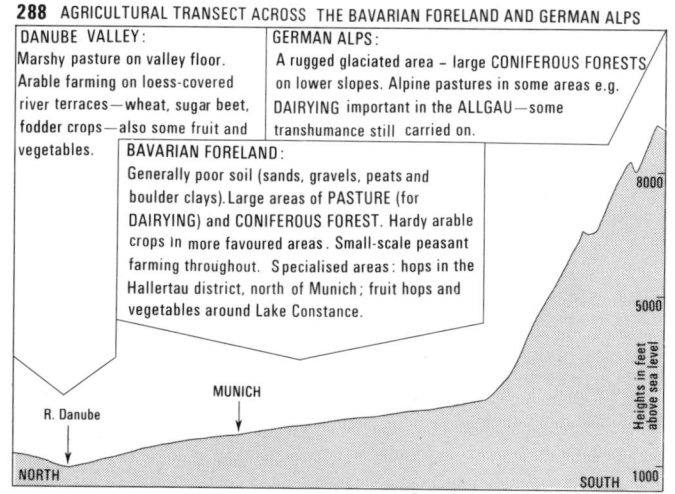

288 AGRICULTURAL TRANSECT ACROSS THE BAVARIAN FORELAND AND GERMAN ALPS

DANUBE VALLEY:
Marshy pasture on valley floor. Arable farming on loess-covered river terraces—wheat, sugar beet, fodder crops—also some fruit and vegetables.

GERMAN ALPS:
A rugged glaciated area – large CONIFEROUS FORESTS on lower slopes. Alpine pastures in some areas e.g. DAIRYING important in the ALLGAU—some transhumance still carried on.

BAVARIAN FORELAND:
Generally poor soil (sands, gravels, peats and boulder clays). Large areas of PASTURE (for DAIRYING) and CONIFEROUS FOREST. Hardy arable crops in more favoured areas. Small-scale peasant farming throughout. Specialised areas: hops in the Hallertau district, north of Munich; fruit hops and vegetables around Lake Constance.

290 MUNICH—Largest city in Southern Germany

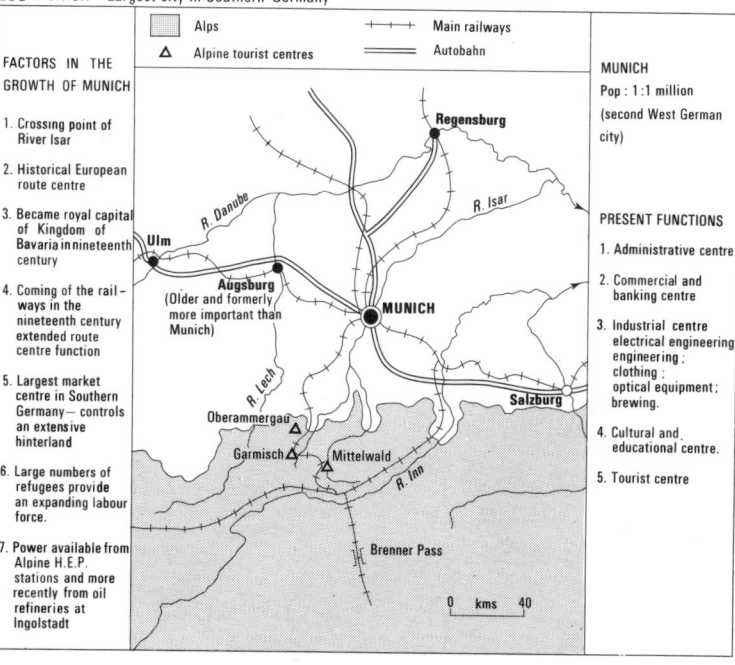

FACTORS IN THE GROWTH OF MUNICH

1. Crossing point of River Isar
2. Historical European route centre
3. Became royal capital of Kingdom of Bavaria in nineteenth century
4. Coming of the railways in the nineteenth century extended route centre function
5. Largest market centre in Southern Germany—controls an extensive hinterland
6. Large numbers of refugees provide an expanding labour force.
7. Power available from Alpine H.E.P. stations and more recently from oil refineries at Ingolstadt

MUNICH
Pop : 1·1 million (second West German city)

PRESENT FUNCTIONS

1. Administrative centre
2. Commercial and banking centre
3. Industrial centre electrical engineering engineering ; clothing ; optical equipment; brewing.
4. Cultural and educational centre.
5. Tourist centre

291 BENELUX COUNTRIES—RELIEF

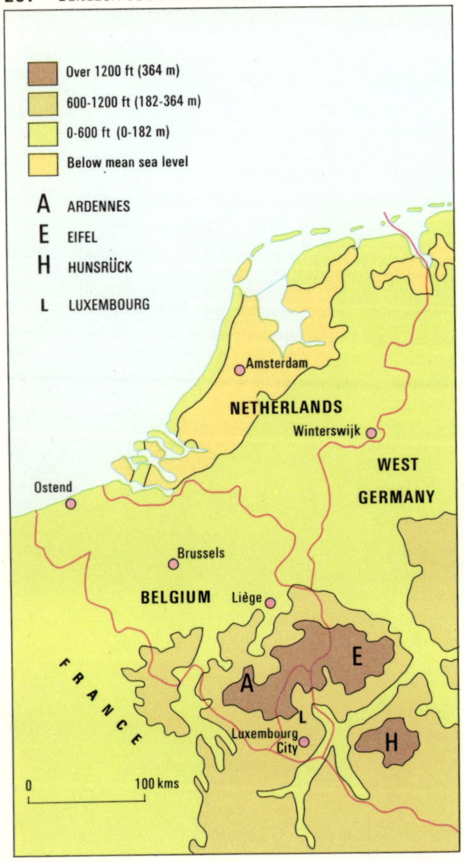

Over 1200 ft (364 m)
600-1200 ft (182-364 m)
0-600 ft (0-182 m)
Below mean sea level
A ARDENNES
E EIFEL
H HUNSRÜCK
L LUXEMBOURG
Amsterdam
NETHERLANDS
Winterswijk
WEST GERMANY
Ostend
Brussels
BELGIUM
Liège
FRANCE
A
E
L
H
Luxembourg City
0
100 kms

292 BENELUX COUNTRIES—DRAINAGE

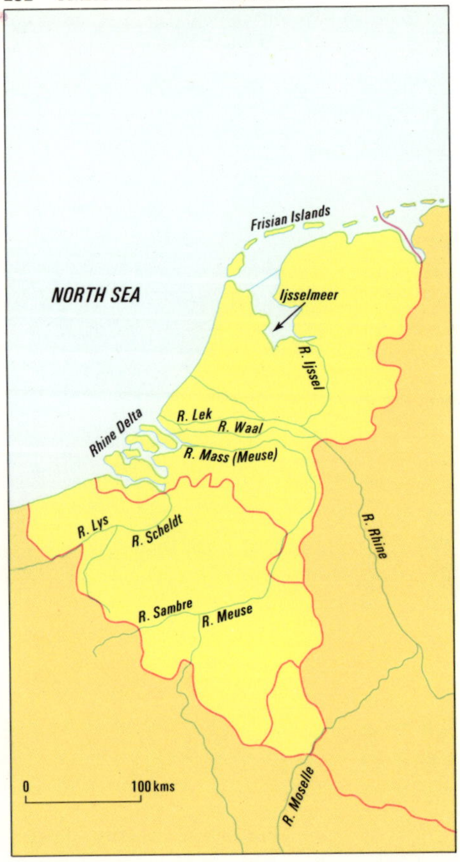

Frisian Islands
NORTH SEA
Ijsselmeer
R. Ijssel
Rhine Delta
R. Lek
R. Waal
R. Mass (Meuse)
R. Rhine
R. Lys
R. Scheldt
R. Sambre
R. Meuse
R. Moselle
0
100 kms

293 BENELUX COUNTRIES—GEOLOGY

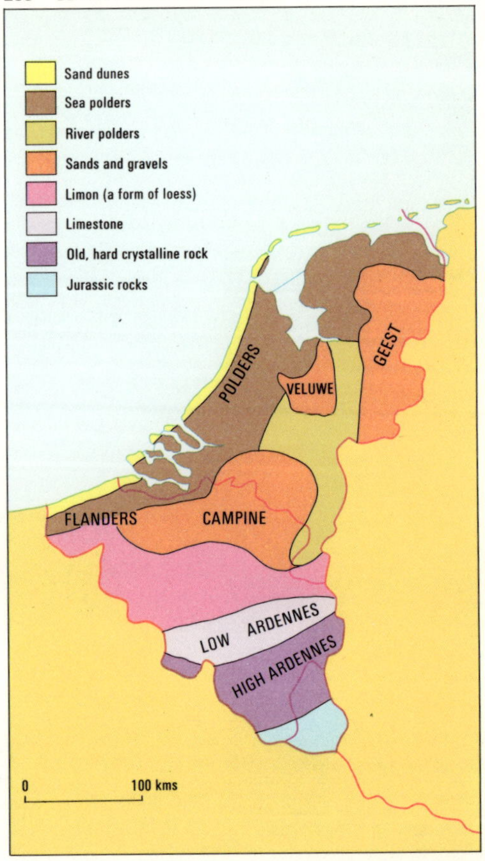

Sand dunes
Sea polders
River polders
Sands and gravels
Limon (a form of loess)
Limestone
Old, hard crystalline rock
Jurassic rocks
POLDERS
VELUWE
GEEST
FLANDERS
CAMPINE
LOW ARDENNES
HIGH ARDENNES
0
100 kms

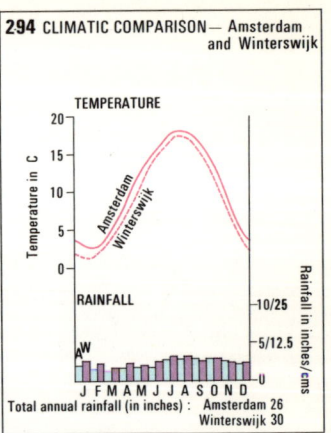

294 CLIMATIC COMPARISON— Amsterdam and Winterswijk

TEMPERATURE
Temperature in °C
20
15
10
5
0
Amsterdam
Winterswijk
RAINFALL
A W
10/25
5/12.5
0
Rainfall in inches/cms
J F M A M J J A S O N D
Total annual rainfall (in inches) : Amsterdam 26
Winterswijk 30

Fig. 291 Relief

291a Which three countries make up Benelux? (Benelux is a combination of their names and was first used to describe the Customs Union formed between these countries in 1948.)

291b Do the Benelux countries occupy a highland or lowland part of Europe?

291c Which of these countries has (i) only a narrow area of lowland in the East associated with the Moselle valley (see also fig. 292) (ii) over half its land surface below mean sea level (iii) highland in the South-East called the Ardennes?

Fig. 292 Drainage

292a (i) Name the three longest rivers that flow through the Benelux countries (ii) Do any of them rise within these countries?

292b Name the piece of coastline where these rivers enter the sea.

292c The River Rhine divides up into three main channels before entering the sea. They are called distributaries. Name them.

Fig. 293 Geology

293a What rocks comprise the highest land in (i) the Netherlands (ii) Belgium.

293b Explain the words (i) polder (ii) limon.

Fig. 294 Climatic comparison - Amsterdam and Winterswijk

294a (i) Describe the relative positions of Amsterdam and Winterswijk (see fig. 291). (ii) How far apart are they?

294b Compare their climates, emphasising the differences, if any.

Fig. 295 Climatic transect across Belgium and Luxembourg

295a Compare the positions and climates of Ostend and Luxembourg.

295b Account for the differences you observe.

295c Does there seen to be any dramatic differences between climates in various parts of Benelux? Give two examples to support your answer.

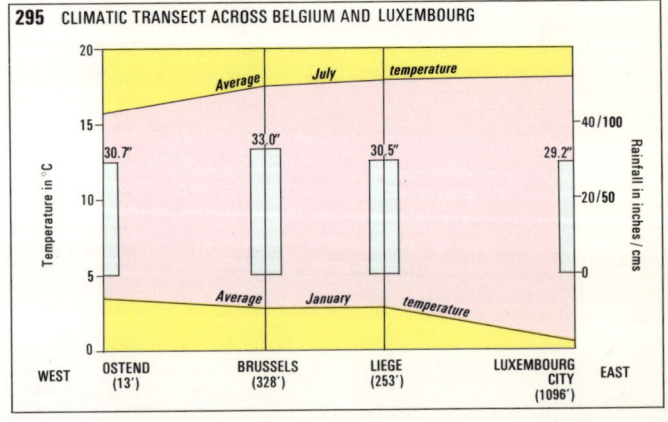

295 CLIMATIC TRANSECT ACROSS BELGIUM AND LUXEMBOURG

Temperature in °C
20
15
10
5
0
Average July temperature
30.7″
33.0″
30.5″
29.2″
Average January temperature
40/100
20/50
0
Rainfall in inches / cms
WEST
OSTEND (13′)
BRUSSELS (328′)
LIEGE (253′)
LUXEMBOURG CITY (1096′)
EAST

Fig. 296   Population figures for selected European countries

296a What is the area of the Netherlands?
296b How many times bigger is Britain?
296c (i) Define population density.   (ii) What is the population density of the Netherlands? (Divide population by area).
296d How does it compare with the other Benelux countries? The Netherlands has the highest population density in the world.

296 POPULATION FIGURES OF SELECTED EUROPEAN COUNTRIES			
COUNTRY	AREA (in sq. miles)	POPULATION (in thousands)	POPULATION DENSITY (per sq. mile)
NETHERLANDS	13,000	12,600	
BELGIUM	12,000	9,500	796
LUXEMBOURG	1,000	335	335
FRANCE	213,000	49,900	234
BRITAIN	93,000	55,000	592

Fig. 297   Main urban centres in southern Netherlands

297a What is the population of the Netherlands (see fig. 296).
297b (i) What percentage of the population live in Randstad Holland? (ii) What towns make up Randstad Holland? Randstad is a planning term meaning ring city. The Dutch planning authorities are trying to prevent it becoming a continuous urban area.
297c Explain the significance of the term 'Greenheart'.

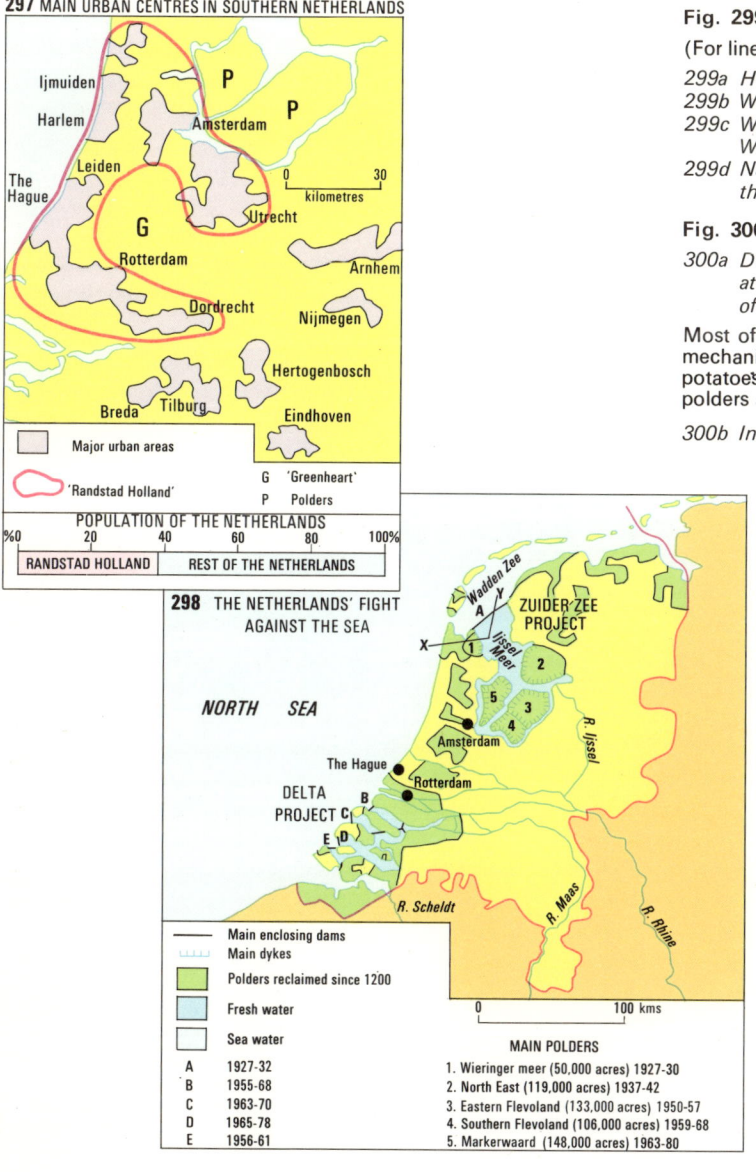

Fig. 298   The Netherlands' fight against the sea

Over the centuries the Dutch have made enormous efforts to reclaim land from the sea—not only to increase land area but also to improve (i) defences against the sea (ii) fresh water supplies (iii) communications, and to reduce salt infiltration into the soil of coastal areas.

298a Name the two main reclamation projects.
298b Which one involves only a small element of land reclamation?
298c How much land will be reclaimed from the Zuider Zee by 1980?
298d What stage has the Delta Project reached?
298e Which sea is likely to be reclaimed next?

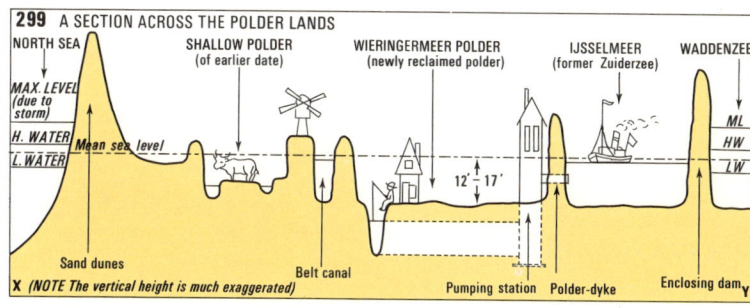

Fig. 299   A section across the polder lands

(For line of section see X-Y fig. 298.)

299a How much below mean sea level is the Wieringermeer Polder?
299b When was it first drained? (See fig. 298.)
299c What protects the polders from   (i) the North Sea   (ii) the Wadden Zee?
299d Name the ancient and modern methods of pumping water in the polder lands.

Fig. 300   The North-East Polder

300a Describe the layout of the North-East polder paying particular attention to the pattern of roads and canals and the location of settlement and pumping stations.

Most of the NE polder is given over to arable farming using modern mechanised methods. Crops like wheat, barley, oats, sugar-beet, potatoes and flax are all grown successfully. The other Zuider Zee polders are similar.

300b Indicate some ways in which the polders favour agriculture.

Fig. 301 Land use

301a (i) What proportion of the Netherlands is devoted to agriculture? (ii) How does this compare with France? (See fig. 177.)

301b Do crops or pasture occupy most land?

Fig. 302 Value of agricultural production

302a What percentage of total agricultural production is made up of (i) livestock products (ii) horticultural products?

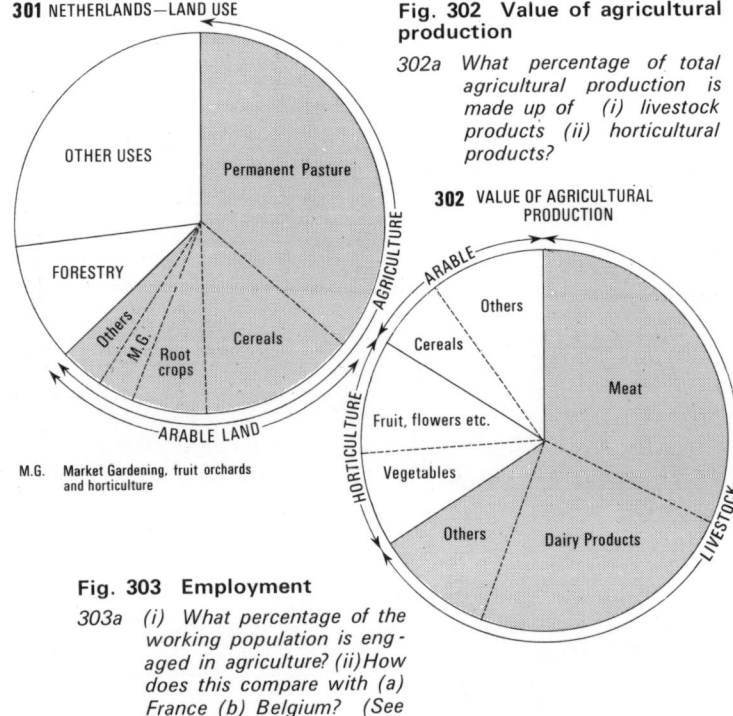

301 NETHERLANDS—LAND USE

OTHER USES
Permanent Pasture
FORESTRY
Others
M.G.
Root crops
Cereals
AGRICULTURE
ARABLE LAND

M.G. Market Gardening, fruit orchards and horticulture

302 VALUE OF AGRICULTURAL PRODUCTION

ARABLE
Others
Cereals
Fruit, flowers etc.
Vegetables
Others
Dairy Products
Meat
HORTICULTURE
LIVESTOCK

Fig. 303 Employment

303a (i) What percentage of the working population is engaged in agriculture? (ii) How does this compare with (a) France (b) Belgium? (See fig. 246.)

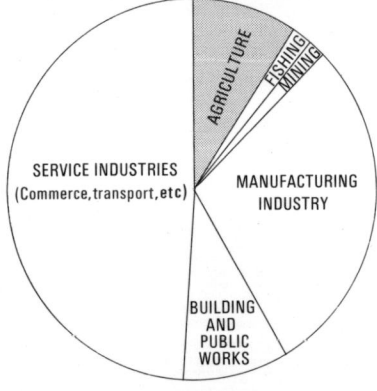

303 NETHERLANDS—EMPLOYMENT

SERVICE INDUSTRIES (Commerce, transport, etc)
AGRICULTURE
FISHING
MINING
MANUFACTURING INDUSTRY
BUILDING AND PUBLIC WORKS

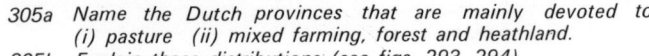

504 NETHERLANDS—FARM SIZES

100%
80%
60%
40%
20%
0%
OVER 50 acres
25-50 acres
UNDER 25 acres

Fig. 304 Farm size

304a Do farms in the Netherlands tend to be large or small?

304b Justify your answer.

Fig. 305 Agricultural land use

305a Name the Dutch provinces that are mainly devoted to (i) pasture (ii) mixed farming, forest and heathland.

305b Explain these distributions (see figs. 293, 294).

305c Most of the pasture is used for dairying. North Holland specialises in dairy products (e.g. butter and cheese (Edam and Gouda) are produced at Alkmaar). Suggest why South Holland specialises more in fresh milk.

305d Name and locate the three main arable regions.

305e The market gardening, fruit growing and horticultural districts are well dispersed. Is there any association between these districts and reclaimed land? Quote two examples.

305f Bulb growing (mainly tulips) is favoured by the sandy soils in district B. Name this district.

305g The most rapidly expanding sector of livestock farming in the Netherlands is pig farming, concentrated in less favourable sandy regions. Name these regions (see fig 293).

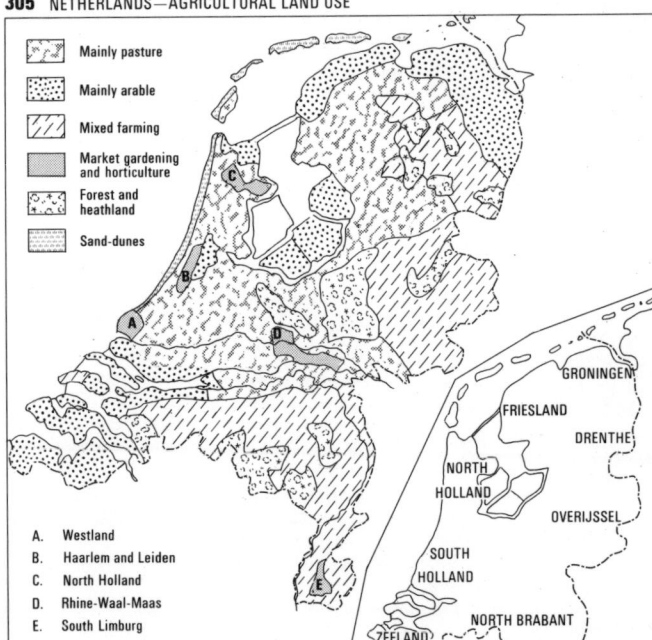

305 NETHERLANDS—AGRICULTURAL LAND USE

Mainly pasture
Mainly arable
Mixed farming
Market gardening and horticulture
Forest and heathland
Sand-dunes

A. Westland
B. Haarlem and Leiden
C. North Holland
D. Rhine-Waal-Maas
E. South Limburg

0 kilometres 100

GRONINGEN
FRIESLAND
DRENTHE
NORTH HOLLAND
OVERIJSSEL
SOUTH HOLLAND
NORTH BRABANT
ZEELAND
LIMBURG

MAIN PROVINCES

Fig. 306 Farming in Westland

306a Locate Westland (see fig. 305).

306b Describe the nature of farming in Westland (pay particular attention to the shape and size of farms and methods of production). Why are boiler houses necessary? Chief products include cut-flowers, tomatoes, cucumbers, early lettuce, peaches and grapes.

306c (i) Compare the area under market gardening, fruit orchards and horticulture (see fig.302) with the contribution they make to total agricultural production (see fig. 303). (ii) Explain your answer.

306d Is farming in this district extensive or intensive?

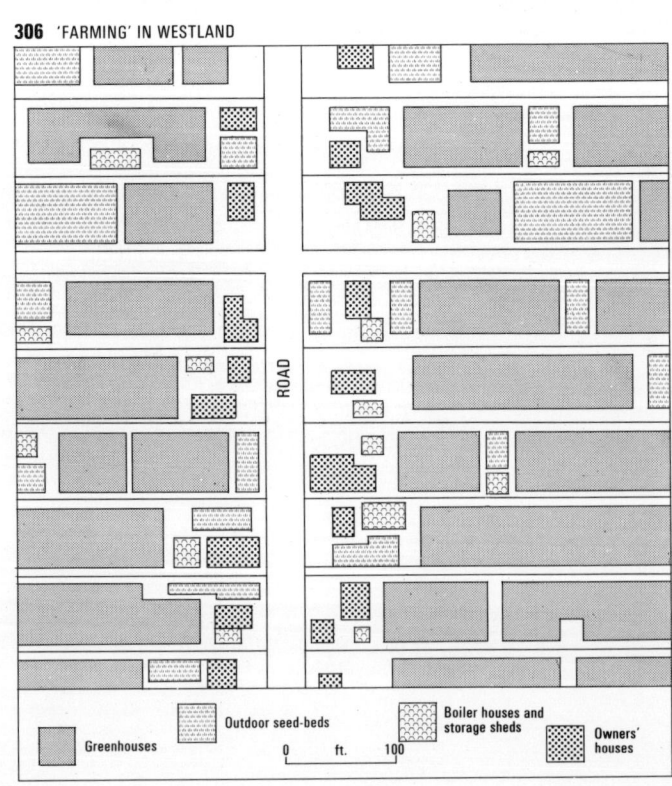

306 'FARMING' IN WESTLAND

ROAD

Greenhouses
Outdoor seed-beds
Boiler houses and storage sheds
Owners' houses

0 ft. 100

307   A COMPARISON OF AGRICULTURAL PRODUCTION AND YIELDS IN SOME E E C COUNTRIES

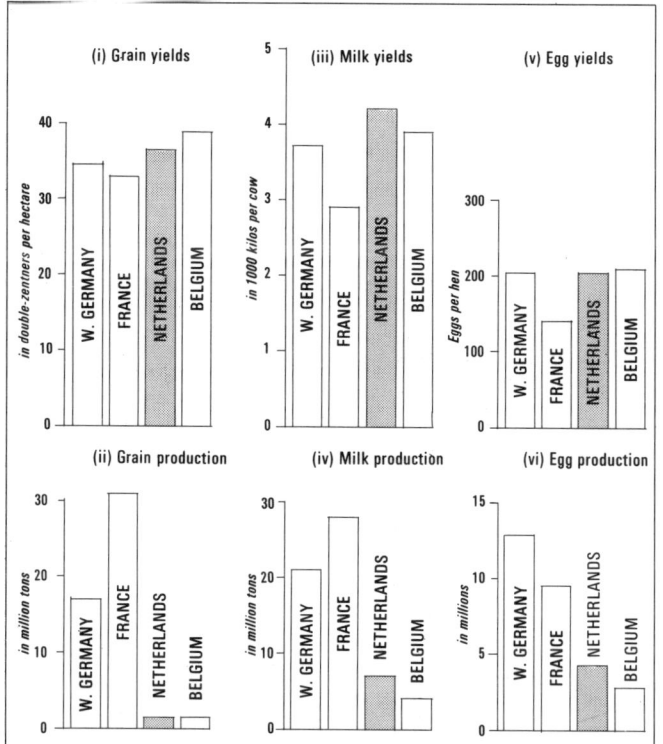

Fig. 307   A comparison of agricultural production and yields in some EEC countries

307a   How do Dutch yields of (i) grain (ii) milk (iii) eggs compare with the EEC countries shown above ?

307b   How does production compare?

307c   Explain the discrepancy.

Dutch agriculture is very much a business. Space is at a premium, and as well as creating new land, 'old' land is continually being revived. Large quantities of fertiliser are applied in some areas, producing what in effect is a completely new soil. The Dutch farmer is also highly mechanised and applies scientific techniques to his farming. These methods are all geared to obtaining as high a return as possible from the land.

Fig. 308   Foreign trade

308a   Compare the value of food exports with the value of all manufactured goods exported.

308b   What sort of foods does the Netherlands need to import?

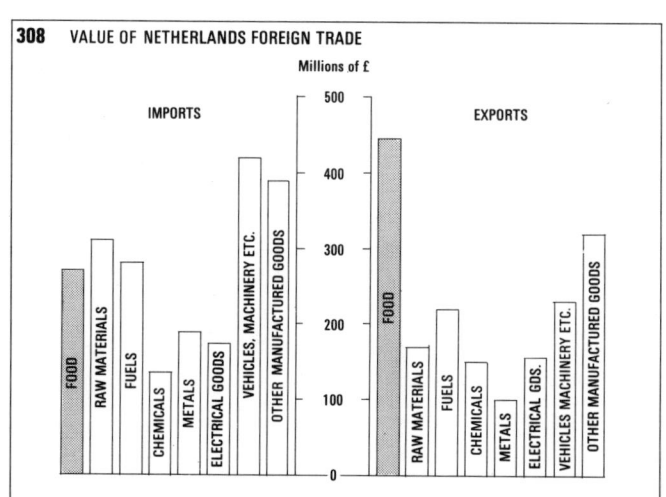

308   VALUE OF NETHERLANDS FOREIGN TRADE

309   NETHERLANDS — AGRICULTURAL EXPORTS (by value)

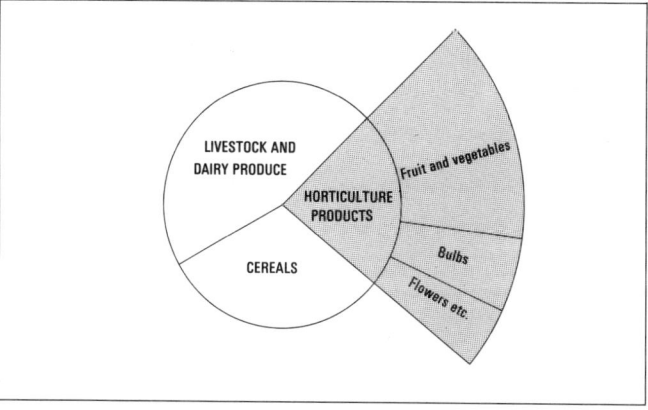

Fig. 309   Agricultural exports

309a   List the three main sectors in order of importance.

309b   Most of the horticultural and dairy products are destined for major European conurbations.   Name some that are near at hand.

309c   What advantage has the Netherlands for distribution of agricultural produce (see fig. 318).

Fig. 310   Fishing

310a   Name the three main Dutch fishing ports.

310b   How does the total Dutch catch compare with that of Britain?

310c   What does the composition of this catch tell you about the location of the main fishing grounds visited by Dutch fishing vessels?

310   NETHERLANDS—FISHING

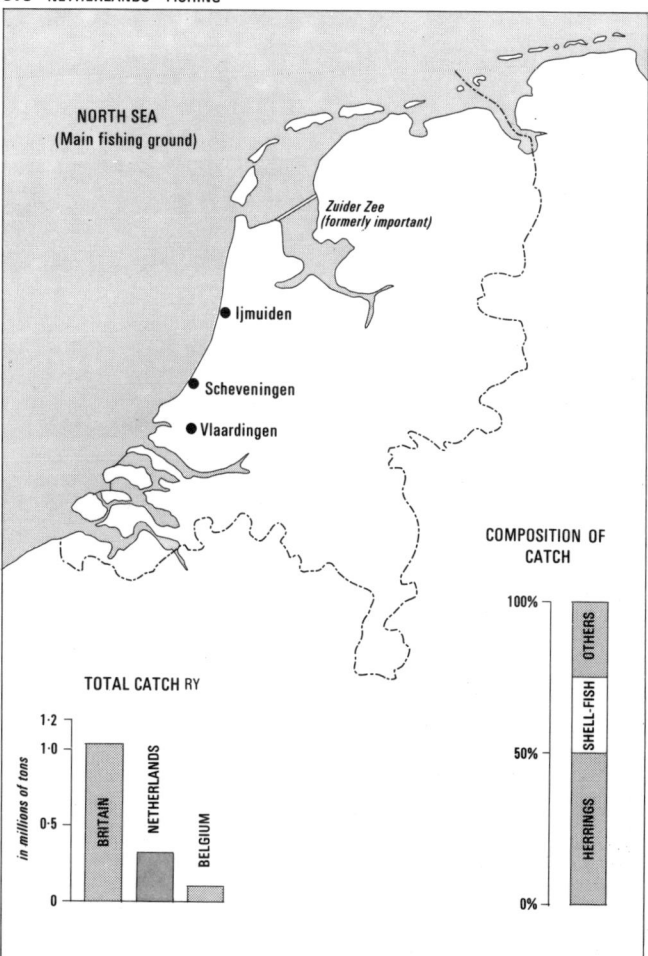

Fig. 311 Petroleum, natural gas and coal

311a Name and locate the main Dutch sources of (i) petroleum (oil) (ii) natural gas (iii) coal.

311b Name the two main oil refining centres and explain their locations.

311c Which parts of Europe do these refineries serve?

311 NETHERLANDS—PETROLEUM, NATURAL GAS AND COAL

312 NETHERLANDS—FUEL AND POWER PRODUCTION IN 1960 AND 1968

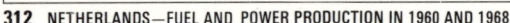
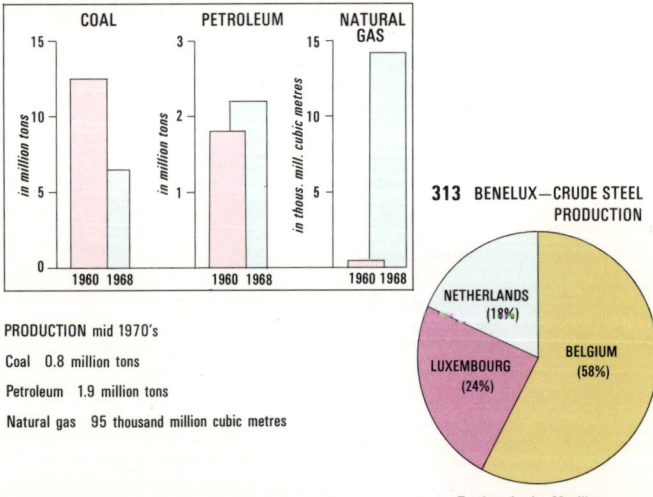

PRODUCTION mid 1970's

Coal   0.8 million tons

Petroleum   1.9 million tons

Natural gas   95 thousand million cubic metres

313 BENELUX—CRUDE STEEL PRODUCTION

NETHERLANDS (18%)

BELGIUM (58%)

LUXEMBOURG (24%)

Total production 20 mill. tons

Fig. 312 Fuel and power production

312a Which form of power has undergone the most dramatic increase in production? The Netherlands is now the major European producer of this fuel.

312b Which form of power has suffered a decline and by how much?

Fig. 313 Benelux - crude steel production

313a Compare steel production in the Netherlands with the other Benelux countries.

313b Belgium used to, and Luxembourg still has, its own supply of iron ore. Has the Netherlands any such supply? (See fig. 311.)

314 NETHERLANDS—IRON AND STEEL

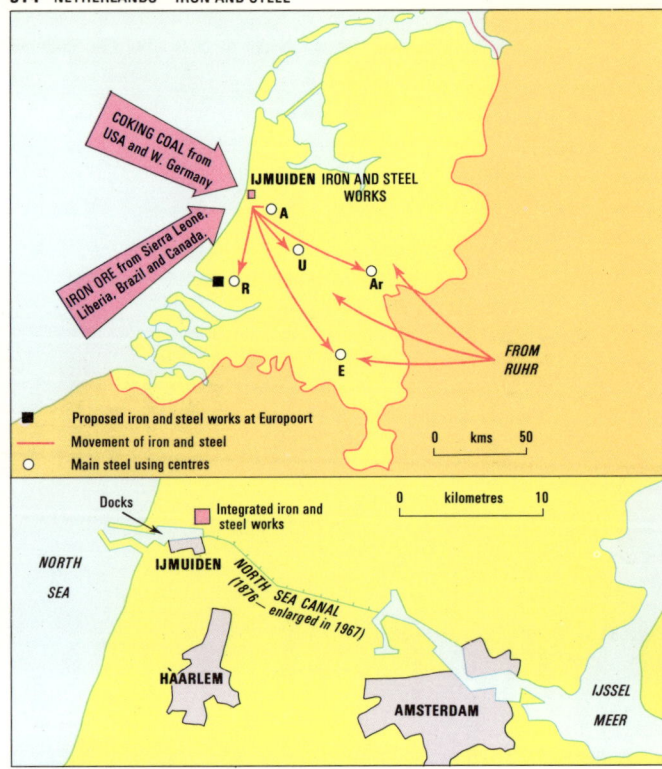

Fig. 314 Iron and steel

314a How and where does the Netherlands obtain its iron ore?

314b (i) Name and locate the main iron and steel works in Netherlands.(ii) Account for its location (consider site, raw materials, power and transport).

314c (i) Name the proposed location of a new iron and steel works. (ii) Explain why.

Fig. 315 Metal and engineering industries

315a Name (i) two main engineering centres (ii) two metal smelting centres, and indicate what they make or process.

315b (i) What industry dominates Eindhoven? (ii) Name the world famous firm involved in this industry. (iii) What does it manufacture? Eindhoven was chosen as the site for its first factory (in 1891) because land was cheap and labour plentiful. Eindhoven's growth since that time is largely due to this firm's expansion. Today it employs a workforce of 25 000.

315 NETHERLANDS—METAL AND ENGINEERING INDUSTRIES

316 NETHERLANDS—CHEMICAL INDUSTRY

0 kms 50

Delfzijl Ⓒ
Emmen Ⓒ
Amsterdam Ⓒ
Utrecht Ⓒ
Arnhem Ⓒ
ROTTERDAM Ⓒ
Flushing Ⓒ
Ⓒ
Terneuzen
Geleen Ⓒ

Ⓒ Premier chemical centre
Ⓒ Important chemical centres
Ⓒ New chemical centres
➜ Large scale imports of petroleum

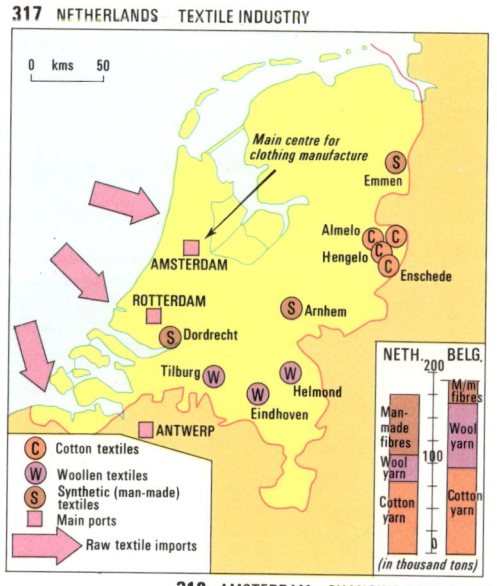

317 NETHERLANDS TEXTILE INDUSTRY

0 kms 50

Main centre for clothing manufacture

Emmen Ⓢ
Almelo Ⓒ Ⓒ
Hengelo Ⓒ Ⓒ Enschede
AMSTERDAM ◼
ROTTERDAM ◼
Ⓢ Dordrecht
Ⓢ Arnhem
Tilburg Ⓦ
Ⓦ Helmond
Eindhoven Ⓦ
ANTWERP

Ⓒ Cotton textiles
Ⓦ Woollen textiles
Ⓢ Synthetic (man-made) textiles
◼ Main ports
➜ Raw textile imports

NETH. BELG.
200
M/m fibres
Man-made fibres | Wool yarn
Wool yarn | 100
Cotton yarn | Cotton yarn
0
(in thousand tons)

Fig. 316 Chemical industry

316a Account for (i) Rotterdam's premier position in the chemical industry (ii) the new chemical industry at Delfzijl (iii) the chemical industry at Geleen (see fig. 311).

316b The chemical industry is expanding more rapidly than any other Dutch industry. Explain why. (See fig. 312.)

Fig. 317 Textile industry

317a Name the main two sectors of the Dutch textile industry.

317b In which provinces is concentrated (i) the cotton textile industry (ii) the wool textile industry? (See also inset fig.305.)

317c (i) Name the three main centres making man-made fibres. (ii) Do these centres also have chemical industries? (iii) Explain the relationship.

The Dutch textile industry has a long tradition but its present structure and distribution is a product of the twentieth century.

318 NETHERLANDS—ROAD AND RAIL TRANSPORT

0 kms 50

Groningen
A
The Hague
U
R Ar
E
An
To Brussels and Paris
To Cologne
To Liege

A Amsterdam
U Utrecht
R Rotterdam
Ar Arnhem
E Eindhoven
An Antwerp

● Main Towns and cities
┼┼┼ Main railways
━━ Motorways

Fig. 318 Road and rail transport

318a Name the main route centre in the Netherlands.

318b With which European cities has the Netherlands direct motorway contact?

318c (i) Is the Netherlands well served by road and rail transport? (ii) Which part is most isolated? (iii) Name two factors favouring easy communications.

Fig. 319 Amsterdam - changing access and growth

319a Describe the site and situation of Amsterdam before 1800.

319b What changes in access have taken place since 1800 and why?

Amsterdam is the capital, premier city and second port of the Netherlands. It has a population of 900 000 and is an important commercial, financial and industrial centre.

Fig. 320 Port of Amsterdam - goods traffic

320a (i) Are imports or exports most important? (ii) Suggest why.

320b What type of goods form the largest proportion of imports? Quote examples.

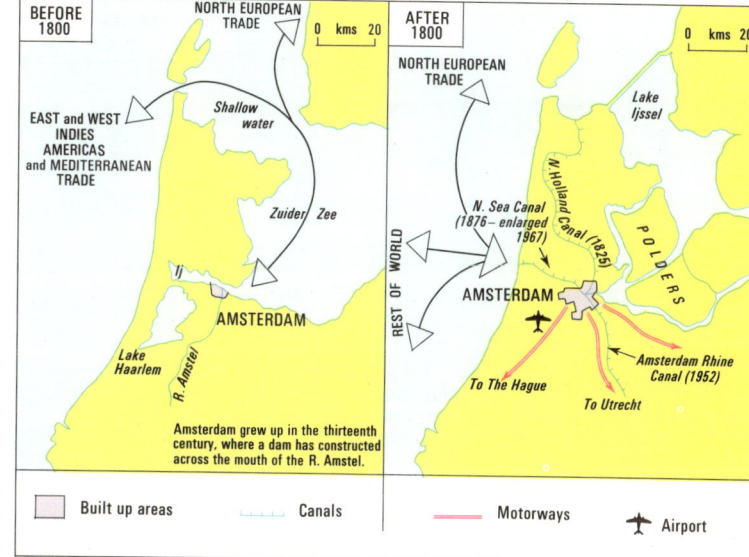

319 AMSTERDAM—CHANGING ACCESS AND GROWTH

BEFORE 1800
NORTH EUROPEAN TRADE
0 kms 20
EAST and WEST INDIES AMERICAS and MEDITERRANEAN TRADE
Shallow water
Zuider Zee
Ij
AMSTERDAM
Lake Haarlem
R. Amstel

Amsterdam grew up in the thirteenth century, where a dam has constructed across the mouth of the R. Amstel.

AFTER 1800
NORTH EUROPEAN TRADE
0 kms 20
Lake Ijssel
N. Sea Canal (1876—enlarged 1967)
N. Holland Canal (1825)
POLDERS
REST OF WORLD
AMSTERDAM
Amsterdam Rhine Canal (1952)
To The Hague
To Utrecht

▢ Built up areas
⋯ Canals
━ Motorways
✈ Airport

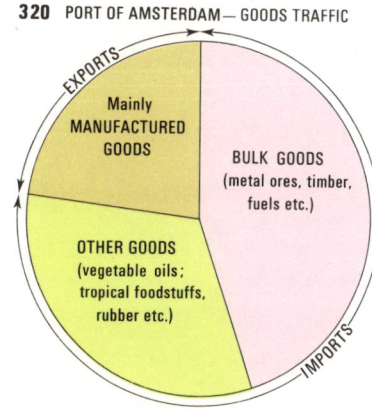

320 PORT OF AMSTERDAM— GOODS TRAFFIC

EXPORTS
Mainly MANUFACTURED GOODS
BULK GOODS (metal ores, timber, fuels etc.)
OTHER GOODS (vegetable oils; tropical foodstuffs, rubber etc.)
IMPORTS

Total traffic=18 million tons

The port and main industry industrial region of Amsterdam is now being extended westwards along the North Sea canal. Amsterdam's industries include oil refining (Mobil), diamond cuttings, sugar refining, printing, clothing, car assembly (Ford and Fiat), tobacco processing, shipbuilding and repairing, saw-milling, chemicals, marine engineering, rubber manufacturing, oil-seed crushing, electronic engineering.

320c List these industries under the following three headings (i) food industries (ii) engineering (iii) other industries.

320d (i) Which industries developed in response to Amsterdam's function as a port? (ii) Of these, which are the result of the Netherland's early trade contacts with the East Indies (now Indonesia)?

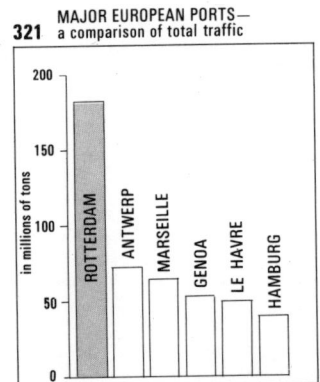

321 MAJOR EUROPEAN PORTS— a comparison of total traffic

Fig. 321 Major European ports

321a Name the premier European (and world) port and indicate its total traffic.

321b Compare its total traffic with that of (i) Antwerp (ii) Hamburg.

Fig. 322 Position and hinterland

322a Explain the term 'hinterland'.

322b Rotterdam's pre-eminence is largely a result of its geographical position.
(i) Describe its position in relation to Europe's waterways.
(ii) Why is it so significant?

322 ROTTERDAM—POSITION AND HINTERLAND

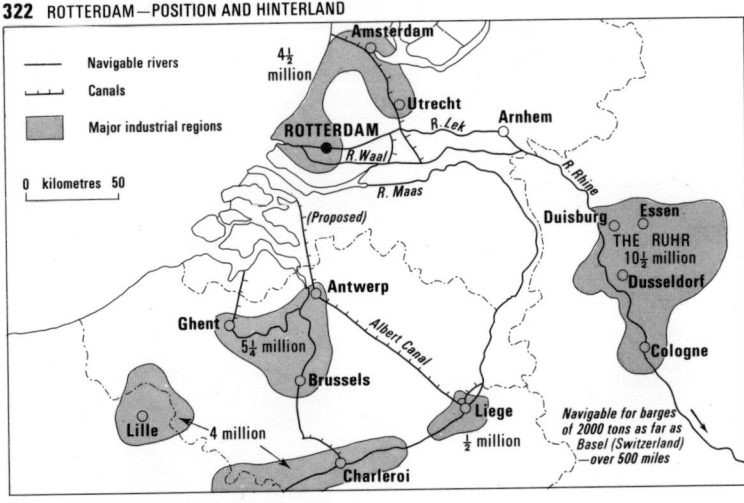

Fig. 323 Europoort

323a (i) List the five main units of the port of Rotterdam in order of construction.
(ii) Find the meaning of the Dutch word 'Europoort' (note: 'poort' is not the equivalent of the English 'port').

323b In what ways has dock lay-out changed since 1940?

323c How does Rotterdam-Europoort manage to accommodate the largest vessels afloat at any state of the tide? State three reasons.

323d (i) What industry dominates the Port of Rotterdam?
(ii) Name some of the main firms.
(iii) Where precisely is it found?

323 ROTTERDAM—EUROPOORT—SITE, DEVELOPMENT AND INDUSTRY

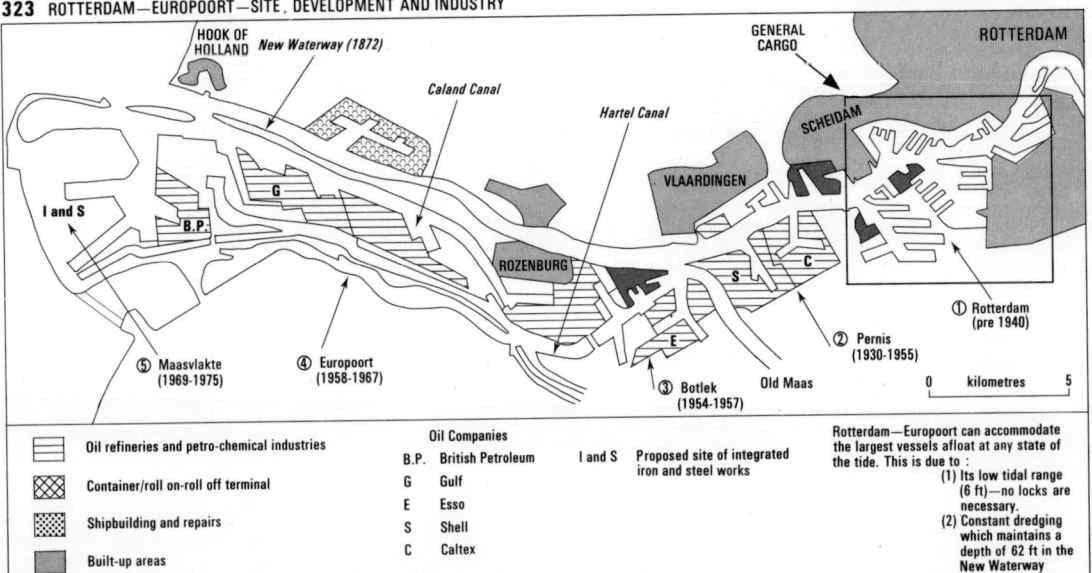

324 ROTTERDAM—SEA-BORNE GOODS TRAFFIC (in millions of tons)

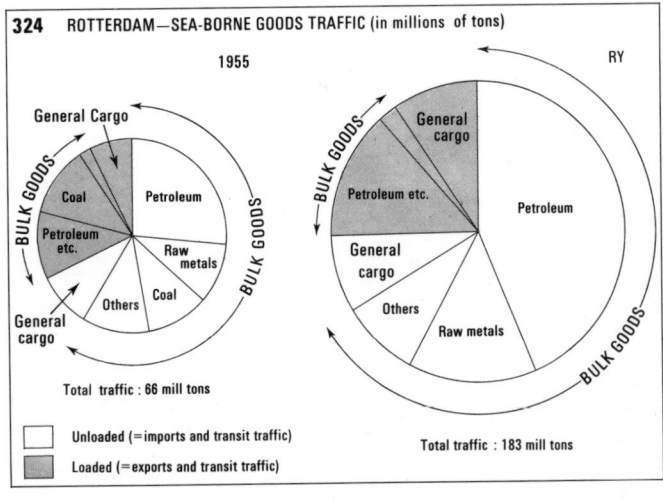

□ Unloaded (=imports and transit traffic)

▨ Loaded (=exports and transit traffic)

Total traffic : 66 mill tons

Total traffic : 183 mill tons

325 ROTTERDAM—CARGO IN TRANSIT

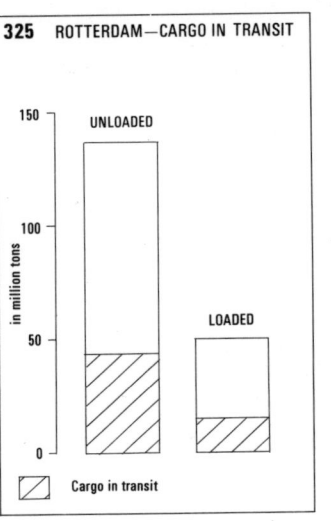

▨ Cargo in transit

326 GOODS TRAFFIC ON THE RIVER RHINE TO AND FROM ROTTERDAM

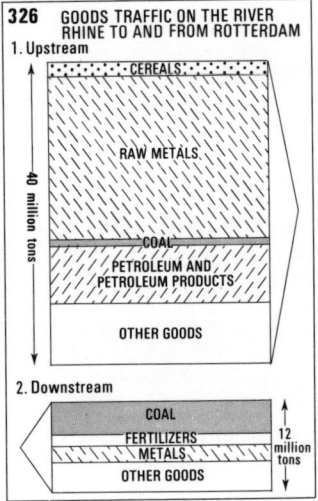

Fig. 324 Seaborne goods traffic

324a By how much did Rotterdam's traffic expand between 1955 and 1969?

324b Are imports or exports more important today? Explain why.

324c List three main changes in the nature of seaborne goods traffic.

Fig. 325 Cargo in transit

325a Explain 'in transit'.

325b What proportion of unloaded cargo is in transit?

Fig. 326 Goods traffic on the River Rhine

Note: 50% of Rotterdam's loaded traffic is by barge.)

326a Describe and explain the main differences between upstream and downstream traffic on the River Rhine.

326b By what other means is cargo transported to and from Rotterdam?

The Hague is the political capital of the Netherlands. It is essentially a residential town but has expanded rapidly during this century, developing light, consumer industries.

Fig. 327   Belgium and France - a comparison of size

327a   How many times bigger than Belgium is France?
327b   What is (i) the total population
*   (ii) the population density of Belgium?*
*   (See fig. 296.)*

Fig. 328   Benelux - population of major towns and cities

328a   (i) Name the largest city in Benelux.
*   (ii) Indicate its population.*
*   (iii) Name the country in which it occurs.*

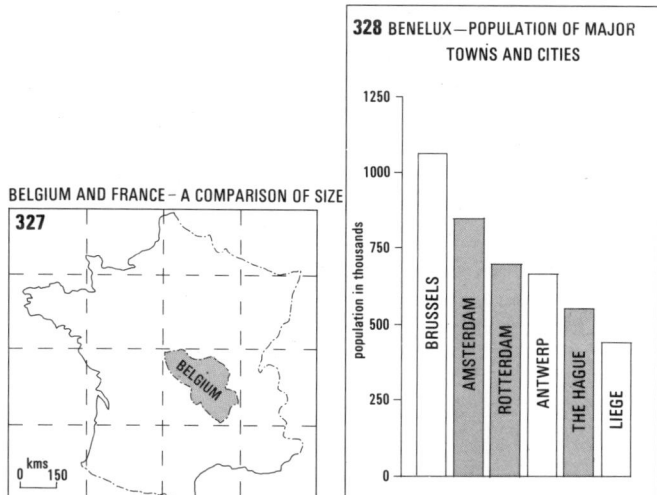

BELGIUM AND FRANCE - A COMPARISON OF SIZE

327

kms 150

328 BENELUX—POPULATION OF MAJOR TOWNS AND CITIES

Fig. 330   Port of Antwerp - sea traffic 1970

330a   How does Antwerp's sea traffic compare with other major European ports? See fig. 321.)

330b   Compare and contrast Antwerp's loaded and unloaded sea traffic.

(Note: a quarter of total traffic is in transit.) Antwerp handles 90% of the overseas trade of Belgium and Luxembourg.

Fig. 331   Antwerp - port and industry

331a   How far is Antwerp from the open sea (North Sea)? (See fig. 329.)

331b   (i) Compare the location of present port facilities with that of the proposed port expansion.
*   (ii) Explain the difference.*

331c   (i) Explain container traffic.
*   (ii) How many times did Antwerp's container traffic increase between 1966 and 1971?*

331d   (i) Name the main group of industries in the port of Antwerp.
*   (ii) Name two other important industries.*

Refining of tropical produce, non-ferrous metal smelting, food processing, electrical engineering and diamond cutting are also important.

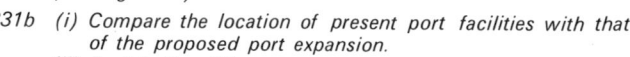

330 PORT OF ANTWERP—SEA TRAFFIC (1970)

329 BELGIUM—POPULATION, SETTLEMENT AND LANGUAGE DIFFERENCES

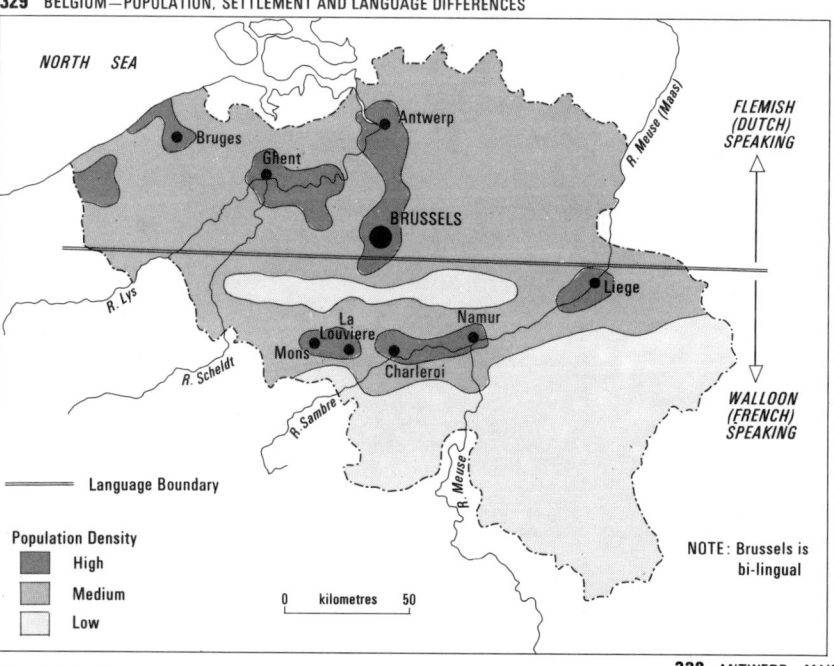

Fig. 329   Belgium - population, settlement and language differences

329a   Copy out the following, filling in the missing words:

'There are two areas in Belgium where population density is high: along the valley of the Rivers .... and .... with towns like C.... and L...., and in the triangle formed by Ghent, ... and .... The most extensive area of low population density is in the South East / North West where the land is highest / lowest. There are two official languages in Belgium: in the North .... is spoken; while in the South .... is the most common language. Brussels is a .... city.'

Fig. 332   Antwerp - main transport links

332a   With which parts of Europe has Antwerp direct contact by (i) road (ii) rail (iii) waterways? (See fig. 322.)

332b   How does Antwerp's hinterland compare with that of Rotterdam? (See fig. 322.)

331 ANTWERP—PORT AND INDUSTRY

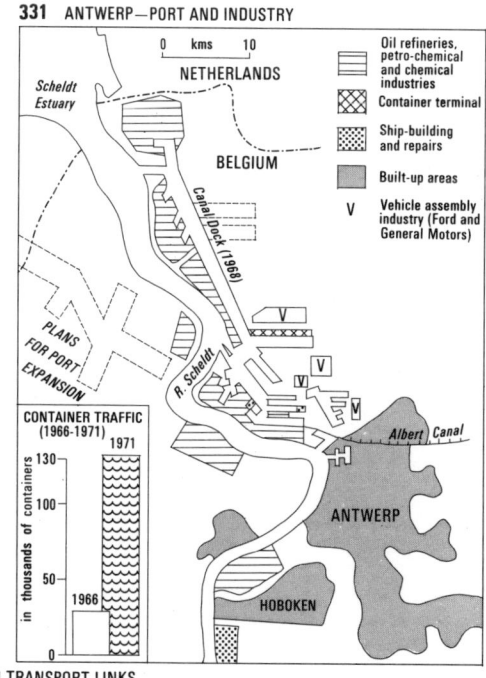

332 ANTWERP—MAIN TRANSPORT LINKS

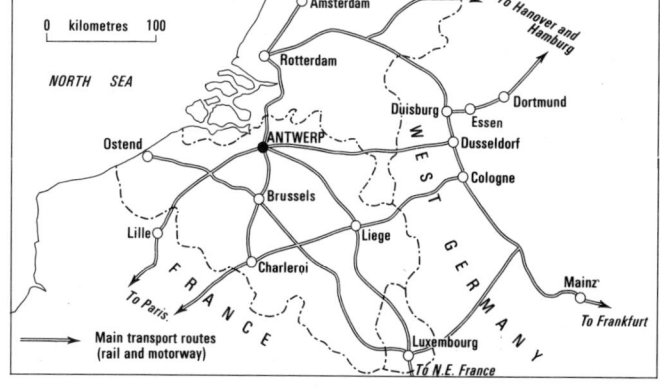

Fig. 333   Land use

333a   What proportion of Belgium is devoted to (i) agriculture (ii) forestry?

333b   Compare land use in Belgium and the Netherlands (see fig. 301).

Fig. 334   Agricultural land use

334a   What proportion of Belgium's agricultural land is devoted to grain crops?

334b   How does Belgium compare with the Netherlands in this respect? (See fig. 301.)

334c   Which is most extensive in Belgium - arable or pasture land?

334d   What percentage of Belgium's labour force is engaged in agriculture? (See fig. 247.)

334e   Compare this percentage with other EEC countries (see fig. 247).

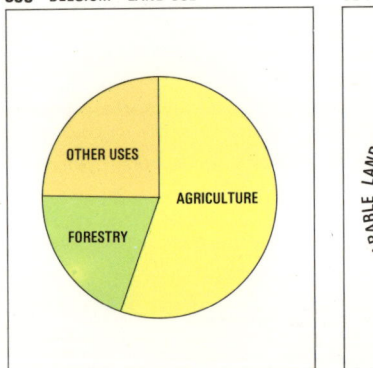

333   BELGIUM—LAND USE

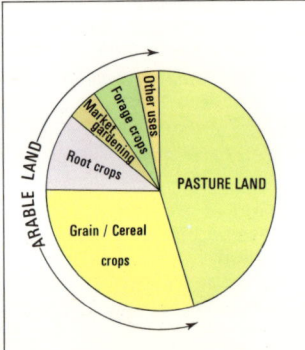

334   BELGIUM—AGRICULTURAL LAND USE

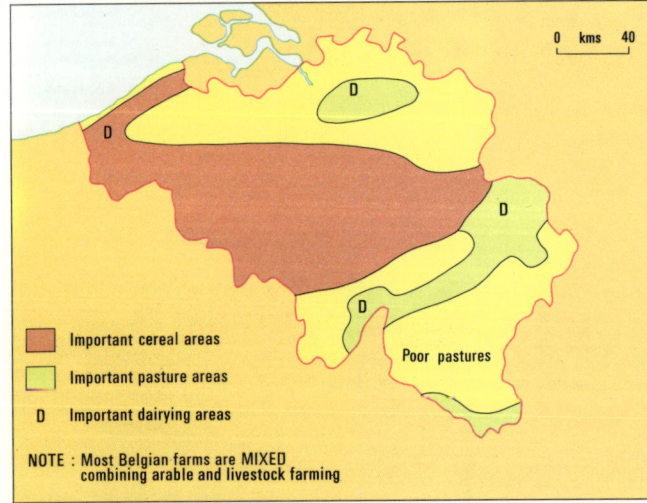

335   BELGIUM—CEREALS AND PASTURE

- ■ Important cereal areas
- ■ Important pasture areas
- D   Important dairying areas

NOTE : Most Belgian farms are MIXED combining arable and livestock farming

Poor pastures

Figs. 335/336   Cereals and pasture: main regions

335/336a   Which region(s) of Belgium are important for (i) cereals (ii) pasture?

335/336b   Suggest reasons why (see p. 52).

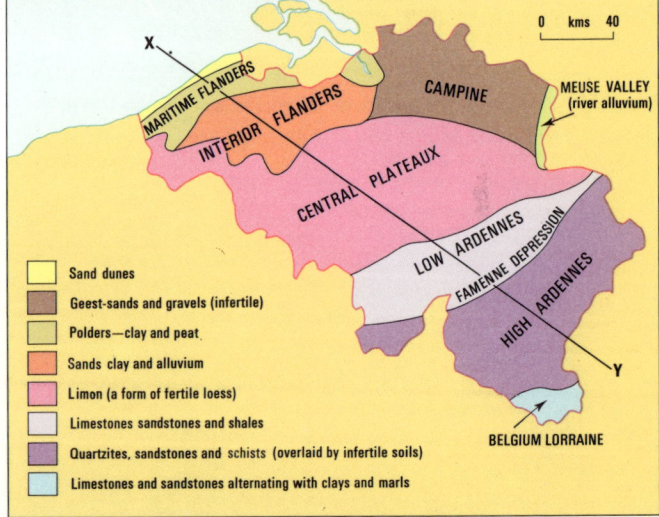

336   BELGIUM—MAIN REGIONS—THEIR ROCKS AND SOILS

0   kms   40

- □ Sand dunes
- ■ Geest-sands and gravels (infertile)
- ■ Polders—clay and peat
- ■ Sands clay and alluvium
- ■ Limon (a form of fertile loess)
- ■ Limestones sandstones and shales
- ■ Quartzites, sandstones and schists (overlaid by infertile soils)
- ■ Limestones and sandstones alternating with clays and marls

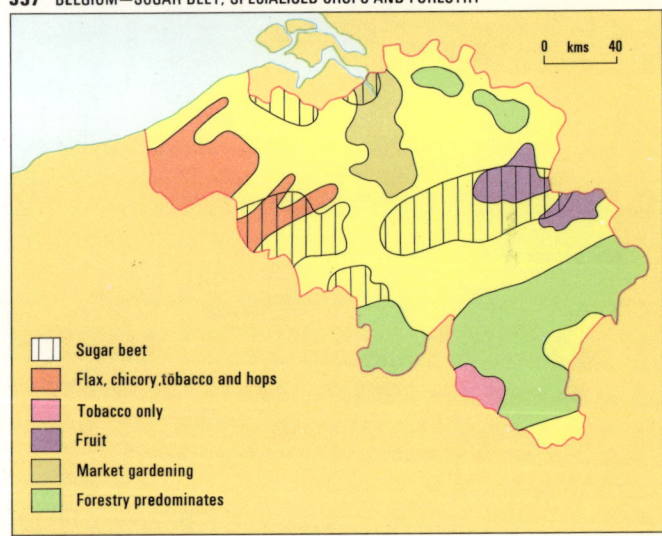

337   BELGIUM—SUGAR BEET, SPECIALISED CROPS AND FORESTRY

0   kms   40

- ▥ Sugar beet
- ■ Flax, chicory, tobacco and hops
- ■ Tobacco only
- ■ Fruit
- ■ Market gardening
- ■ Forestry predominates

Figs 336/337   Specialised crops and forestry: main regions

336/337a   (i)   Where is sugar beet grown? (ii) Which other crops are grown in the same areas? (See also fig. 336.)

336/337b   Which river valleys are important for specialised crops like flax, chicory, tobacco and hops? (See fig. 292.)

336/337c   (i)   Locate the main Belgium market gardening district. (ii) Explain this location (see fig. 322).

336/337d   (i)   In which two regions is forestry predominant? (ii)   Suggest three reasons why (see also p.52).

Fig. 338   Section across Belgium

338a   Use the section to construct a transect diagram of agriculture in Belgium. Include notes on soil and climate where possible (see figs. 336 and 295).

338   SECTION ACROSS BELGIUM

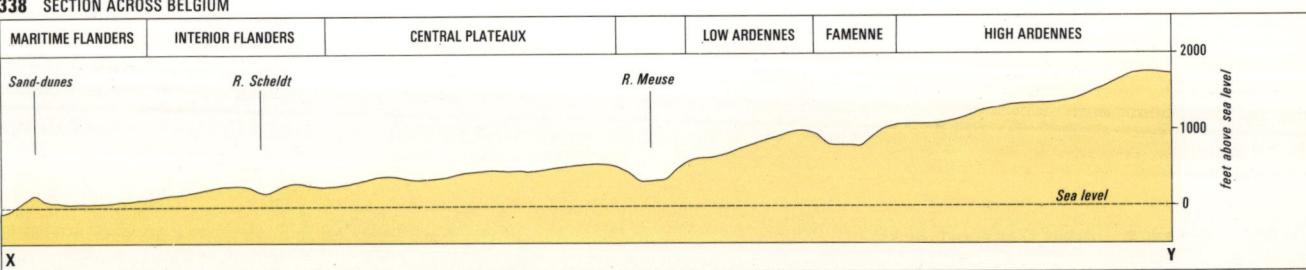

339 BELGIUM—MAIN SOURCES OF POWER

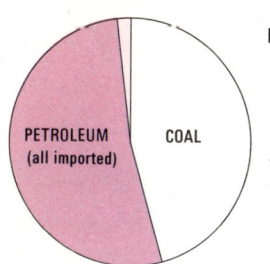

Fig. 339 Main sources of power

339a (i) Name Belgium's main source of power.(ii) How is it obtained? (iii) What port is used? (See fig. 332.)
339b (i) Name Belgium's main domestic source of power.(ii) Compare its importance with that of petroleum.

Fig. 340 Main coalfields

340a The Sambre-Meuse valley is the traditional coal mining region. It is divided into four parts - name them and their respective coal mining centres.
340b Name the other Belgian coalfield. It has been developed during the twentieth century and much of production is state controlled.

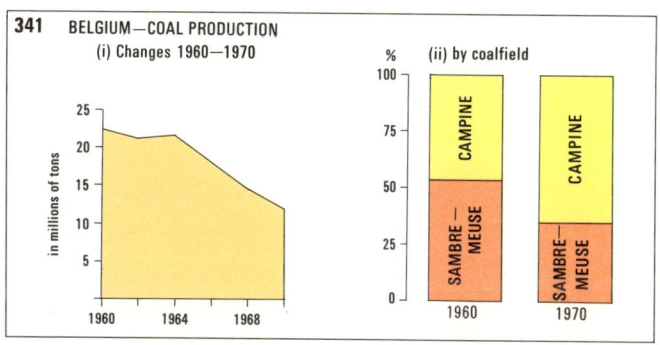

Fig. 341 Coal production

341a What happened to Belgian coal production between 1960 and 1970?
341b Which coalfield produces most coal today and how much?

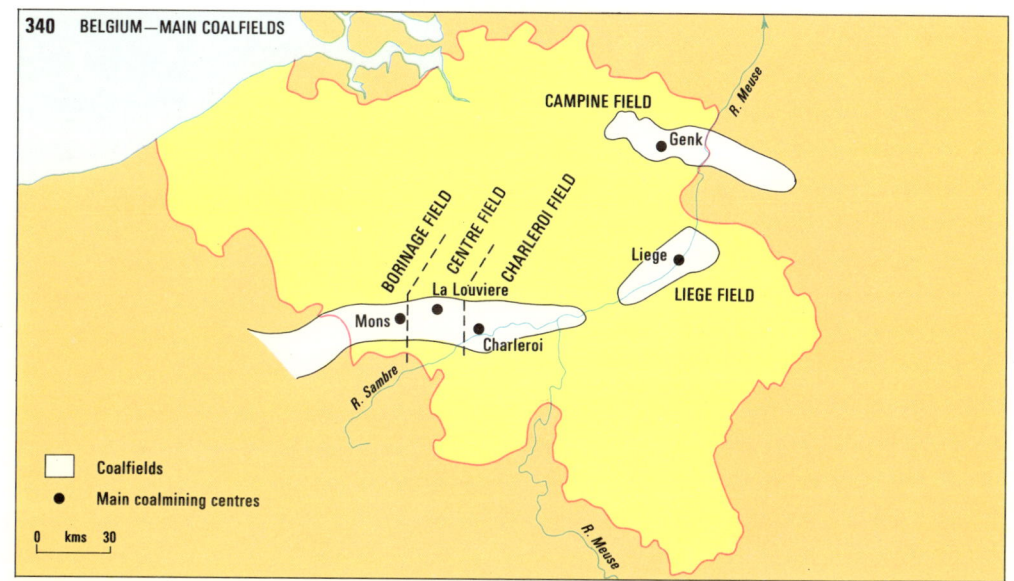

Fig. 342 Population changes in old and new coal mining areas

342a (i) Which of these groups of provinces incorporates (a) the old (b) the new coalmining regions? (ii) Explain your decision.

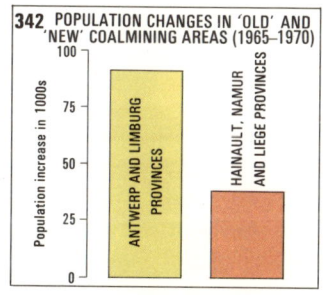

Fig. 343 Borinage coalfield

343a Locate the Borinage field and name its main centre (see fig. 340).
343b How many collieries (i) existed in 1950 (ii) remain open today?
343c Suggest some of the consequences of such a rapid decline.

The Sambre-Meuse coalfield (and the Borinage in particular) has suffered increasingly from deep, thin, contorted seams and foreign competition. In the 1950s the Belgian government was forced to support this industry with grants and subsidies but pit-closures, unemployment and emigration increased. In 1959 the Borinage was declared a development area and since that time light industries have been attracted to newly established industrial estates, transport facilities improved and daily commuting to Brussels encouraged. However the situation today is still far from perfect.

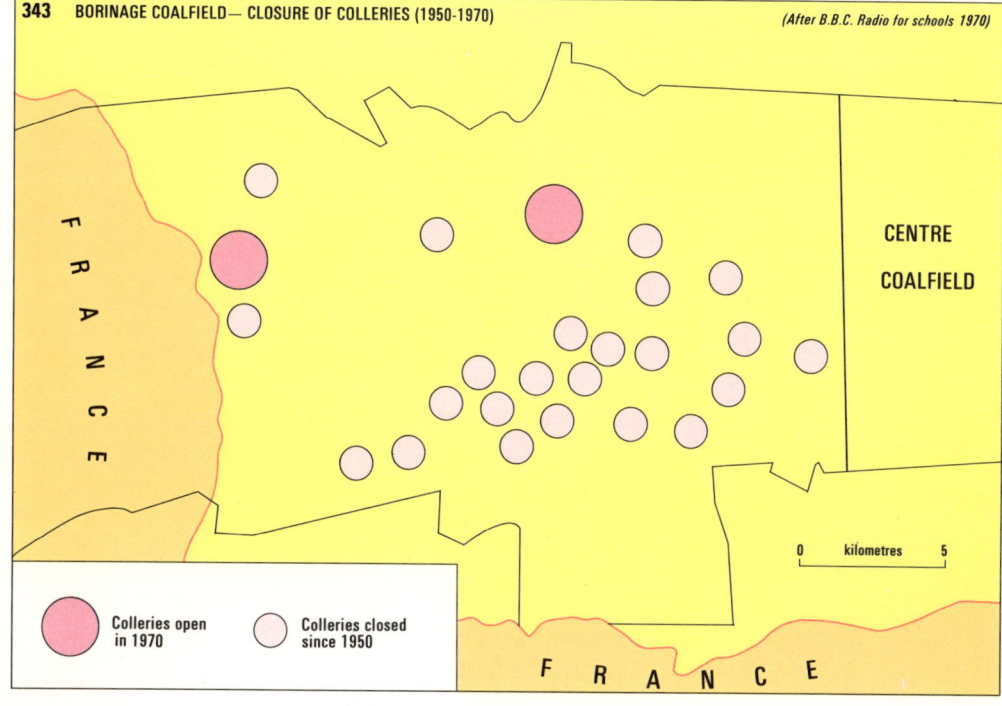

Fig. 344 Exports

344a What type of goods makes up 70% of Belgium's exports?
344b What proportion of Belgian exports is in the form of metal and metal goods?

Fig. 345 Benelux - crude steel production

345a How much crude steel does Belgium produce each year?
345b How does this output compare with (i) the Netherlands (ii) West Germany? (See fig. 266.)

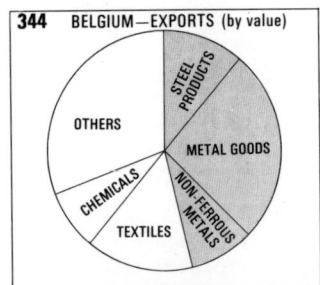

344 BELGIUM—EXPORTS (by value)

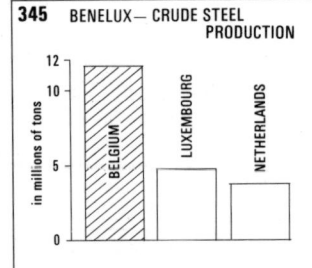

345 BENELUX — CRUDE STEEL PRODUCTION

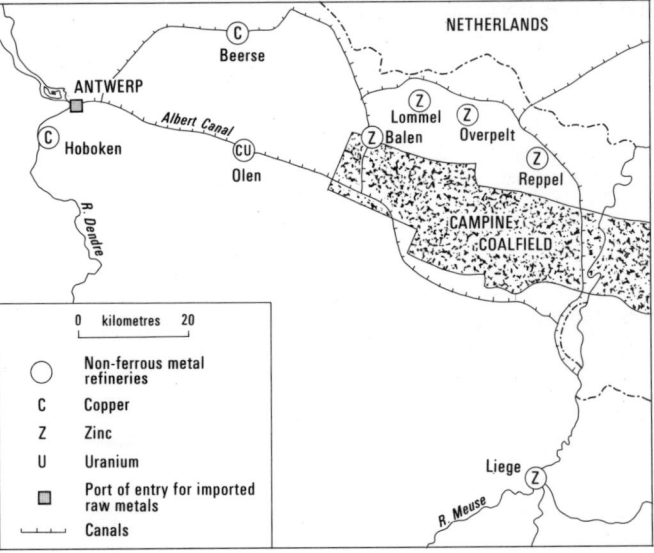

348 BELGIUM—NON-FERROUS METAL INDUSTRY

Fig. 348 Non-ferrous metal industry

348a The traditional centres of this industry are Hoboken and Liege. In which region are the remaining centres located? See fig. 336.)
348b In the 1920's this region was remote and unpopulated and provided cheap, level land. Hence the Belgian government encouraged development here.
Suggest (i) two other factors favouring industrial development (transport and power) (ii) one disadvantage (labour).

Fig. 349 Engineering industries

349a Name the main engineering centre in Belgium.
349b (i) Name the other three important centres for heavy and light engineering.
(ii) How well located are they in respect of supplies of semi-finished metals? (e.g. crude iron, steel, copper, etc.)
349c (i) Locate the main car assembly plants.
(ii) Are they in the traditional (Sambre-Meuse) or new industrial areas?

349d Account for the location of the electrical engineering industry at Antwerp and Brussels.

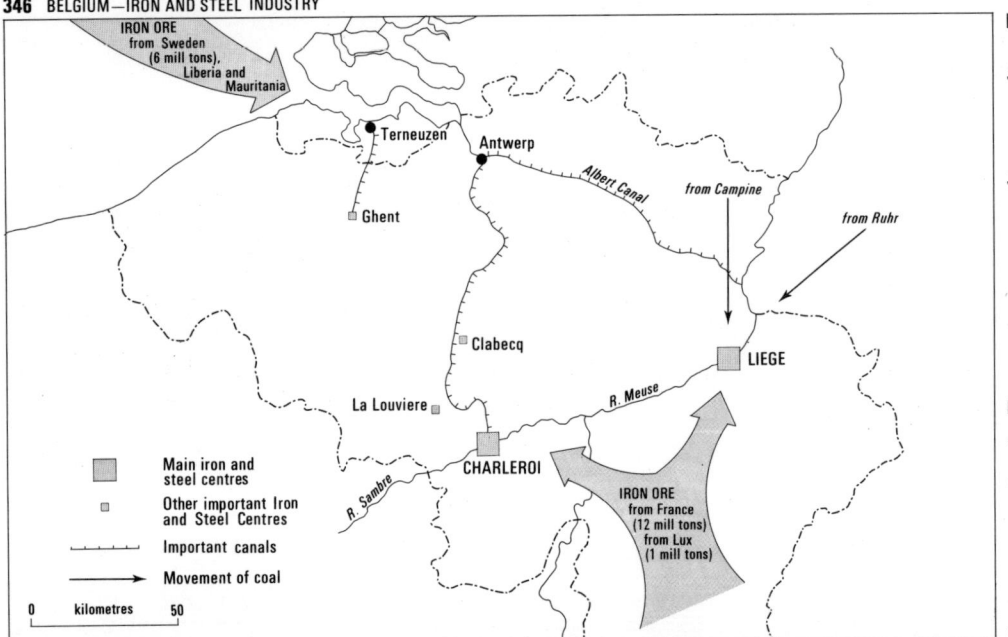
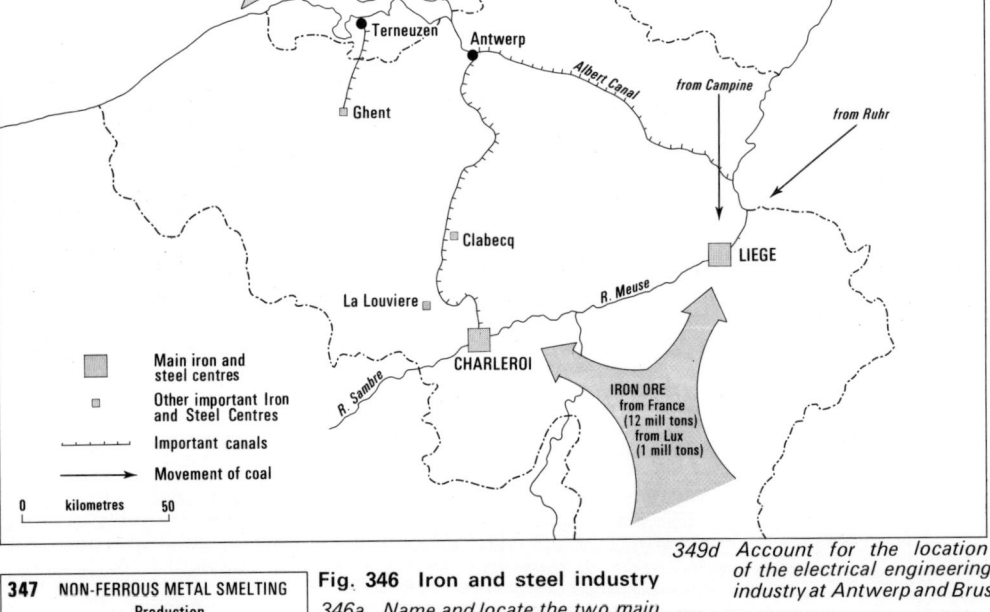

346 BELGIUM—IRON AND STEEL INDUSTRY

Fig. 346 Iron and steel industry

346a Name and locate the two main Belgian iron and steel centres.
346b Where do they obtain their main raw materials?
346c All the important iron and steel centres in Belgium have access to one common form of transport.
(i) Name it.
(ii) Quote two examples.

Fig. 347 Non-ferrous metal-smelting-production

347a (i) Define non-ferrous.
(ii) Quote three examples of non-ferrous metals.
347b West Germany is one of the world's major smelters of non-ferrous metals. How does Belgium compare?

347 NON-FERROUS METAL SMELTING Production

349 BELGIUM — ENGINEERING INDUSTRIES

Fig 350 Textile industry of Flanders

350a (i) In which part of Belgium is Flanders?

(ii) Which three river valleys contain most of Flanders textile towns?

350b Name the two main textile centres and the textiles they produce.

350c Where does Ghent obtain its raw materials for making (i) cotton textiles (ii) linen textiles (iii) synthetic (man-made) textiles? (See fig. 352.)

350d Flanders has been a very important European textile region since the Middle Ages. In which two ways was water important in the early development of this industry?

350e Where is the main Belgian wool textile centre located?

350 TEXTILE INDUSTRY OF FLANDERS

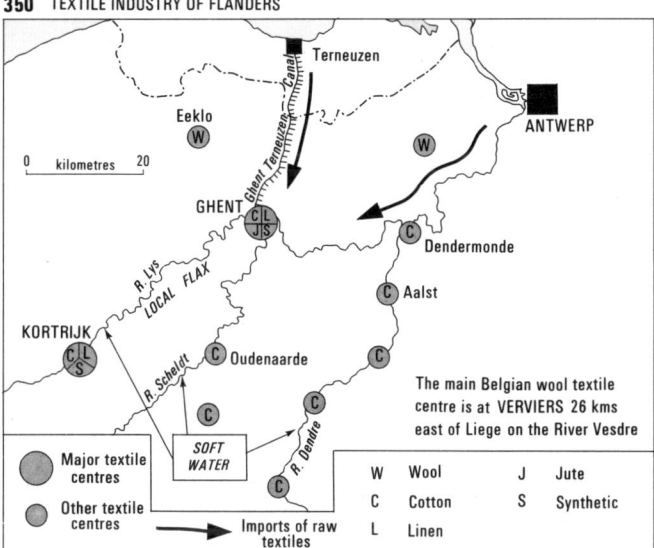

Fig. 351 Production of textiles

351a Name the most important textile produced in Belgium.

351b Examine and explain the changes in the Belgian textile industry.

354 BRUSSELS — EMPLOYMENT

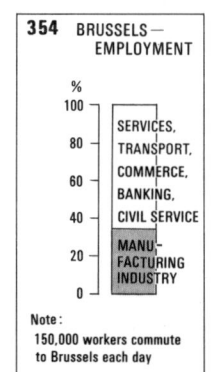

Note: 150,000 workers commute to Brussels each day

352 BELGIUM—CHEMICAL INDUSTRY

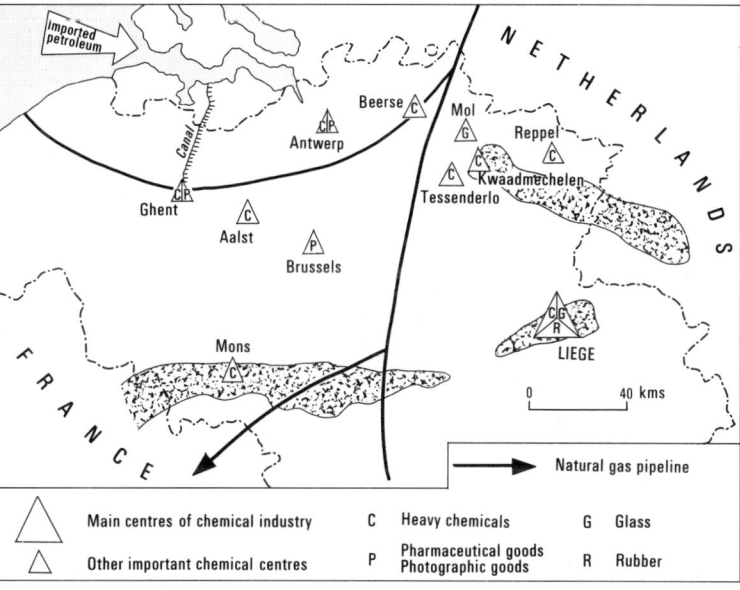

Symbol	Meaning	Symbol	Meaning
△ (large)	Main centres of chemical industry	C	Heavy chemicals
△ (small)	Other important chemical centres	P	Pharmaceutical goods Photographic goods
		G	Glass
→	Natural gas pipeline	R	Rubber

Fig. 352 Chemical industry

352a Name the main centre of the Belgian chemical industry.

352b The newest chemical industries are located in the Campine. Name two examples.

352c Local raw materials are available in the Campine (i) name two (one is used for making glass). They can also be easily imported (ii) by what means of transport?

The non-ferrous metal industry provides many by-products as well as using raw chemicals itself.

352d Explain the location of the chemical industry at Antwerp.

Fig. 353 Liege industrial region

353a (i) Describe the site and situation of Liege (see fig. 332).

(ii) What is its population? (See fig. 328.)

353b (i) Name three types of industry common in Liege.

(ii) Indicate in which districts they are found.

353c Liege is one of Europe's foremost industrial cities. What factors have favoured its development?

353d Compare the industrial geography of the following three regions: Sambre-Meuse Valley, Antwerp-Ghent-Brussels region, Campine.

Fig. 354 Brussels - employment

Brussels is Belgium's capital and leading administrative, industrial, financial and commercial centre.

354a What is its population? (See fig. 328.)

354b What percentage of its labour force work in (i) manufacturing industry (ii) services (e.g. banking, transport, shops, etc.)?

354c Name some of Brussels' industries (see figs. 346, 349 and 352). Other industries include paper-making, food processing and clothing manufacturing.

354d Brussels' position as a route centre is a significant factor in its importance. Describe this position with reference to (i) lowland Belgium (ii) North-Western Europe.

351 BELGIUM-PRODUCTION OF TEXTILES (1963 and 1968)

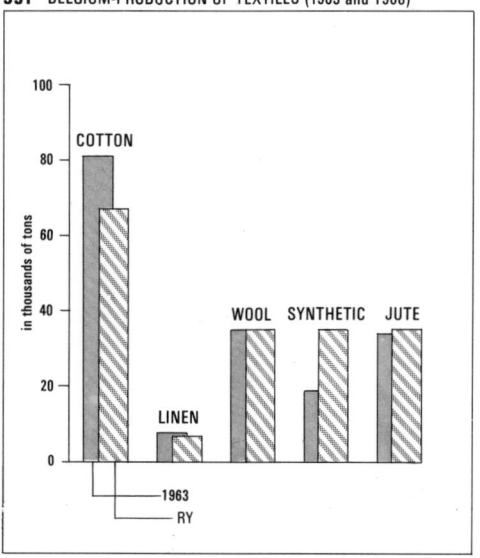

353 LIEGE INDUSTRIAL REGION

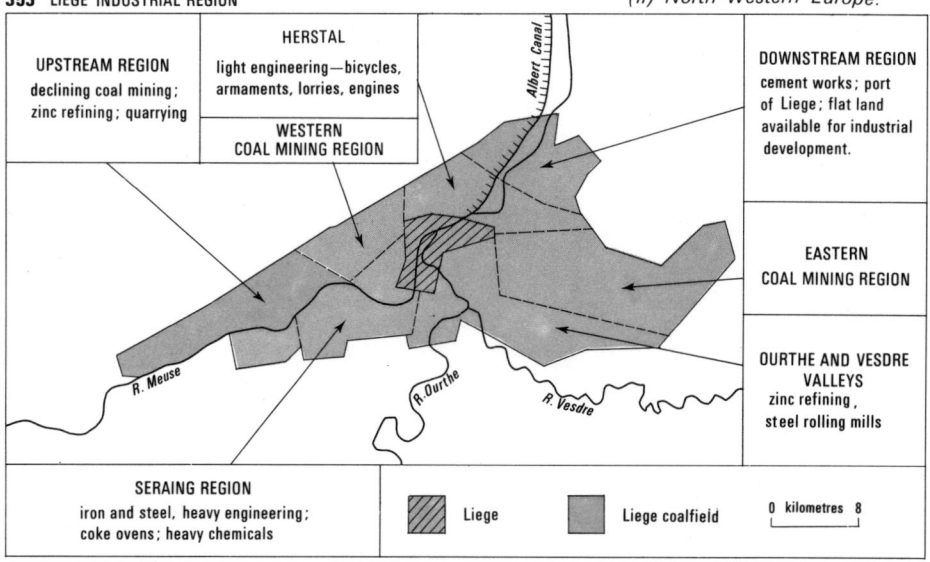

355 LUXEMBOURG—GENERAL

- ○ Main towns
- +—+ Main railways

0 kms 10

BELGIUM

To Liege

Wiltz

Vianden

R. Sûre

WEST

To Cologne

To Frankfurt

R. Alzette

Mertert

To Namur

LUXEMBOURG CITY

GERMANY

R. Moselle

Differdange

To Longwy

Esch Dudelange

To Thionville and Metz

FRANCE

ARDENNES REGION—Extensive woodland; pasture (beef and dairy cattle); some arable.

BON PAYS—More important farming region—pasture (beef and dairy cattle); arable—wheat, barley, potatoes and vines.

Fig. 355 General

355a (i) What are the maximum North-South and East-West dimensions of Luxembourg?
(ii) How many people live there? (See fig. 296.)
(iii) Compare the size of Luxembourg with your home town.

Figs. 355/356 Land use

355/356a List, in order of importance, the main uses of land in Luxembourg.
355/356b (i) Locate and describe the two main regions of Luxembourg.
(ii) Account for their differences.

Fig. 357 Employment

357a What proportion of Luxembourg's working population is engaged in (i) agriculture (ii) mining and manufacturing industry?
357b How does employment in Luxembourg compare with the Netherlands? (See fig. 303.)

357 LUXEMBOURG—EMPLOYMENT

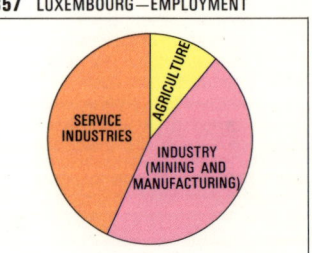

SERVICE INDUSTRIES

AGRICULTURE

INDUSTRY (MINING AND MANUFACTURING)

Fig. 358 The importance of the iron and steel industry

358a How important is the iron and steel industry to Luxembourg's economy?

Fig. 359 Iron and steel industry

359a Name and locate the four main iron and steel centres.
359b (i) How much iron ore is smelted each year?
(ii) What proportion is imported?
(iii) Where is it obtained?
359c Where does this industry obtain its coking coal? Some iron and steel is used in the engineering industry of Luxembourg City but most of it is exported.
359d Luxembourg City has a population of 80 000. In addition to being the capital it is becoming an important centre for European finance and administration. Suggest one reason for its importance (see fig. 355).
359e Being small, Luxembourg has always endeavoured to join itself economically with other countries. (i) Of what economic union is Luxembourg now a part? (ii) In what way does economic union benefit Luxembourg?

358 LUXEMBOURG—THE IMPORTANCE OF THE IRON AND STEEL INDUSTRY

(i) Value of total industrial production

IRON AND STEEL INDUSTRY

(ii) Value of total exports

IRON AND STEEL INDUSTRY

(iii) Total labour force

IRON AND STEEL INDUSTRY

% 0   20   40   60   80   100%

356 LUXEMBOURG—LAND USE

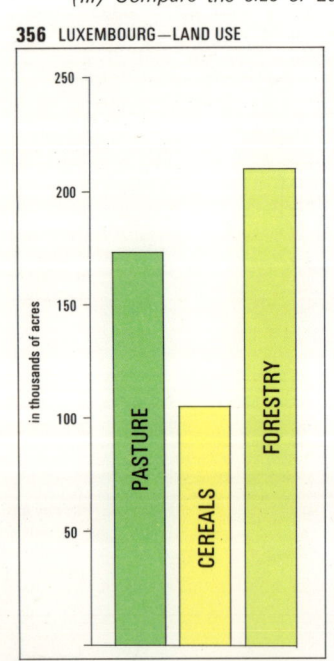

250

200

150

in thousands of acres

100

50

PASTURE

CEREALS

FORESTRY

359 LUXEMBOURG—IRON AND STEEL INDUSTRY

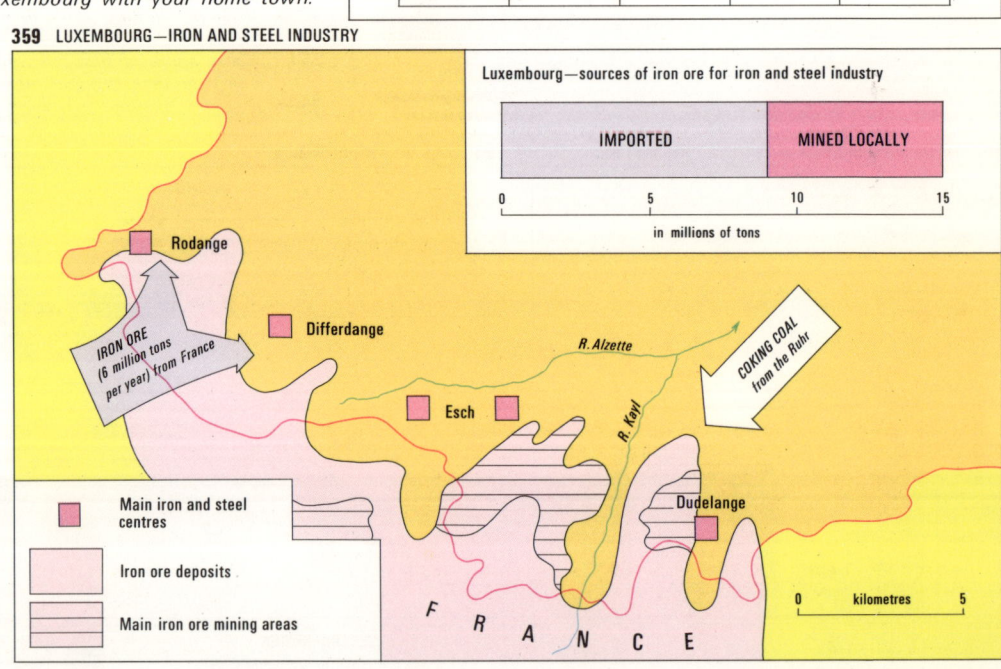

Luxembourg—sources of iron ore for iron and steel industry

IMPORTED   MINED LOCALLY

0   5   10   15

in millions of tons

Rodange

IRON ORE (6 million tons per year) from France

Differdange

R. Alzette

COKING COAL from the Ruhr

Esch

R. Kayl

Dudelange

■ Main iron and steel centres

Iron ore deposits

Main iron ore mining areas

F R A N C E

0   kilometres   5